# LABOR RELATIONS IN NEW DEMOCRACIES

# Labor Relations in New Democracies

## East Asia, Latin America, and Europe

José A. Alemán

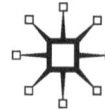

LABOR RELATIONS IN NEW DEMOCRACIES
Copyright © José A. Alemán, 2010.

All rights reserved.

First published in hardcover in 2010 by PALGRAVE MACMILLAN® in the United States—a division of St. Martin's Press LLC, 175 Fifth Avenue, New York, NY 10010.

Where this book is distributed in the UK, Europe and the rest of the world, this is by Palgrave Macmillan, a division of Macmillan Publishers Limited, registered in England, company number 785998, of Houndmills, Basingstoke, Hampshire RG21 6XS.

Palgrave Macmillan is the global academic imprint of the above companies and has companies and representatives throughout the world.

Palgrave® and Macmillan® are registered trademarks in the United States, the United Kingdom, Europe and other countries.

ISBN: 978–1–137–44563–6

Library of Congress Cataloging-in-Publication Data is available from the Library of Congress.

A catalogue record of the book is available from the British Library.

Design by Newgen Knowledge Works (P) Ltd., Chennai, India.

First PALGRAVE MACMILLAN paperback edition: August 2014

10 9 8 7 6 5 4 3 2 1

*To Viany*

## Contents

| | |
|---|---|
| *List of Figures* | ix |
| *List of Tables* | xi |
| *Foreword* | xiii |
| *Acknowledgments* | xvii |
| Introduction | 1 |
| 1  Industrial Relations after the Third Wave | 11 |
| 2  Democratization and Socioeconomic Security | 25 |
| 3  Labor Market Regulation and Industrial Conflict: An Empirical Baseline | 41 |
| 4  Labor Market Regulation and Social Dialogue: A Qualitative Comparative Analysis | 65 |
| 5  Protest and Social Dialogue in South Korea, 1987–2007 | 81 |
| 6  Protest and Social Dialogue in Democratic Chile, 1988–2006 | 115 |
| Conclusion: Participation, Flexibility, and the Future of the Third Wave | 137 |
| *Appendixes* | 149 |
| *Notes* | 157 |
| *References* | 173 |
| *Index* | 189 |

# Figures

| | | |
|---|---|---|
| 1.1 | Labor Regime and Labor Market Policies | 16 |
| 1.2 | Industrial Conflict as a Function of Social Dialogue | 21 |
| 2.1 | Average Wage Rates in New and Established Democracies, and Autocracies, 1983–2003 | 26 |
| 2.2 | Median Wage Rates in New and Established Democracies, and Autocracies, 1983–2003 | 26 |
| 2.3 | Outcome RSI and EPSI by Country | 35 |
| 2.4 | Voice Representation as a Function of Employment Protection | 36 |
| 2.5 | Overall Voice Representation as a Function of Overall Employment Protection | 38 |
| 2.6 | Outcome Voice Representation as a Function of Income Inequality | 39 |
| 3.1 | Conditional Effect of Wage Deregulation on Overall Unit Labor Costs, 1994–2003 | 58 |
| 5.1 | Labor Disputes, 1975–2001 | 85 |
| 6.1 | Percent of the Labor Force Involved in Strikes in Chile | 136 |
| C.1 | Quality of Industrial Relations by Country | 140 |

# Tables

| | | |
|---|---|---|
| 2.1 | Presence of Tripartite Boards Dealing with Labor Issues or Policies | 32 |
| 3.1 | Regression of Overall Unit Labor Costs in New Democracies, 1994–2003 | 55 |
| 3.2 | Conditional Negative Binomial Models of Industrial Conflict in New Democracies, 1994–2003 | 60 |

# Foreword

How are labor and relations between labor, capital, and the state affected by democratization processes? At first sight, one might believe that democratization should lead to more peaceful relations because it creates rights and more opportunities for participation and the articulation of interests. However, this does not reflect the trajectory of labor relations in new democracies. We observe great variation in labor behavior and relations with regard to the peacefulness of labor groups and the extent to which they benefit from democratization.

*Labor Relations in New Democracies* sets out to explain this variation. This is an important goal because we need to understand how labor fares under conditions of democratization, as this has the potential to feed back on the success of democratization processes and a country's stability. José Alemán develops a simple, but powerful theory that is able to account for the variation across countries and additionally specifies the underlying mechanisms. The theory receives empirical confirmation from multiple angles by a well-crafted multimethods design that includes bivariate analyses, time-series cross-section regression, Qualitative Comparative Analysis (QCA), and comparative process tracing.

Empirical research across different disciplines in political science fruitfully combined regression analysis and case studies in the 1990s, that is, when the battle between qualitative and quantitative methods was at its peak. At that point, the methods field was far from viewing large-n and small-n methods (n being the number of cases) as complementary instead of competing methods. Empirical research was rushing ahead of development of methods.

In the late 1990s, Coppedge (1999) laid the foundation for a multimethod framework with his discussion of thick and thin concepts in regression analysis and case studies. Lieberman (2005) followed him a few years later with his seminal article on nested analysis. To a degree, the discussion of nested analysis was a post hoc rationalization of existing practices, accomplished through highlighting the synergistic potential of multi-method research for causal analysis from a fundamental point of view. At the same time, the elaboration of nested analysis set new standards yet to be reflected in empirical research, specifically by focusing on the rationale of selecting cases based on regression results. In the field of methods, nested analysis set the standards for further research on case selection, concept formation, and commensurability of causal inference in multi-method research. Nested analysis was absorbed by empirical research following the guidelines on how to systematically select cases in follow-up case studies. After some delay, the idea of combining two methods operating on different levels of analyses was also transferred to the realm of set theory and the integration of QCA and process tracing in particular.

In this context, José Alemán's book *Labor Relations in New Democracies* nicely reflects the state of the field of multi-method research and the potential of using multiple methods to substantiate a theoretical argument. Based on his theory of industrial conflict, Alemán first explores the data and takes a look at bivariate patterns in chapter 2. What might strike one as (too) low-tech and an unnecessary step prior to multivariate regression is in fact valuable because it delivers interesting insights that might easily remain undetected in a multivariate setting.

In chapter 3, Alémán proceeds with a time-series-cross-section regression building on the state-of-the-art in this field. While this might all be done in a single journal article, the merits of book-length multi-method research come to bear in the following chapters. The analysis of social pacts with QCA in chapter 4 shows that not every nail (data) needs to be hammered with statistics. Given that the regression and QCA are not run with the same data, chapters 3 and 4 combined show that both varieties of cross-case analyses can peacefully coexist with one another in empirical research and deliver a broader picture than each method does on its own.

Drawing together the insights of the regression analysis and QCA, Alemán moves forward with a detailed discussion of his choice of cases. Here, we again see that empirical multi-method research can move ahead of the methods literature because he selects two off-lying, that is, deviant cases. To my knowledge, the deviant-case-only strategy has not thus far been discussed in the methods literature. The debate about case selection has only been about whether one should exclusively focus on typical cases or if a comparison of typical and deviant cases is in order, but not whether we can discard the typical cases in the process tracing part. However, by looking at a plot guiding case selection (such as figure 2.4 in this book), the deviant-case-only strategy suggests itself just because it seems interesting to explore why two cases do not conform with the general trend, yet are located on different sides of it.

Chapters 5 and 6 contain the process tracing studies and close the circle by complementing the cross-case analyses with within-case evidence. Empirical multi-method research has been proliferating in recent years in books and articles alike, a development that should be welcomed. Nevertheless, the process tracing chapters show that process tracing works best when it has room to breathe and covers more pages than are available in (print) journals. In total, this book is witness to the promise of multi-method research, namely, that the combination of multiple methods produces rich and complementary insights from different angles that, taken together, allow for a comprehensive approach toward the advancement of theory.

INGO ROHLFING
Bremen International Graduate School of Social Sciences,
University of Bremen and Jacobs University Bremen

# Acknowledgments

This book, which grew out of my doctoral dissertation, represents the culmination of a very long intellectual and personal journey. As the manuscript goes to press in the winter of 2009, it is hard to believe that it has been seven years in the making. As my single most consuming project, it would not have been possible without the ongoing support of a wide network of family, friends, and colleagues, in Princeton, New York and elsewhere. Their encouragement, dedication, and understanding have made this book possible.

For financial and logistical support, I would like to thank a number of organizations, in particular the Fellowship of Woodrow Wilson Scholars for funding my final year of graduate studies. Funding from the Institute for International and Regional Studies, the East Asian Studies Program, the Center for International Studies, the Mellon and Macarthur Foundations, and the Princeton Council for Regional Studies supported my various trips to the field. I would also like to thank The Korea Foundation for its monetary and institutional support in Seoul and the Office of Faculty Research at Fordham University for awarding me a faculty fellowship in the summer of 2007 that allowed me to do additional data collection. Wiley InterScience and Sage deserve credit for allowing me to reuse some of the material featured in chapters 3 and 4.

For intellectual support and encouragement, a number of individuals deserve credit, beginning with my dissertation committee. To an extent I only fully recognize now, their distinct talents and interests have allowed me to define myself within the discipline in particular and academia at large. From my first days on campus when I took his seminar on Society and Development, Lynn White has been a constant source of encouragement. His enthusiasm and warmth have made the academic burden a little more bearable than it would have otherwise been. Deborah Yashar's sharp intellect and insightful advice was decisive in the early stages of the project. Kosuke Imai could not imagine when I first barged into his office how much I would call upon his help. His accessibility and genuine collegiality have made it very easy for me to seek out his counsel. Gilbert Rozman has been extremely receptive to my work and ideas. From the very first days of my dissertation, he took the time to read and reply in a timely fashion to every single chapter draft I produced. I thank him for his commitment to country and area expertise.

The research featured in this book has benefited from the various scholarly venues in which it has been presented, including presentations at various universities and academic conferences. The first two chapters benefitted from the probing eyes of participants at the CUNY Workshop on Politics and Protest in New York City, who made numerous suggestions for sharpening my arguments and improving presentation. Colleagues in the Political Science Department at Fordham University and participants in the "New Empirical Applications of Qualitative Comparative Analysis" panel at the 2007 American Political Science Association annual meeting quizzed me intently on some of the ideas elaborated in chapter 3 of the manuscript. I also want to thank Andra Olivia Miljanic for organizing the "Labor Relations and the Effects of Globalization on Inequality-Addressing Institutions" panel at the 2008 American Political Science Association annual meeting.

A number of individuals and organizations deserve special mention. The staff at the Yonhap news agency in Seoul tolerated my scavenging for news wires. In the Princeton Politics and Sociology departments, John Londregan and Bruce Western provided crucial inputs at various times on particular aspects of this project. The consultants in the Data Services Unit in Firestone Library at Princeton University—in particular Dan, Kristi, Julie, and Fabio—have endured countless hours of probing questions. Without their patient assistance with the mundane and not so mundane, this project would have taken much longer to complete. The economics librarian at Princeton, Bobray Bordelon, was instrumental in locating crucial sources of data. I would also like to thank David Gibian for help in compiling the index, and the able team at Palgrave Macmillan for so skillfully shepherding the book through the publication process.

In the Political Science Department at Fordham, I have benefitted from the good spirits of Bob Hume, who has been my tenure track companion since we both arrived in the summer of 2005. Bob has patiently endured my commiserating for the past four years and provided the perspective necessary to stay focused on the task. Jeff Cohen has been a great mentor, at one point reading various drafts of book proposals and making suggestions for improvement. Susan Berger also took the time to read the entire manuscript. I also want to thank John Entelis, Rich Fleisher, and Costas Panagopoulos for showing interest in the evolution of the book.

Various parts of the book have benefitted from generous feedback and help from a number of scholars. Nita Rudra patiently answered my questions regarding the construction of one of the variables in chapter 3. Thomas Plümper and Bruce Western provided crucial methodological advice. Charles Ragin saved me from my own ignorance in chapter 4. Mark S. Anner, Charles H. Blake, Teri L Caraway, Matthew Carnes, Abhishek Chatterjee, Sebastián Guzmán, James Jasper, Jai Kwan Jung, Sun Chul Kim, John Krinsky, Roy Licklider, Margarita Mooney, David Yang, and Elke Zuern read and commented on draft chapters or conference papers adapted from these chapters. James Jasper went beyond the call of duty by offering advise on the intricate process of book publishing.

My deepest love and gratitude go to my family, in particular my parents José and Maryté Alemán and my grandparents Amparo and Nene. I am indebted to them for their sacrifice, including giving me the opportunity to immigrate to the United States. By teaching me the most valuable lessons in life, I have been able to chart my own path, fully knowing that I would have their unconditional support, emotional as well and financial. At times, they have believed in me more than myself. My sister Lourdes and her new family, the Berzins, have been a terrific source of empathy. I have been truly blessed in these past four years to be living so close to them.

Last but not least, my wife Viany has been truly indispensable. Although she was not present at its inception, it is truly an understatement to say that without her this manuscript would have never journeyed from dissertation to book. I am at once grateful and sorry to have had her at my side as the manuscript went through more changes and revisions than I care to remember: grateful to her for being a friend, lover, colleague, editor, and *media naranja*; sorry for the huge burden she carried for me, a burden that she never asked for but gracefully accepted. It is to her that I dedicate this book.

# Introduction

> *The steady bombardment of televised images of militant strikers wearing red headbands, defiantly raising their fists in the air while sitting cross-legged and chanting menacing slogans, has become indelibly etched in the minds of wary foreign investors... In comparison to other advanced countries, Korea's industrial relations have been marred with violent protests, exhibited by inflexible and uncompromising behavior between labor and management in response to the government-led restructuring efforts in the corporate sector.*
>
> —Korea Herald, *January 31, 2001*

Democratic institutions that give a voice to workers are typically associated with harmonious industrial relations. The quote, however, captures an important observation: the variation in levels of labor conflict new democracies have experienced.[1] While regional experts have found this variation puzzling, this book builds a theoretical framework that accounts for these findings. Like their predecessors in previous waves, capital and labor in late-developing countries have favored democratic institutions when these institutions are perceived as advancing their material interests (Bellin 2002, 2000). Labor in particular stands to gain from negotiations with employers and government representatives over wages and other benefits.

While democratization is associated with increased workers' voice, economic reforms in recent decades have called into question democracy's ability to deliver economic benefits to workers. First, as many scholars and practitioners have noted (e.g. ILO 1997), the decentralization of collective bargaining in the 1980s and 1990s has meant that in practice unions do not exert real leverage with employers in many emerging democracies. Similarly, changes in labor contracts and the diversification of the types of contracts employers can offer have been the main objectives of labor reforms in many countries (Bronstein 1995, 1997; Córdova 1996; Cazes and Nesporova 2001;

Tokman 2002). Some countries did not deregulate their labor markets in any meaningful sense and a number of them actually reregulated their collective bargaining and employment statutes (Pagés 2004: 67; Murillo 2005; Cook 2007). Many governments in the developing world, however, have made their labor regulations more flexible (ILO 2004: 140; Standing 2008).

I argue in this study that democratization and labor market reforms have resulted in a twist on an old adage when applied to workers: "*The strong do what they can and the weak suffer what they must.*"[2] That is, in countries where labor market institutions have become more inclusive and protective, labor has the resources both to cooperate in an extended way with employers and the state, *and* to press for economic and political gains using industrial action. As a result, labor conflict in these new democracies has been higher than in countries where workers and unions have benefitted the least from democratization, both economically and politically. In the latter set of countries, workers' ability to cooperate with employers and the state *and* to prosecute industrial action has suffered, even though the economic benefits they derive are not generous. Precisely because the working class in these countries enjoys few organizational and political resources, their ability to contest their situation has declined.

These findings not only explain a significant amount of variation in the extent of labor conflict, but also address an interesting puzzle in this important group of countries: it is precisely in those countries where labor market institutions are more inclusive and protective where workers are most militant. The key to resolving this contradiction lies in another observation: that instances of social dialogue in new democracies may result in agreements among workers, employers, and state representatives, but these agreements do not usually amount to lasting compromises of the type observed in advanced industrialized democracies (Przeworski 1985; Buchanan 1995). Such compromises ensure that workers behave in such a manner as to make positive rates of profit possible, and employers commit themselves to some rate of transformation of profits into wage increases and some rate of investment out of profits (Przeworski 1985: 182).

This difference in the character of working class compromises lies in the distinction between the social dialogue practiced in many emerging democracies in the late twentieth century and the classical variety of corporatism exemplified by Western European economies before the 1980s.[3] In countries where corporatist policymaking has been institutionalized, workers *can* demand wage and other benefits commensurate with their organizational strength, but they pursue moderation in the overall interest of all involved. In contrast, in new democracies that feature inclusive labor market institutions and protective labor regulations, workers do not refrain from using industrial action in pursuit of their goals even as they strike pacts with employers and government representatives.

One could argue that a certain level of militancy is not only expected but desired in stable democratic polities (Przeworski 1980). Even in societies in which labor is politically influential, industrial disputes can sometimes occur. In emerging democracies where unions have little political voice, sustained militancy can also lead over time to more effective labor representation in the political process (Alemán 2005). Strikes, however, often hurt the interests of other workers. When corporatist policymaking is institutionalized, moreover, unions tend to pursue long-term interests as opposed to narrow sectoral ones, and this implies that they have an interest in moderation on the part of their members.

The problem many new democracies face, and one that this book systematically documents, is that it is difficult for workers, employers, and their representatives to come to agreements over wages and other benefits. The roots of this predicament lie in the interaction of two recent trends specific to these countries: the short-lived nature of democracy as a political regime and the global context in which these countries have democratized. According to scholars of Latin America and Western Europe, the general attitude of trade unions toward employers and governments in the 1980s was one of distrust after years of repression or exclusion. While unions and employers lacked experience in negotiation and compromise, governments used social dialogue in a self-serving way and attempted to impose it by decree. Union leaders were generally reluctant to accept compromises with potential rather than concrete advantages for workers. These attitudes stood in the way of far-reaching labor agreements and meaningful implementation (Blake 1994, 1996; Bronstein 1995; Buchanan, 1995; Marshall 1999: 24).

Arguments of this sort suggest that with enough time and experience, labor, employers, and the state will learn to trust one another and embark on a path of consensual and mutually beneficial bargaining. In the last two decades of the twentieth century, however, workers in the East and South, to borrow Przeworski's (1991) terminology, have experienced slumps in real wages, job security, social insurance, public sector employment, and union densities that are probably more dramatic than anything seen in the established democracies of North America, Western Europe, and Japan (Glyn 2006). By any conventional metric, workers in the semi-periphery and periphery of the global economy suffered drastic declines in their material fortunes (Deyo and Agartan 2003; Kurtz 2004b; Ost 2000). The inability of democracy to deliver economic benefits to millions of workers has called into question its ability to serve as a foundation for harmonious industrial relations.

## Theoretical Contributions

Scholars have documented labor's contribution to democratization, both in earlier democratic waves as well as in the Third Wave of democratization that began in 1974 (Collier and Mahoney 1997; Collier 1999; Foweraker and Landman 1997; Kim 2007; Sandoval 1998; Seidman 1994). My concern in this project is with the period after the initial transition to democracy, and more specifically the relationship between labor inclusion in policymaking, the extent of labor (de)commodification, and the quality of industrial relations. Recent studies assume that political representation closes a channel for dissent on the part of workers, so that if labor is meaningfully incorporated in policymaking, it is also able to block reforms that would result in further decommodification of the labor market (e.g., Etchemendy 2004). The result is then labor cooperation with the government. Where labor is excluded or repressed, on the other hand, governments can afford to push for more labor market flexibility. To buy acquiescence from unions, governments also increase compensatory programs such as unemployment insurance.

These accounts assume that unions can either moderate their behavior in response to favorable policies, or protest when labor market reforms and their associated outcomes are not favorable to their interests. Organized labor, however, is not always in a position to contest a general lack of protections, particularly in countries where it lacks economic and political voice. In addition, labor incorporation in policymaking does not always foreclose the possibility of protest precisely because corporatist policymaking is not institutionalized in most new democracies. In emerging democracies then, the decision to protest is not independent of the resources available to workers.

This book also evaluates power resources theories linking labor market regulations and policies to the partisanship of the government. These theories depart from the assumption that political parties based in socioeconomic categories relatively disadvantaged in terms of economic resources are expected to push for modifying outcomes related to market distributive processes (Korpi 1983; Stephens 1979). Accordingly, the foremost emphasis of this approach has been on how social democratic, socialist, and leftist parties transform the logic of industrial relations under capitalist democracy.

> When the working class has control of the government, the locus of conflict over the distribution of resources, the national income in particular, shifts from the labor market and the private sector, where strike activity is the typical means of pressure, to the public sector, where political exchange prevails. Thus, redistributive, welfare policies instituted by labor governments reduce conflict. (Franzosi 1994: 11)

Exponents of the power-resources approach expect labor to be more accommodating under left leaning governments. Left parties typically favor extensive labor market regulations (Botero 2004). Conservative parties, on the other hand, favor allowing the market to determine the most efficient equilibrium between labor supply and demand (Hicks 1999). This book presents extensive evidence documenting the fact that labor regulations in new democracies are not epiphenomenal to the party or political force in control of government—in this case parties to the left of the political spectrum. On the contrary, while some conservative parties have supported or at least maintained protective labor regulations, many left-of-center parties have failed to regulate the labor market in workers' favor. In some cases, they have even pushed for more flexibility.

In emphasizing effective incorporation and protective labor regulations as key resources in the arsenal of workers and their unions then, I claim that labor market regulations cannot be treated as epiphenomenal to the presence of labor leaning parties in emerging democracies. Accordingly, I demonstrate that the level and enforcement of labor market regulations is a crucial explanator of when and how workers and their unions enjoy meaningful political incorporation. Not only do labor regulations increase the ability of workers and unions to forge pacts with employers and government representatives over wages and other policies, they also affect labor compensation and in so doing explain differences in the frequency of labor conflict.

## The Dual Transitions Reconsidered

Polanyi's (1944) metaphor of the "double movement" nicely captures the contradictions embedded in the politics of labor incorporation in many new democracies. These contradictions are evident in reforms that attempt to incorporate subjects politically while relying on market relations to exclude them and/or demobilize them as a group. Polanyi spoke of the countermovement by state or societal actors to provide protection from or redress for the insecurities associated with the commodification of labor, land, and services. This protection typically entails forms of state intervention that insulate certain spheres of social relations from perfect competition.

Governments have traditionally recognized that labor is not just any commodity, that is, it does not come into being through the expectation of its saleability and it cannot be separated from its owner (Itzigsohn 2000: 15–16). Consequently, they have subjected outcomes like employment opportunities, wages, and pensions to authoritative collective decisions involving politics rather than, or in addition to, private market exchanges. Polanyi suggests then that democratization should not become a vehicle for subordinating a broad range of social outcomes to market competition. Recent work also suggests that state action is necessary both to expand political representation and regulate it (Kurtz 2004a; Shadlen 2004).

My examination of recent transitions calls then for a reconsideration of how labor market reforms have been received by two important groups, labor and capital. New democracies present a natural laboratory for the study of these questions, given the variation in the dependent variable—levels of labor conflict/cooperation—as well as the common starting point for many countries, namely, authoritarian regulation of labor markets with extensive state intervention. The book is thus motivated by the policy implications of how interest groups behave in the face of incomplete or partial institutional consolidation.

One problem confronted by comparative researchers is how wide to cast their theoretical net. As Western (2001: 366–67) argues, complex explanations make diffuse predictions, but simple explanations concentrate their predictive probability in narrow regions. As a result, predictions will usually be available that are consistent with one theory but highly unlikely under the other. The approach I follow in this study is to derive explanatory propositions from close observation of two countries (South Korea and Chile) that can then be tested systematically in a large-N framework (Hyman 2001).

The approach recognizes that the scope conditions for the research question can only be ascertained through a rigorous dialogue of theory and empirical data. As Collier and Collier (1991: 13–14) argue, a principal challenge of comparative research is "to push the systematic comparison of cases as far as possible without pushing it to the point where it does violence to the distinctive attributes of each case." Likewise, Ragin (2000) argues in favor of intensive explanation and correct specification of the population of cases in comparative analysis. As such, the study requires a thoroughly inductive approach that is able to build on empirical regularities.

Looking for empirical regularities, however, does not entail giving up on deductive reasoning. Throughout the book, the experience of established democracies is used to formulate hypotheses and guide the analysis. In selecting cases for in-depth examination, the strategy I follow is based on the nested approach to comparative research (Lieberman 2005; Rohlfing 2008). Nested analysis provides a strong foundation for adjudicating among the competing goals and inferential logics of large-N analysis and case oriented comparative research, namely, to establish associations among a large number of observations while remaining attuned to atypical cases.[4] In both instances, the approach is explicitly cross-regional, a research strategy still underutilized in comparative politics.

**Plan of the Book**

Chapter 1 presents a theory that relates political incorporation and labor market regulation to the quality of industrial relations. The literature on democratization has emphasized changes in the political arena but has not fruitfully explored how these changes shape the ability of workers to bargain with employers and the state over wages and other benefits.[5] Political economists, on the other hand, have emphasized the constraining logic of globalization but have not fully explored the implication of these competitive pressures for labor market policy. This chapter then begins to integrate the literature on democratization with studies of corporatism.

Chapter 2 compares trends in monthly wages for male workers in new and established democracies from 1983 to 2003. This comparison reveals that levels of labor compensation in new democracies continue to lag behind levels of labor compensation in established democracies. The comparison conveys the challenge of delivering wage benefits to workers in new democracies. The chapter then evaluates the extent of labor incorporation and labor market regulation in emerging democracies. The question I ask is whether protective labor market regulations are indeed linked to effective voice representation in this important group of countries, setting the stage for the analysis of wage costs and industrial conflict in the following chapter.

Chapter 3 studies the effect of wage compensation on industrial conflict in new democracies. The empirical analysis reveals that workers in new democracies, compared to their counterparts in established democracies, are less likely to accept wage moderation even when wages are the product of negotiations among state, employers, and union representatives. The results are robust to the inclusion of important variables such as the size of the labor force, the partisanship of the government, and the level of economic development. The analyses also reveal that levels of wage regulation are the main predictors of wage compensation in new democracies.

Chapter 4 examines in a more explicit fashion the mechanisms linking cooperation among trade unions, employer associations, and governments to social peace. After introducing an original dataset of labor agreements in new democracies, I conduct a Boolean analysis of the determinants of these agreements, also known as social pacts. If chapter 3 shows that industrial conflict is explained by lower levels of labor market regulation, chapter 4 demonstrates that most cases of successful labor agreements in new democracies are explained by higher levels of wage and employment regulation.

Chapter 5 looks at the evolution of the labor regime in the Republic of Korea under the Sixth Republic (1988–present). South Korea makes a good case study because favorable legislation for workers and labor unions is usually present in countries with labor-based parties, whereas conservative governments typically endorse legislation favoring employers. Yet South Korea retained significantly more protective labor laws than many new democracies until 1998. Of particular importance for the theory the book presents is the relationship between changes in levels of employment protection and industrial relations. The South Korean case demonstrates that the flexibilization of employment regulations can result in more labor militancy and industrial conflict even when the labor regime is becoming more politically inclusive.

Chapter 6 examines the evolution of social dialogue under the center left *Concertación* government in Chile since 1990. Despite being governed by a nominally pro-labor government, Chile had one of the most flexible labor markets in the developing world in the 1990s. Wage bargaining was conducted primarily at the firm level and job security provisions remained extremely limited. The Chilean case shows how low (albeit increasing) levels of wage and employment regulation result in more labor-government and labor-business conflict. Industrial conflict would have been even higher if the labor market were not so flexible already.

The concluding chapter brings the evidence of the book together. It concludes that social dialogue has finally arrived in the emerging democracies of Latin America, Eastern Europe, and East Asia. The chapter, however, reveals important regional differences in the political economy of labor incorporation. The oldest new democracies, all located in Southern Europe, have experienced relatively high levels of labor conflict in recent years. These countries—Greece, Portugal, and Spain, to be precise—share a history of political incorporation and protective labor market policies.

At the other end of the spectrum, East European countries, characterized by low levels of incorporation and flexible labor market regulations, have experienced declines in strike activity. This chapter is then able to account for something students of contentious politics have not successfully explained: the region-specific variation in patterns of labor and social-movement mobilization many have uncovered in new democratic regimes. In so doing, I demonstrate that many new democracies remain far from having established anything resembling institutional consolidation in the labor arena.

## Chapter 1

# Industrial Relations after the Third Wave

The late twentieth-century wave of global democratization brought formal democracy to a greater number of countries than ever before (Doorenspleet 2005). The advent of competitive regimes in much of the Second World and parts of the Third coincided with important changes in the institutions and practices of worker representation.[1] For many labor movements, however, this has been a mixed blessing. In most if not all new democracies, labor has been afforded formal recognition as an organized interest group; worker organizations and their representatives, moreover, participate in the formulation and implementation of economic and social policies.

At the same time, governments in many new democracies have taken the lead in reducing many of the protections workers have historically enjoyed. This has made it more difficult for workers to overcome their collective action problem and for labor unions to play a meaningful role in policymaking and implementation. This raises the first question addressed in this study: have changes in the structures and practices of labor representation increased workers' ability to bargain over wages and other benefits? Or, conversely, have these changes decreased labor's bargaining power vis-à-vis employers and governments?

Democracy as a political regime is known to be more favorable than autocracy to the interests of wage earners (Rodrik 1999). In a democratic regime, political institutions can work in favor of trade unions and workers by increasing political representation and granting workers rising levels of income and employment. One prerequisite for these outcomes, however, is the existence of institutional and regulatory support for workers and their organizations. Economic reforms in recent years have dramatically constrained the ability of new democratic regimes to provide institutional and regulatory support to workers. This raises the second question posed in this book: have changes in the structure and practices of labor representation moderated or radicalized labor movements in new democracies?

The experience of established democracies demonstrates that well functioning labor market institutions are characterized by long-term cooperative ties among employers, unions, and state representatives. These ties typically manifest themselves in the presence of centralized collective bargaining or national "tripartite" boards/labor councils in which public policies are discussed and agreements concluded among employers, workers, and state representatives. The purpose of these institutions is typically to keep wage growth in accordance with productivity improvements, so that the highest possible level of wages and work-related benefits can be maintained (Crouch 1982; Schmitter and Lehmbruch 1979; Lehmbruch and Schmitter 1982; Goldthorpe 1984; Garrett 1998: 9).

These outcomes are more easily obtained when peak associations of labor and employers can negotiate on behalf of their respective constituencies. In this situation, consultation, bargaining, and negotiations transcend narrow economic issues such as wages to include macroeconomic and social welfare policies. When national level discussions between the government and representatives of peak employer and trade union confederations lead to agreements on public policy, scholars refer to the phenomenon as corporatism (Compston 2003: 791).[2] The term pluralism is used then to characterize a system in which interest associations are either fragmented or do not engage in concerted dialogue (Siaroff 1999).

Schmitter (1981) claimed that corporatism was more successful in containing political discontent in advanced industrialized democracies because of its ability to create and enforce a "social contract" between labor and capital. As a result, neo-corporatist democracies experienced less protest than pluralist ones. Nollert (1995), on the other hand, argued that neo-corporatist practices narrowed the gap between societal demands and state capabilities.[3] Because neo-corporatism improves macroeconomic performance and reduces income inequality, it reduces political protest.[4]

Negotiations involving representatives of labor, business, and the government have featured prominently in processes of democratic transition and consolidation (Encarnación 1997; Iankova 2002). All Central and East European countries have managed their transition from socialist to market economies through national level dialogue among labor, business, and government representatives (Borisov and Clarke 2006). Social dialogue has played a prominent role in the reform and reorganization of labor market policies and institutions in Latin America (Cook 2007: 11).[5] Examples of African and Asian countries featuring tripartite social dialogue include South Korea, South Africa, and the Philippines (Ishikawa 2003).

In both the number of countries that embraced it and the scope of its reach, the 1990s witnessed a resurgence of national social dialogue. Some attribute this development to the positive sum nature of the process. According to the ILO, social dialogue facilitates the negotiation of wage pacts as well as more encompassing agreements over labor market and social policy reforms.[6] The case for social dialogue, however, rests on two important assumptions: that the system of interest representation is sufficiently democratic, and that labor market regulations provide some degree of protection to workers from the volatility of the market.

Historically, social dialogue and labor market flexibility have been negatively correlated (Honeybone 1997: 493). That is, the more centralized and institutionalized the process has been in established democracies, the more regulated labor markets have been. Studies of labor politics, however, do not fully investigate the effect of labor regulations on workers' ability to make collective demands. It is important then to pay attention to the interplay between the rules and policies governing a labor regime at the national level and the regulations that govern industrial relations at the firm and industrial levels.

## Corporatism and Labor Market Regulations

Repressive policies are obviously one of the ways in which governments exclude interest groups from policymaking, and many scholars have placed them at the heart of their conceptualizations of labor regimes.[7] Cook (1998, 2007), for example, distinguishes between liberal and restrictive labor codes in Latin America. Liberal codes grant workers a great deal of autonomy to organize and run their organizations and participate in politics. Restrictive codes, on the other hand, impose restrictions on the formation, administration, and activities in which unions engage, particularly political activities. Similarly, Itzigsohn (2000: 19) distinguishes between repressive and protective policies. Protective regulations are those achieved by workers negotiating with employers and the state as a result of the strength of their organizations. Repressive regulations are designed to limit collective action on the part of workers.

Constraints by themselves, however, are insufficient to fully characterize a labor regime. As Collier and Collier (1979) note, regimes that seek to exclude labor from policymaking can impose restrictions on workers even as they provide some inducements to win their cooperation. These incentives (which can be provided in a selective way), include official recognition, monopoly of representation, compulsory membership, and group subsidies.

Collier and Collier (1979: 979) envision tripartite institutions as an inducement that provides "the opportunity for certain groups to be represented on functionally organized, semi-public entities such as wage-price councils and economic planning boards." Their framework, however, is derived from formal labor legislation and does not explicitly account for these institutions.[8] They justify their exclusion by claiming that wage-price councils and economic planning boards were not consistently present in countries that otherwise extended inducements to organized labor. In many new democracies, tripartite institutions have operated in the absence of other inducements typically associated with these channels of participation. Tripartite institutions, however, have become too common in new democracies to justify their omission.

When it comes to new democracies then, I adopt Wiarda's (1997: 118) distinction between inclusionary and exclusionary corporatism. This distinction captures differences not only in labor legislation, but also in policy instruments designed to bring (or exclude) certain groups into (from) the political process. While compatible with the different labor regimes Collier and Collier (1979) found, the exclusionary/inclusionary distinction highlights the reality that both laws and channels of formal participation are necessary to increase labor's collective voice.

At one end of the political spectrum, exclusionary labor market regimes combine high constraints with low inducements. A prominent example is the institution of "corporatism without labor" found in all export-oriented East Asian Newly Industrialized Countries (or NICs), with the exception of Singapore (Deyo 1987, 1989; Deyo,

Haggard and Koo 1987; Gereffi and Wyman 1990; McNamara 1999: 11; Pempel 2002). These countries exhibited fragmented policymaking processes, low levels of union participation in collective bargaining, and narrow and specialized—largely industry-specific—employer and trade union associations.[9]

The opposite is the situation found in many European coordinated market economies (CMEs) that combine low constraints with high inducements: employer and trade union associations are encompassing and centralized, and labor inclusion is usually reflected in union officials' positions in the executive branch of the government (Garrett 1998). In between are the Latin American corporatisms combining high constraints with high inducements, and pluralist economies like the United States combining low constraints with low inducements.

While it is important to keep the overall character of the labor regime separate from specific labor market regulations, a great degree of overlap is present between the two. This is because government policies and labor market regulations usually converge in their objectives. The South Korean government, for example, banned union political activities and excluded one labor federation from peak level tripartite bargaining before 1998. In addition, until the late 1990s, the Korean government prohibited third-party mediation in labor disputes and plural unionism at the workplace. The political bans coupled with the flexible regulations effectively denied unions a collective voice in society.

### Labor Market Regulations

The other pillar of most industrial relations systems in the "South" and "East" before democratization was extensive regulation of employment contracts and other components of the employment relationship. These policies generally embodied a philosophy that individual workers needed state protection vis-à-vis employers (Cook 2007: 42), or that governments served as caretakers for the interests of the working class (Portes 1994). Neoliberal structural adjustment policies, however, have led to the flexibilization of individual and collective labor regulations in many emerging democracies (Cook 1998, 2007).

To capture differences in the extent of labor market regulation, I follow Cook (1998, 2007) in distinguishing between flexible and protective labor market regulations. These terms may apply to both employment (individual) and collective labor law. Flexibility denotes a weakening of economic regulation to the advantage of market forms of coordination (Esping-Andersen and Regini 2000: 21). Lower levels of unionization and less centralized wage bargaining, less government intervention in the wage-setting process, fewer restrictions on hiring and firing of employees, and lower social insurance charges and other nonwage labor costs are typically symptomatic of flexible labor market regulations (IMF 1994: 36). Flexible regulations decrease unions' market power, whereas protective regulations increase it.

Examples of protective regulations in the realm of wage setting include employers' legal duty to bargain with unions as opposed to loose collectives of workers, collective agreements that are extended to third parties by law, and mandatory workers' councils allowing workers to participate in plant level management. Examples of protective employment regulations include fixed-term contracts that are granted for specific situations and are temporary in nature, laws requiring fair grounds for termination of employment, high premiums for overtime work, generous annual leave, caps on the amount of overtime worked per year, and strict regulation of minimum notice and severance periods.

Figure 1.1 juxtaposes Wiarda's distinction between inclusionary and exclusionary labor regimes with Cook's characterization of labor market regulations as protective or flexible. The vertical dimension in figure 1.1 depicts government strategies that range from high constraints and low inducements in authoritarian settings to democratic settings that combine low constraints with high inducements. The horizontal dimension depicts the degree of

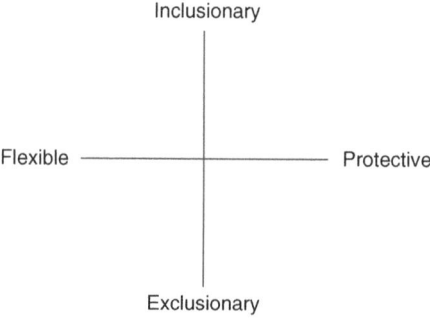

**Figure 1.1** Labor Regime and Labor Market Policies

protection that results from government enforcement of existing labor regulations.

How does this framework compare with others advanced in the literature? Schmitter (1974) distinguishes between "state" and "societal corporatism." In the first case, interest associations are dependent on state organs and penetrated by them. In the second, they are autonomous and penetrative, in the sense that the legitimacy and functioning of the state derives from its ties to interest associations (Schmitter 1974: 102–103). While Schmitter's concern with the autonomy of interest associations captures an important difference between democratic labor regimes and authoritarian ones, the framework is primarily typological. As a result, it misses the dynamic trajectory many emerging democracies undergo as workers exchange constraints on their ability to organize and participate in politics for inducements to lobby the state and partake in policymaking, a trajectory illustrated in figure 1.1 by the vertical axis.

Similarly, Valenzuela (1989: 448) suggests two labor control strategies used by authoritarian regimes: the state corporatist strategy and the repressive market mechanism.[10] In state corporatism the state subordinates organized labor to its authority by co-opting the leadership of unions. Unions, which are organized in a top-down manner, gain organizational and material resources from the government in exchange for political subordination. In the market strategy, the government relies on market mechanisms to weaken unions. These mechanisms decrease workers' bargaining power vis-à-vis employers. Examples of market strategies include decentralized collective bargaining, voluntary association between workers and their unions, and plural unionism at the firm level (Valenzuela 1989: 448).

Unlike Valenzuela, my theoretical framework does not assume a priori that only authoritarian governments seek to exclude trade unions from the political process, whether indirectly through market mechanisms, or more directly through the political process. Indeed, Valenzuela's characterization is blind to nonmarket forms of government repression. More fundamentally, if corporatism is seen as a consciously chosen strategy of the government (Woldendorp 1995: 124), one can evaluate its success in terms of its ability to resolve labor-employer and labor-government conflicts in a way that is not reducible to the structure of interest representation. For Third Wave democracies then, the key question is whether labor is in fact meaningfully incorporated in the political process. As many new democracies attest, unions in some cases lack effective bargaining power even while they take part in tripartite negotiations.

In the past two and a half decades in particular, many new democracies appear to combine inclusionary labor strategies with flexible regulations in the labor market arena. During the 1990s most new democracies had in place national/sectoral level bargaining institutions, in addition to company level bargaining.[11] In eighteen of the twenty-nine new democracies profiled, however, the dominant level of bargaining from 1985 to 1995 was the company or plant. In Central and Eastern Europe, wage bargaining takes place for the most part at the firm level.[12] Collective bargaining in many parts of Latin America is limited mainly to employees in large companies.[13] Finally, it still plays a relatively minor role in Asia.[14] Indeed, while nine countries moved toward more national/sectoral level collective bargaining, company level bargaining increased in twenty countries.

The erosion in workers' voice many countries have experienced (ILO 2004: 273) creates asymmetries between workers, who are fragmented into multiple bargaining units, and employers, who retain their capacity to speak with one voice. When bargaining is decentralized to the local or plant level, the national trade union might not be in a position to assure that wage guidelines will be implemented (Hassel 2006: 84). This asymmetry has severe consequences for the generalized exchange logic of social dialogue. Przeworski (1992: 126) argues, for example, that trade unions usually participate in social and economic pacts only if they are "strong, centralized, and politically influential. Otherwise, they have no reasons to expect that they would benefit from their underutilized power."

Another way to look at the erosion in workers' voice is by examining trends in unionization rates. Unions in developing countries have been particularly weak and have been further weakened by government action (ILO 2004: 249). Hopes that traditionally weak or nonexistent employment security would strengthen have also not materialized in many countries (ILO 2004: 138). The ILO (1997) profiled levels of trade union membership as a percentage of total labor force between 1985 and 1995. The starting point, the mid 1980s, marks the time when developing countries began to undergo profound, globalization-induced economic reforms (Rudra 2005). Whether referring to the nonagricultural labor force, wage/salary earners, or formal sector employees, most countries (nineteen in number) experienced drops in union membership. Only four countries

(Chile, Korea, Philippines, and Spain) registered net increases throughout the period. One should note, however, that unionization rates in these countries were artificially reduced at the outset of democratization as a result of exclusionary strategies.[15]

For students of labor politics, democratization, and industrial relations, these trends in labor market practices and regulations pose several important questions. First, under what circumstances do inclusionary policies benefit workers economically? Political representation is certainly correlated with a number of important social and macroeconomic indicators, such as the Human Development Index (or HDI) and the ILO's measure of income security. It is also inversely related to the Gini coefficient of income distribution, implying that it is associated with lower levels of inequality (ILO 2004: 273). These correlations, however, are based on data collected on new as well as established democracies, raising the possibility that voice representation is beneficial to workers mostly in established OECD democracies.[16]

Second, to what extent has labor market deregulation been direct, or policy-based, and to what extent has it been the unintended result of economic liberalization or lack of enforcement of existing laws and regulations? Labor market deregulation is sometimes direct, as when governments ease state regulation of collective and individual labor laws. Very often, however, deregulation takes indirect forms, as when governments fail to enforce existing labor regulations. Latin America in the 1980s and 1990s, for example, experienced a process of de facto deregulation that did not result from institutional changes (Itzigsohn 2000: 18).

This study sees the relationship between labor regimes and labor market regulations as being mutually constitutive. In so doing, it differs from other studies of labor politics in new democracies in at least two ways: it highlights the interplay between political incorporation and labor market regulation, and it questions rather than assumes the positive sum nature of this process. The corporatist literature assumes particular outcomes such as increased wage and consumption levels for workers, restraint on the prerogatives of employers, and state intervention favoring compensation (Ost 2000). Instead, I open for empirical examination the assumption that participation in policymaking is Pareto-optimal for workers and unions. In the following section, I present a theory that relates political incorporation and labor market regulation to the quality of industrial relations. I refer to this argument as the political economy of labor incorporation.

## The Political Economy of Labor Incorporation

Schmitter (1981) presented evidence from advanced industrialized democracies showing a strong negative correlation between corporatism and civil unrest. In his account, the glue that keeps labor, employers, and governments together is predominantly embodied in the formal institutions of social partnership. Corporatist institutions reduce labor conflict both because they represent a more consensual mode of policymaking and because social partnership results in better economic performance. This is particularly the case when, in the face of changing economic conditions, the economy needs to move from one equilibrium to another.

Economic benefits, however, also make workers more likely to cooperate. As Nollert (1995) observed, social partnership reduces conflict because it increases wages for workers, allowing employers and unions to forge class compromises. Labor market flexibility, however, can undercut wage gains since it reduces the bargaining power of workers. The level of regulation in the labor market should then be a crucial determinant of the ability of the social partners to come to mutually satisfactory agreements. Workers benefit the most when labor regulations are protective. When regulations are flexible, employers can more easily ignore unions (Buchanan 1995: 37). In this situation, workers cannot expect the highest possible level of disposable income (in the form of wages and other benefits). On the contrary, competitive pressures call for wage and employment flexibility as a way to control costs and increase competitiveness.

From the perspective of class compromises, however, bargaining strength cannot by itself explain variation in strike activity. As Oskarsoon (2003: 145) has observed, changes in the relative bargaining power of capital and labor resulting from the business cycle, or shifts in the organizational or political environment, should be reflected in wages, not strikes. Chapter 3 reveals, however, that it is precisely in those countries where workers receive the highest wages and benefits, in Western Europe, where the working class is also most militant. Why workers are more militant in circumstances where they enjoy more collective resources is then tied to the reality that social dialogue, not being properly institutionalized, fails to provide a coordinated solution in which social agents are able to impede the direct realization of the other's interests while refraining from imposing their own preferences unilaterally. When a flexible labor market results in lower compensation, therefore, some workers are more likely to pursue their goals unilaterally through industrial action. At the other end of the spectrum, in Eastern European new democracies, workers are in a weak position organizationally and politically. In this situation, unions cannot overcome their collective-action problem. Lacking political and economic power, they lose their ability to make economic demands or to press for regulatory and policy changes that would increase their bargaining power. Neocorporatist bargaining involving weak unions then raises the question why employers and governments should bother to negotiate at all. Why not simply ignore unions? One reason is that, as Crouch (2006: 53) has argued, if employers and governments have experienced or have reason to think that stable neo-corporatist relations can produce positive-sum outcomes, they may not want to foreclose that possibility for what may prove to be a temporary weakening of labor. Instead, employers may negotiate with trade unions, but not follow through on implementation, as the Eastern European experience demonstrates (Borisov and Clarke 2006: 628). On the labor side, unions may cooperate with employers and governments in a sporadic way, to avoid becoming even more irrelevant.[17]

Figure 1.2 illustrates a stylized model of corporatist policymaking in a country in which social dialogue is well institutionalized.

As the diagram demonstrates, social dialogue leads to the inclusion of organized labor into the political process. To be meaningful, however, political representation has to be accompanied by protective

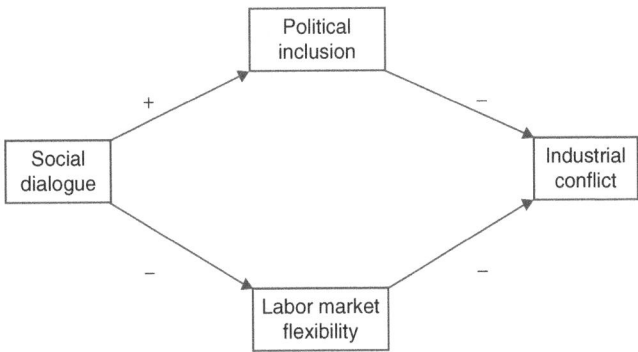

**Figure 1.2** Industrial Conflict as a Function of Social Dialogue

wage and employment regulations that render employers more constrained in their behavior. If unions are politically included, reducing the flexibility of labor regulations should then result in a decline in labor conflict. Conversely, labor regulations should increase the ability of trade unions to obtain favorable terms from employers and government representatives.

The problem with social dialogue in new democracies stems in some cases from labor's inability to fashion "social contracts." As chapters 3 and 4 make clear, labor is not in a position to engage in meaningful negotiations with employers and state representatives in some countries. Where workers are politically included and regulations are protective, on the other hand, the lack of institutionalization of corporatist policymaking presents an additional obstacle. Unions, employer organizations, and individual firms have an incentive to free ride on collective commitments or break away from their respective confederations. As a result, even where political incorporation is real, pacts among workers, employers, and the state may not necessarily foreclose the possibility of strikes by workers.

In asking then how well corporatism works in new democracies, this study sheds light on the challenge of consolidating inclusive and protective labor market institutions. Social partnerships have a tendency to break down. While corporatist institutions may lead to harmonious labor relations in some countries and/or periods of time, this cannot be assumed of all countries and time periods.

Labor protest frequently manifests itself in slowdowns, absenteeism, sabotage, demonstrations, riots, and factory occupations, in addition to strikes (Silver 2003: 35). All these events take place outside the routine parameters of conflict resolution in society. Since reliable cross-national datasets of non-strike forms of labor protest do not exist, students of industrial relations tend to focus primarily on strikes and lockouts. A *strike* is defined as a work stoppage by one or more groups of workers whereas a *lockout* refers to the temporary closure by employers of one or more firms. The International Labour Organization collects information on the number of strikes and lockouts in a given country and year, the number of workers involved in these events, and the number of days of work lost to strikes. I will return to this data in chapter 3 where I provide empirical tests of the effects of labor market regulations on wage costs and strike activity.

## Conclusion

With democratization, unions in most new democracies have pushed for political inclusion and meaningful participation in policymaking. This has manifested itself in the frequency with which they engage in consultations with employers and the state over economic and social policies. Once labor is incorporated in the policymaking process, the expectation is that workers will benefit materially from this inclusion. Few studies, however, have explicitly evaluated the extent to which political inclusion has benefited workers, particularly in light of the economic reforms many new democracies have experienced.[18]

To assess the extent to which political inclusion has benefited workers, this chapter has argued in favor of decoupling the nature of the political regime—politically inclusive or exclusive—from the level of regulation in the labor market. The following chapter undertakes a systematic evaluation of the extent of labor incorporation and labor market regulation in emerging Third Wave democracies. The question I ask is whether protective labor market regulations are indeed linked to effective political representation in this important group of countries. I leave for chapter 3 an evaluation of how the two shape the level of benefits workers receive.

## Chapter 2

# Democratization and Socioeconomic Security

In this chapter, I evaluate to what extent democracy has benefitted workers economically. A comparison of trends in monthly wages in autocracies, new democracies, and established democracies (1983 to 2003) reveals that levels of labor compensation in new democracies continue to lag behind levels of compensation in established democracies. The chapter then evaluates the extent of labor incorporation and labor market regulation in emerging democracies. This begins to shed light on why compensation has lagged or remains stagnant in some countries.

Economic security is positively associated with political freedom and democracy (ILO 2004). Along with processes of democratization and democratic inclusion, however, many new democracies have undergone sustained and sometimes forcefully imposed market liberalization.[1] Figures 2.1 and 2.2 illustrate what is at stake for organized interest groups and governments in new democracies. Consistent with the literature, the figures show that labor compensation increases in established democracies but stays flat in autocracies (Rodrik 1999). In many new democracies, however, levels of compensation do not seem to differ very much from those found in autocracies.

Figure 2.1 plots normalized average monthly wage rates from the Occupational Wages around the World (OWW) database (Freeman and Oostendorp 2005).[2] Keeping with standard practice, a country is considered a democracy the year in which it obtains a score of 6 or more in the Polity scale.[3] All country-year observations that correspond to countries with polity scores of less than 6 are classified as autocracies. Finally, all observations in which the authority of the

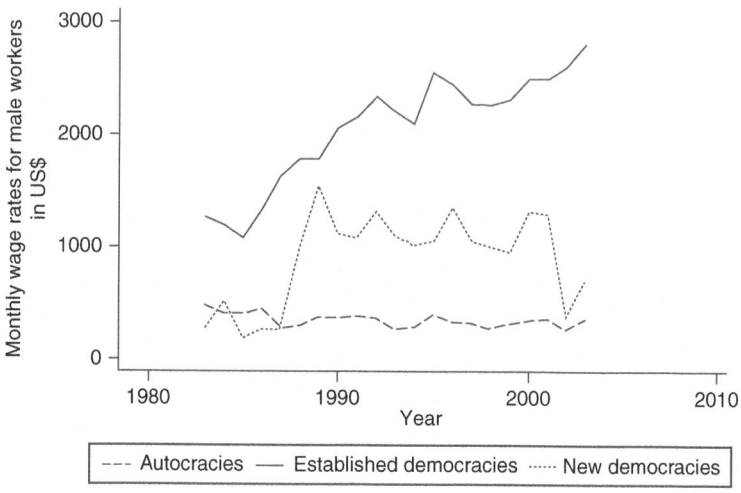

**Figure 2.1** Average Wage Rates in New and Established Democracies, and Autocracies, 1983–2003
*Source:* http://www.nber.org/oww/.

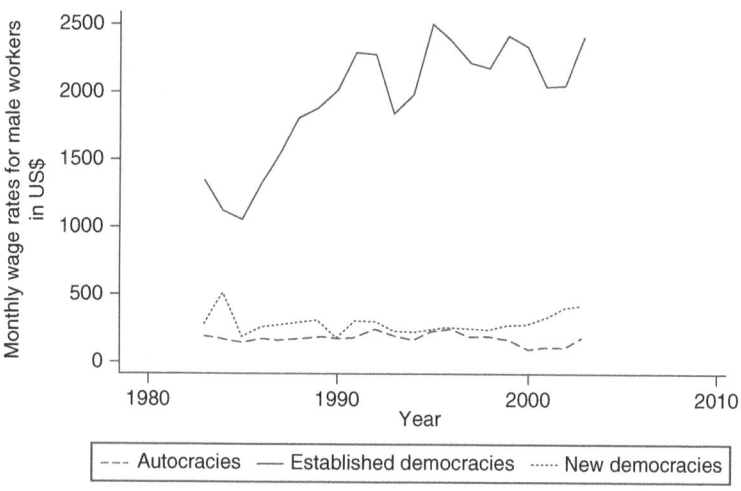

**Figure 2.2** Median Wage Rates in New and Established Democracies, and Autocracies, 1983–2003
*Source:* http://www.nber.org/oww/.

central government has collapsed due to a civil war, a protracted regime transition, or a military occupation have been excluded from the analysis.

The first group in the figure includes seventeen OECD established democracies typically grouped together in the comparative political economy literature: Australia, Austria, Belgium, Canada, Denmark, Finland, France, Germany, Ireland, Italy, Japan, the Netherlands, New Zealand, Norway, Sweden, the United Kingdom, and the United States. The second group includes observations from countries that became part of the Third Wave of democratization, that is, countries whose democratic transitions began on or after 1974, the year most commonly used as the beginning of this wave (Huntington 1991). Most of these countries were not democratic in 1983 and some subsequently reverted back to autocracy. Almost all, however, were democratic as of 2003.[4] These countries are: Argentina, Bolivia, Brazil, Bulgaria, Chile, Czechoslovakia (the Czech Republic after 1993), the Dominican Republic, Estonia, Honduras, Hungary, South Korea, Latvia, Lithuania, Mexico, Moldova, Nicaragua, Peru, the Philippines, Poland, Portugal, Romania, Russia, Slovakia, Slovenia, South Africa, Taiwan, Thailand, Turkey, the Ukraine, and Uruguay. The third group is reserved for autocratic country-year observations.

Figure 2.1 demonstrates that average monthly wages for male workers in new democracies remain below that of their OECD counterparts. In some new democracies, labor's share of national income increased after democratization. These gains, however, appear modest and most certainly reversible. In fact, these averages probably understate the nature of the problem, since the informal sector grew dramatically in many new democracies in the 1990s (ILO 2004) and female workers, who are disproportionately present in the informal sector, are omitted from these calculations.[5]

Admittedly, these calculations average over observations belonging to countries with different levels of development and, as such, they may not be very informative. Some important countries—such as Greece and Spain—are also not included in the series due to lack of data. Using averages, moreover, risks providing a misleading picture, since averages are disproportionately influenced by outliers. Plotting instead the median monthly wage rates in figure 2.2, a different picture emerges. Levels of labor compensation in new democracies do not seem to differ very much from those found in autocracies.

The figures above raise an important question: how can labor raise its share of national income in new democracies? Unions obtain higher wages and other benefits when they effectively negotiate with employers and the state. Some scholars note, however, that unions cannot secure favorable policies when they are organizationally weak and politically marginal. According to this view, the ability of unions to obtain benefits is a function of important attributes of the political system and society.

In this chapter, I first examine the conditions under which labor and capital come to mutually satisfactory agreements as posited in the literature. These agreements are a function of labor participation in policymaking, since union compliance with the need of national economic policy requires the conversion of industrial into political power, which unions can trade for a variety of favorable policies from the government. This characterization of the political relationship between trade unions and governments has been predominantly described by the notion of political exchange (Pizzorno 1978; Streeck and Kenworthy 2005). That is, in order for workers to engage in positive sum bargaining with employers, they have to wield extensive power over public policymaking.

I then propose an alternative explanation, namely, that existing studies of labor politics have neglected the role of labor market regulations. I hypothesize that a high level of regulation in the labor market is a prerequisite for lasting compromises in new democracies. I also provide preliminary evidence linking effective labor market regulation to political incorporation. Admittedly, the theories I review are merely descriptive at this stage and do not explicitly account for variation in patterns of labor conflict. I leave for chapters 3 and 4 an account of how they explicitly explain cross-national variation in the extent of labor militancy.

## Corporatism and Industrial Relations: Existing Arguments

Scholars of corporatism tend to emphasize "the co-ordinated, co-operative, and systematic management of the national economy by the state, centralised unions, and employers" (Siaroff 1999: 177). This emphasis on policy effectiveness in terms of macroeconomic performance necessarily implies specific patterns of behavior: from the government, an "active state involved at least moderately in the economy" (Siaroff 1999: 178), which facilitates bargained and/or voluntary income policies rather than state-imposed ones; from organized interest groups, a long term outlook that entails cooperation and coalescence and, consequently, low levels of strike activity. Particular institutions are thought to facilitate cooperation in the areas of labor market policy, macro-economic policy, and social welfare policy. Since corporatism is a multi-dimensional concept, different theories place their explanatory weight on particular institutions.

### Resource Mobilization Theories

Corporatism is said to work well when employers and labor federations enjoy monopoly of representation. Monopoly of representation minimizes coordination problems and facilitates formulation of a common bargaining strategy. Conversely, fragmented union and employer organizations decrease the ability of the two respective groups to behave strategically and speak with one voice.

The experience of established democracies demonstrates that when labor unions are encompassing, corporatist institutions facilitate a political exchange of moderation for economic rewards, a finding I have already alluded to. Employers have their own reasons to organize in groups that help overcome the limits to collective action (Swank and Martin 2001). When capitalists are organized in encompassing organizations, they are more willing to forgo maximum profits in the short term in exchange for more stability and predictability in the business climate.

But as important as monopoly of representation is for overcoming the collective action problem within and between the social partners, it also affects how the government relates to these groups. Monopoly of representation increases the weight of functional interests on the economy and hence the government's initiative to follow a pragmatic, responsive strategy to facilitate the inclusion of organized interests in policymaking. A single, encompassing union federation is not only more likely to uphold agreements but to also use its higher capacity to disrupt the normal functioning of the economy should the government fail to take union interests into account (Avdagic 2005: 42–43). The government also has incentives to take employers seriously, since the willingness of capitalists to invest is a prerequisite for low unemployment, low inflation, and high economic growth (Przeworski and Wallerstein 1986).

By contrast, where two or more national confederations exist, union centrals tend to compete for members, support from rank and file workers, control over financial flows, posts on public bodies, and other forms of state support and legitimation (Robertson 2004). Rivalry and hostility between unions not only increases coordination problems but also strengthens the government's position vis-à-vis organized labor. A high degree of interunion conflicts, in other words, can be used by the government as an excuse to minimize the role of organized labor in policymaking (Avdagic 2005). The government in such cases might either opt for weakening national corporatist structures, or it might attempt to use specific organizational or political issues to play unions off against each other, thus deepening their division and further reducing their role in policymaking.

Most advanced industrialized democracies fall into two distinct institutional clusters: "corporatist" or "pluralist" (Siaroff 1999: 176). This neat dichotomy, however, is unlikely to work well outside of the OECD zone, particularly with the spread of globalization. Consequently, while it is still possible to talk about corporatism as a distinct form of policymaking, it is important to open up the box of underlying structural attributes to empirical investigation.

### Partisan Theories

Alliances between political parties and interest associations have featured prominently in studies of labor relations under corporatism. The starting model proposed that parties on the left tend to draw their support overwhelmingly from the ranks of workers and unions. As a result, they devote their energies to advancing a redistributive, decommodifying agenda. Parties on the right represent more affluent classes and hence prefer to subject collective outcomes to the competitive pressures of the market (Hibbs 1977). Both formulas assume that governments choose policies congruent with their electoral needs and the desire to maintain economic competitiveness (Boix 2000; Hicks 1999; Rueda 2005).

The partisan approach is also useful in characterizing government policies and strategies in emerging democracies. In Eastern Europe, for example, establishment of corporatist institutions has been a consistent feature of left government strategies for economic transformation (Orenstein and Hale 2001: 260). Right-wing politicians, on the other hand, have tried to undermine corporatist institutions, accepting their role in society only after periods of massive social unrest (Ekiert and Kubik 1998, 1999). In Latin America, populist regimes also granted some inducements to organized labor, particularly in the formal sector.

Pro-labor rules and policies, however, have never been the exclusive domain of left-wing politicians, as South Korea and other countries with relatively rigid labor markets attest. In recent years, moreover, alliances between left parties and organized labor weakened in many new democracies (Burgess 1999, 2004). The limits of statist development and the rise of a neoliberal policy paradigm paved the way for the electoral rise of leaders committed to economic reforms opposed by their labor allies (Murillo 2000, 2001).

It is not entirely clear then what weight one should assign to partisan alignments and interest organizations in the globalizing context of the late twentieth century. Theories of corporatism, as we have seen, also assume that countries can be neatly divided between those where labor market institutions provide extensive protections to unions and workers, and those where these protections are minimal. Among emerging democracies, however, there may not be a strict connection between the structure of interest representation and the way the labor market is regulated. Consequently, I open to empirical analysis the relationship between labor participation in policymaking and labor market regulation.

### Political Inclusion and Labor Market Flexibility

Assessing labor's responses to economic and political reforms requires evaluating the flexibility/protection of labor market regulations. The problem with labor regulations in many emerging democracies is that they did not originate in the gradual expansion of the power resources of labor through the latter's incorporation into the polity. Quite the contrary, these regulations were the result of political opportunism and the diffusion of certain values about modern labor relations (Portes 1994). While labor codes look good on paper in many countries, enforcement is a different reality.

Fortunately, the ILO has created a global database of Socio-Economic Security (SES) that allows us to compare labor market regulations and policies cross-nationally while overcoming problems of data compatibility and use of different concepts/definitions (ILO 2004). Its main drawback, however, is that the data is only available for one year, 1999. As such, the SES database cannot be used to make rigorous causal claims. If a time has to be chosen to study a collection of countries, however, the late 1990s is probably the most preferable, since labor market policies and institutions do not change much from year to year. Many emerging democracies had by then begun to consolidate the economic and political reforms they had carried out earlier.

With those caveats in mind, I created a list of countries that democratized after 1974 and hence meet the criteria for being considered new democracies (Huntington 1991). I then looked for evidence in the SES of the existence of a formally recognized national board or council that is tripartite in character—that is, one that includes representatives of employers, trade unions, and government. These councils should have formal rules and procedures, and should have delegated authority or powers over a range of labor or social policy issues, in terms of consultation, cooperation, or negotiation over substantive issues. The first clear pattern to emerge in table 2.1 is that, like most of their counterparts in established democracies (Grote and Schmitter 2003, Hassel 2006: 19–20), almost all new democracies had established national tripartite boards or councils to deal with labor policies or issues.

Table 2.1 Presence of Tripartite Boards Dealing with Labor Issues or Policies

| Country | Tripartite Board | Country | Tripartite Board |
| --- | --- | --- | --- |
| Albania | Yes | Lithuania | Yes |
| Argentina | Yes | Mexico | Yes |
| Brazil | Yes | Moldova | Yes |
| Bulgaria | Yes | Panama | Yes |
| Chile | Yes | Philippines | Yes |
| Croatia | Yes | Portugal | Yes |
| Czech Republic | Yes | Romania | Yes |
| Ecuador | Yes | Russia | Yes |
| Estonia | Yes | Slovakia | No |
| Greece | Yes | South Africa | Yes |
| Honduras | No | Spain | Yes |
| Hungary | Yes | Thailand | Yes |
| Korea | Yes | Turkey | Yes |
| Latvia | Yes | Ukraine | Yes |

*Note*: The information above refers to the latest year for which data is available.

To what extent has this been beneficial for workers? The SES database identifies seven forms of security associated with work for ninety-nine countries (ILO 2004: 14). Three types of indicators—input, process, and outcome—are constructed for these forms, and indexes provided for these indicators (ILO 2004: 51). Input indicators assess the formal commitment of the state to socioeconomic security, leaving aside the question of whether this commitment is actually effective. Once again, this commitment would be established through a political process. The outcome indicator captures how much real socioeconomic security actually exists. Depending on their scores for each index, countries are then classified into four clusters: Pacesetters, Pragmatists, Conventionals, and Much-to-be-done. "Pacesetters" are the best performers, "Much-to-be-done" countries, the worst.

I will focus on two of the indexes contained in the SES database corresponding to two of the seven forms of economic security: representation security and employment security.[6] The Representation Security Index (RSI) measures the protection of collective voice in the labor market (ILO 2004: 14), and as such it can be taken as a measure of how effectively labor is included in the policymaking process. The second index, the Employment Protection Security Index (EPSI), takes into account policy commitments made by governments, existing institutions, or mechanisms designed to give effect to these policies, and actual levels of employment security (ILO 2004: 160–62).

Regarding the first index, RSI combines measures of bargaining scope, the percentage of those employed covered by collective agreements, the share of employees in total employment, information on unionization rates, the existence of laws allowing multiple unions and collective bargaining, the presence of a national tripartite council, and information on whether several international conventions on workers' rights have been ratified (ILO 2004: 269–70). As such, RSI is a measure of political representation as well as bargaining coordination.

Regarding the EPSI, employment security exists when there is protection against unfair and arbitrary dismissal, and when workers can obtain redress if they are subject to unfair dismissal. The strength of employment security is also a function of the type of economy and structure of employment, so that it tends to be stronger where large-scale firms predominate and where the public sector is large (ILO 2004: 160). While no particular regional pattern emerges with respect to the RSI, three West European countries—Portugal, Spain, and Greece—come out as "Pacesetters" with respect to the EPSI. These are the countries that launched the Third Wave of democratization and as such are the world's three oldest new democracies.

To return to the argument laid out in chapter 1, we can think about labor regimes and regulations as intersecting axes defining a two-dimensional space in which each country can be located. The advantage of using a two-dimensional space is that it is hard to distinguish in practice the flexibility or protection of the wage regulatory regime from the level of voice representation. The RSI, as we have seen, combines these two dimensions in ways that make a strict separation of the two impractical.

The RSI, while containing information on the presence of a tripartite labor council, does not provide information on whether these councils include all relevant labor confederations. Nevertheless, it is as close as we come to capturing the distinction between inclusionary and exclusionary labor market regimes. For our purposes, it is important to know not just what inducements and protections the government formally grants, but whether they actually empower workers. Consequently, from the three indicators provided for RSI and EPSI (input, process, and outcome), we are interested in how the outcome indicators relate to one another.

While the process indicators provide mechanisms for strengthening voice,[7] outcome RSI measures how effective that voice is likely to be. Accordingly, the unionization rate and the presence of various freedoms, such as the right to organize and strike, comprise the outcome RSI. The unionization rate is the percentage of the workforce belonging to trade unions, and for many developing countries this rate has been estimated by the ILO. The figures have been adjusted using the percentage of the workforce who are wage earners and those on salaried employment (ILO 2004: 270). For the EPSI, the outcome measure assesses the presence of full-time, wage or salaried employment associated with rights and benefits. If employment is insecure, it is primarily part-time or temporary, or included in activities covered by the term "self-employment." Figure 2.3 plots this two-dimensional space, introduced in figure 1.1, with the position of each country overlaid on the two-by-two grid.

The distribution of the data is consistent with theories of labor politics and industrial relations—in particular the power resources approach—which sees labor as stronger politically when it is also

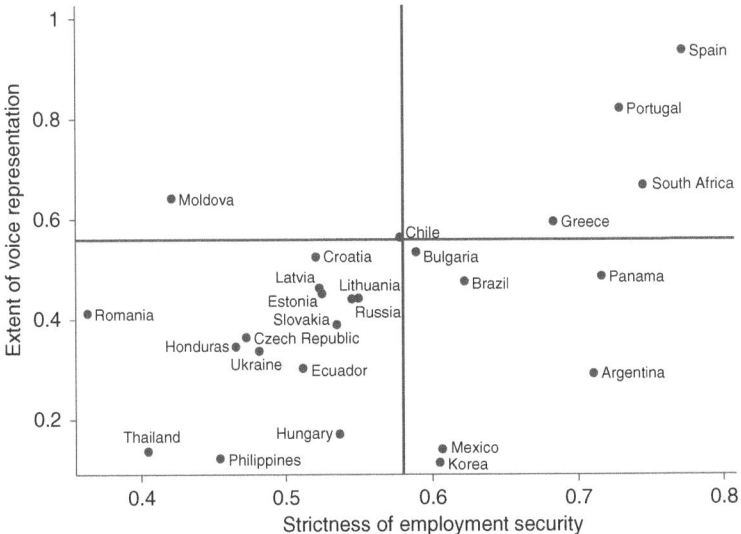

**Figure 2.3** Outcome RSI and EPSI by Country

strong in society (Korpi and Shalev 1979, 1980; Esping-Andersen 1990). The reader may note that, compared to the other three quadrants, the upper left quadrant is sparsely occupied. This quadrant corresponds to countries where labor should be influential politically but labor market regulations are flexible. In reality, however, this is rarely the case. The stricter the regulation of the employment process for a particular country, the higher the degree of collective voice its workers appear to enjoy. Conversely, the more flexible the employment regulatory regime, the more difficult it should be for unions to voice their demands and participate in the policymaking process alongside employers and the state. This simple relationship can be expressed as follows,

$$\text{RSIoutcome}_i = \text{EPSIoutcome}_i + e_i$$

where the outcome RSI for country $i$ is a function of its outcome EPSI and other factors that have been excluded.

Having a panel of countries observed over multiple years would allow us to formulate a more complicated model; this relationship, however, is highly significant ($p < 0.01$) statistically and explains one quarter of the variation in the extent of voice representation.[8] The slope of the relationship can be expressed graphically in figure 2.4, with the position of each country overlaid on the two-by-two grid introduced in figure 2.3. As the figure reveals, there seems to be a clear pattern linking protective labor market regulatory regimes to the ability of labor unions to make demands and have their voice heard in the political arena. The logic behind this relationship can be expressed as follows: when employment is stable, it is easier for workers to unionize. The presence of unions in workplaces contributes to higher wages, more benefits, a narrower wage differential, and a reduced likelihood of non-compensated layoffs and redundancies (ILO 2004: 258).

As unions grow in strength at the firm level, they also increase in strength at the national level. If corporatism is well institutionalized, strong unions should be associated with harmonious industrial relations, the reason being that as unions increase in size and power, their preferences change, making the struggle for marginal wage increases no longer rational (Olson 1982). Similarly, as the size of the labor supply under union control increases, firms' willingness to engage in conflict with workers falls (Western 1997: 3). Poorly institutionalized

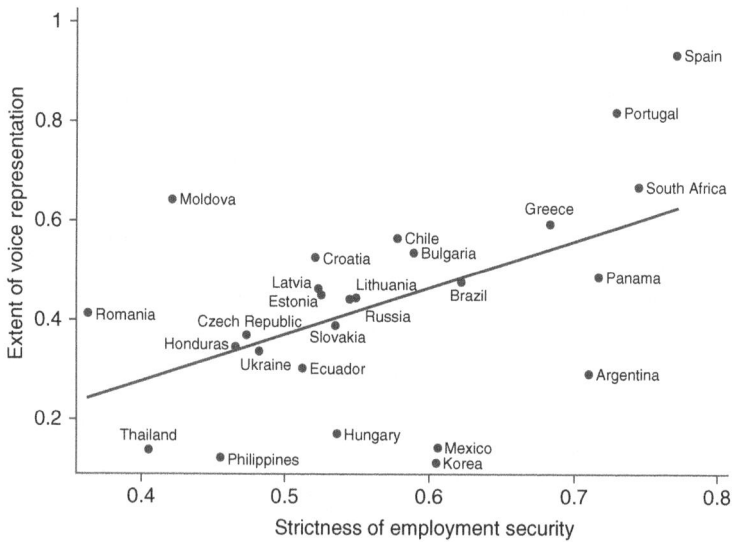

**Figure 2.4** Voice Representation as a Function of Employment Protection

corporatist bargains, however, break down when individual unions and firms defect from pacts forged at the national level by their respective confederations. Defection can lead to strikes, which can be isolated, as in the case of wildcat strikes, or coordinated by union centrals.[9]

It would also help if the SES database contained information on employer associations and their organizations. Unfortunately, this data has not been systematically collected. This omission is also characteristic of the corporatism literature, which tends to pay far more attention to the labor side of the equation (Swank and Martin 2001). I do not wish to imply that labor poses the biggest problem for institutional consolidation. It can be assumed, however, that whenever unions are politically incorporated, so are employer associations, and of the two, labor is the weaker partner and, consequently, the one most likely to be in need of political representation.

The reader may object that the relationship displayed in figure 2.4 could well reflect the effect of economic development on both labor market regulations and voice representation. Formal regulations are not significantly associated with the level of development, although a high level of development is associated with favorable job attributes such as high wages and short working hours (Flanagan 2006: 148). If economic development is indeed responsible for both, moreover, the discrepancy between formal and observed levels of voice representation and employment regulation would be small. When overall RSI and EPSI are plotted against one another in figure 2.5, however, no significant relationship between the two emerges. As the graph clearly shows, countries with high levels of development (e.g., Portugal and Spain) lie on opposite sides of the line capturing the slope of the relationship between these two variables. Countries with low levels of development (e.g., Honduras and Thailand) also lie on opposite sides of the line. What figure 2.5 demonstrates then is that actual levels of employment security, not formal levels of employment regulation, give rise to the *observed* relationship between labor market regulation and voice representation.

Another possibility worth exploring is that income inequality exerts a systematic effect on labor market outcomes. It is entirely plausible that labor market regulations and the patterns of representation they give rise to are both products of the underlying distribution of income and assets in society. In countries where employers enjoy much higher incomes than workers, for example, there may be little societal support

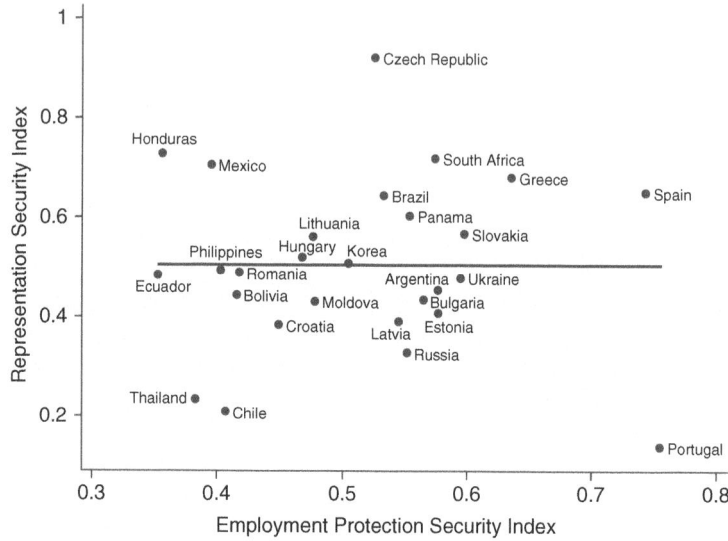

**Figure 2.5** Overall Voice Representation as a Function of Overall Employment Protection

for high levels of redistribution. Conversely, in countries with relatively equal income distributions, there may be broad public support for programs that guarantee a certain level of income and work-related benefits to workers. Figure 2.6 plots outcome voice representation as a function of the gini coefficient, showing again no systematic relationship between the two.

Finally, it is important to consider the possibility of reverse causality. It is conceivable that stronger labor movements are better positioned to obtain more favorable regulations. While unions used their strength and numbers to demand a gradual expansion of rights and benefits in established democracies (Collier 1999), labor market protections in new democracies, if they existed at the onset of democratization, were introduced in a top-down fashion as inducements to win the cooperation of pivotal labor groups (Collier and Collier 1979). Most Latin American countries, for example, initiated and extended pro-labor regulations much earlier in the development process than OECD countries (Flanagan 2006: 154). As a result, collective

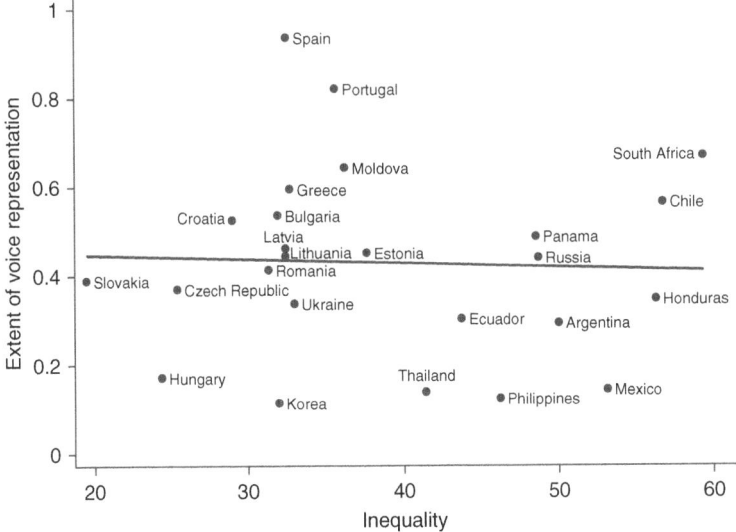

Figure 2.6  Outcome Voice Representation as a Function of Income Inequality

voice is more likely to follow stronger regulation of the labor market in emerging democracies than the other way around.

## Conclusion

The chapter has documented a trend that is at once puzzling and a matter of concern, namely, the failure of wages to grow appreciably in new democracies, especially in contrast to wage trends in established democracies. To be sure, democracy does seem to have increased wages for some workers in some countries, but more than three decades after the Third Wave began, these gains seem modest at best. A number of factors, including flexible or ineffective labor regulations and low or ineffective political representation, could explain these trends. Studies have revealed, for example, that workers in Eastern Europe and Latin America gained little economically in the aftermath of democratization (Greskovits 1998; Kurtz 2004b: 287–99).

This chapter has begun to relate employment security to the economic gains associated with democracy. The analysis demonstrated a systematic relationship between labor market regulation and voice representation in this group of countries. The relationship is more systematically elaborated in the next two chapters. Chapter 3 explains how labor market regulation shapes wage compensation in new democracies and, in so doing, shows how labor conflict varies cross-nationally. In chapter 4 I ask whether those factors that result in conflict also explain the frequency and extent of labor agreements in this important group of countries.

# Chapter 3

# Labor Market Regulation and Industrial Conflict: An Empirical Baseline

Chapter 1 introduced a theory of industrial relations in new democracies that drew on two main factors—the extent of labor participation in economic and social policymaking, and the level of protection afforded by labor market institutions. Industrial cooperation referred primarily to bipartite and tripartite accords on wages and other benefits, and industrial conflict, to strike activity. In this chapter, I demonstrate empirically that employment and wage flexibility lead to decreases in compensation for workers *and* more industrial conflict in new democracies (in the case of wage flexibility). In so doing, the analysis establishes a firm empirical baseline behind these associations.

Strikes are simultaneously an economic weapon and a response to the political environment (Hibbs 1987). The experience of established democracies suggests that corporatist institutions facilitate a political exchange of moderation for economic rewards. The reader may recall that one of the rationales for the existence of these institutions is that they help moderate wage costs. This is certainly in the interest of employers and governments, particularly during inflationary or recessionary periods. Under a favorable political and institutional environment, workers may follow the path of moderation even if they can maximize wage increases and other benefits.

One would expect workers then to stage few strikes when wages increase by modest amounts. In advanced industrialized democracies where corporatist policymaking is institutionalized, labor quiescence went hand in hand with relatively modest increases in earnings. This chapter reveals however, that modest wage increases are generally linked to more labor militancy in new democracies even when wages are subject to negotiations among worker, employer, and state representatives. The analysis I conduct is able to establish these relationships net of the other resources available to workers, such as the level of economic development and the numerical strength of the labor force.

By studying wage moderation, we thus get a better sense of what factors affect the ability of employers, workers, and the government to arrive at compromises. These agreements are not explicitly included in the models I present but are the subject of the analysis in chapter 4. What I wish to examine here is the proposition that labor market flexibility shifts the balance of power and resources from workers to employers, undercutting the ability of unions to enforce class compromises and consequently resulting in more labor conflict.

My contention is not that low levels of regulation are sufficient to foreclose class compromises. Instead, I argue that the more flexible the labor market, the lower the likelihood of a pact holding, even if a compromise is agreed to in the first place. In eighteen of the twenty countries selected, the national minimum wage rates are set by the government or a tripartite body.[1] To the extent the countries in the analysis share this commonality, the sample of country observations provides some confidence in the results. When combined with other pieces of evidence provided throughout the book, the findings largely converge in the hypothesized direction.

The analysis that follows should then be taken as a partial test of the argument laid out in chapter 1 about the relationship between political inclusion and labor market regulation. Corporatism, as we have seen, is a multidimensional concept. Scholars have had difficulty capturing all its relevant dimensions empirically. This is particularly true in the countries I examine. Consequently, the models tested assess the effect of levels of wage and employment regulation, and changes in these levels, on wage costs and strike activity. To some extent, labor regulations are determined endogenously by the political process, as the case studies in chapters 4 and 5 demonstrate. Since these regulations do not change very much from year to year, however, the arguments I make and the tests I provide take levels of labor market regulation as exogenous and evaluate their effects on labor relations.

The chapter proceeds as follows. First, I review the links drawn in the literature between labor market institutions and labor conflict. Second, I consider mechanisms linking wage costs in new democracies to industrial conflict. In section three, evidence of the relationship between wage costs and industrial conflict is presented.

## Labor Market Institutions and Industrial Relations: Existing Measures

Generally speaking, the literature has not agreed on how best to operationalize the concept of corporatism. The International Labour Organization itself defines social dialogue broadly, reflecting the wide range of processes and practices found in different countries. Its working definition includes negotiation, consultation, or simply exchange of information between representatives of governments, employers, and workers on matters of common interest (Ishikawa 2003: 3).

As a result, scholars have created measures that reflect the various mechanisms thought to affect workers' bargaining power and political voice. One of the first indicators of corporatism, Schmitter's index of "societal corporatism," coded labor organizations based on the number of national labor confederations, the presence or absence of stable factions within these confederations, and the presence or absence of separate organizations for manual and nonmanual workers. In addition to associational monopoly, Schmitter provided a measure of union centralization, assessed as the ability of labor confederations to engage in collective bargaining, provide strike funds, maintain a staff, and collect dues from members (Schmitter 1981: 294).

Cameron's (1984) index of corporatism considered three additional institutional aspects of the labor movement: union density, institutions for worker participation in decision-making on the plant floor and on company boards, and the scope of collective bargaining. The latter was measured on a seven-point scale ranging from company-level bargaining to industry- and nationwide agreements (Cameron 1984: 164). While Schmitter (1981) and Cameron (1984) did not provide information on the scope of employer associations, Swank and Martin (2001) constructed measures of the centralization and cohesion of employer associations and the extent of enterprise economic cooperation. Their study was the first to operationalize corporatism as a bundle of institutions including employer and worker organizations and the formal level of collective bargaining.

More recent indicators have assessed the extent of government involvement in the wage setting process (Wallerstein, Golden, and Lange 1997). In general, a high degree of government intervention in the wage setting process should contribute to wage bargaining coordination, since governments foster organizational structures of wage bargaining that are conducive to centralization (Hassel 2006: 83). According to Kenworthy (2001: 70), if the outcome to be explained is wage restraint, government involvement in wage setting is theoretically preferable to indicators of bargaining centralization or coordination. Government intervention in wage matters is usually aimed at encouraging or mandating this restraint.

Turning now to developing countries, McGuire (1999: 10–12) constructed a Labor Strength Index (LSI) for sixteen Latin American and East Asian countries using data from the ILO (1997). He included four dimensions in his index: (1) union members as a proportion of the nonagricultural labor force; (2) the proportion of formal-sector workers covered by collective contracts; (3) the dominant level of collective bargaining (national/sectoral, company/plant, or both); and (4) the number of major ILO conventions ratified. Because of data limitations, however, the LSI is only available for the mid 1990s.

In all these efforts, one can detect Olson's (1965) framework for understanding the political and economic consequences of group organization. Since gathering data on all relevant dimensions of corporatism can be very daunting, many scholars rely instead on unionization rates. As we saw in chapter 2, actual voice representation is best exemplified by this measure. While unionization rates do not provide direct evidence of the existence of corporatist institutions, they are typically good proxies of labor's ability to bargain with employers and the government on an equal footing. That is, high densities are typically found in countries where interest associations are also highly encompassing. One problem with high density rates is that they tend to increase wage pressure. Greater encompassiveness, however, partially compensates for this pressure by exerting a moderating effect on wages (Ebbinghaus and Kittel 2005).

Standardized datasets of unionization rates do not exist for new democracies. Another difficulty with these measures is the legacy of state corporatism—involuntary or compulsory union membership resulting in inflated unionization rates (Rudra 2002: 425, Cook

2007: 21).[2] Consequently, I rely on Rudra's potential labor power (or PLP) indicator. PLP captures the capacity of workers to form centralized, powerful labor organizations that are able, in turn, to form alliances with other interest groups, as well as more effectively negotiate with government and business representatives (Rudra 2008: 33). It is calculated as the ratio of the numbers employed in skill-intensive manufacturing industries relative to numbers employed in low-skill manufacturing industries divided by surplus laborers in the economy.

PLP is inspired by the observation that the bargaining potential of labor is likely to increase with the ratio of skilled to unskilled workers, and to decrease with the size of the surplus labor population (Esping-Andersen 1990, Silver 2003). The political mechanism behind this can be briefly sketched out. Lower levels of surplus labor reduce the asymmetry between the organizational power of wage earners and those whose primary source of income is capital. Moreover, because low-skilled workers are notoriously difficult to organize, larger unions generally include both white- and blue-collar workers. High ratios of skilled workers relative to low-skilled workers reduce returns to skill (Carbonaro 2006: 1821), allowing unions to speak with one voice. I further infer that if different sectors of the labor movement can speak with one voice, labor is in a better position to monitor its own behavior and moderate its demands.[3] As a result, I expect this measure of marketplace bargaining power to be associated with wage and strike moderation.

Rudra's PLP can be compared to unionization rates for 1997, a year for which twenty-six emerging-democracy observations are available (Botero et al. 2004). The correlation coefficient between these two variables is 0.46, indicating that unionization rates are not the most valid measures of labor's marketplace bargaining power in new democracies. Rudra's PLP, however, shows a fairly strong correlation (0.61) with James McGuire's (1999) labor strength index (LSI), the only other cross-national index of labor power available for developing countries.

With respect to partisan factors, political accounts emphasize the strength of the left in the political arena. The gist of this argument is that only when labor-oriented parties have acquired stable and lasting control of governments does the incidence of strikes decline. Partisan accounts suggest that countries governed by socialist, social-democratic, and more generally leftist parties feature extensive labor market regulations (Botero 2004). Conservative parties, on the other hand, favor allowing the market to determine the most efficient equilibrium between labor supply and demand (Hicks 1999).

Another important effect of government partisanship is on macroeconomic performance. Cameron (1984: 161) claims that left governments allied with organized labor gave social democracy its comparatively better macroeconomic performance. Between 1965 and 1982, advanced industrialized democracies in which leftist parties most frequently and most extensively controlled government tended to experience labor quiescence and acceptance of relatively modest increases in earnings. Nations dominated by non-leftist parties, on the other hand, were prone to experience labor militancy and large increases in earnings despite relatively high levels of unemployment. Others suggest, however, that conservative governments are just as capable of moderating wages in the presence of decentralized wage bargaining (Alvarez, Garrett, and Lange 1991; Garrett 1998; Garrett and Lange 1985, 1989).[4]

Turning our attention now to resource mobilization factors, these theories emphasize union competition: unions will be more militant when a number of unions compete with each other for members and resources. One version posits an inverse monotonic relationship between the strength of organized labor and worker militancy (Hibbs 1977; Cameron 1984; Esping-Andersen 1990). Other models of strike activity envision the relationship between union centralization and strikes as curvilinear, that is, countries with strong or weak labor will have low levels of strike activity and countries with intermediate strength will have high levels of strike activity (Tsebelis and Lange 1995: 116; Calmfors and Driffill 1988).[5]

Rudra's PLP indicator, as we have seen, explains how labor market conditions affect labor's ability to coordinate its behavior and make demands from employers and the government. Rudra (2005: 30) claims that labor in low- and middle-income LDCs is not necessarily in a better bargaining position despite certain economic gains. In contrast, labor in high-income countries enjoys both greater economic benefits and an improved bargaining position. This relationship between labor power and gains reduces then to the effect of economic development on labor's ability to coordinate its behavior and bargain with employers and the government. As a result, I use a linear rather than a curvilinear specification for this variable.

## Data and Measurements

Many workers in new democracies do not take part in collective bargaining (Rudra 2002). Employers are also poorly organized and fundamentally heterogeneous (ILO 1997: 145). Collective rights and the enforcement of a minimum wage law, moreover, cannot by themselves guarantee unions a level playing field with national and international capital. Union wage premiums, for example, are small in some countries.[6] As a result, workers may not be receiving the wages and social benefits they expect. This, I hypothesize, may prompt some workers to probe how much employers and the government can afford in wages and other benefits. Workers who choose the strike, however, opt for militancy at the expense of workers in the informal sector who may not be able to act collectively.

Furthermore, to the extent cohesive and independent interest organizations are deemed necessary for corporatist political exchanges, workers and employers in some countries may not be in a position to engage in long-term social cooperation on a voluntary basis. As a result, it is important to ask if labor regulations strengthen labor's position in wage negotiations. As argued in chapter 1, bargaining decentralization has deprived some unions of the possibility to fulfill their most basic aim—to function as a bargaining cartel (Oskarsson 2003: 40). Given the institutional asymmetries just described, labor market flexibility, especially if accompanied by a weakening of alliances between left parties and organized labor, may decrease the ability of workers, employers, and governments to reach mutually satisfactory compromises.

As chapter 2 indicated, no longitudinal measure of voice representation exists for new democracies. As an alternative, I could use the Representation Security Index (RSI) for 1999 and assume it hasn't changed during the period under examination. This, however, would create two problems that would severely bias the ensuing analysis. The first problem results from the fact, already alluded to in chapter 2, that the RSI is simultaneously an indicator of wage regulation and political representation. The second problem occurs when a measure that is time-invariant is included in a multivariate analysis where units are observed at multiple points in time.

Since the indexes contained in the Socio-Economic Security (SES) database are not longitudinal, I rely on two indicators from the Economist Intelligence Unit (EIU) Market Indicators and Forecasts database. I will first attempt to establish the validity of the EIU indicators with respect to the SES indexes. The indicator of wage regulation used is the "Extent of Wage Regulation." The measure reflects how effectively the government determines the prevailing wage rate. Accordingly, 1 denotes a situation in which governments set the wage rate and 5 its opposite, when wages are determined exclusively by supply and demand. This indicator will be compared to the RSI introduced in chapter 2.

The indicator used for employment regulation, "Restrictiveness of Labor Laws," reflects the regulatory environment for hiring and firing workers. This measure is coded on a 1 to 5 ordinal scale, where 5 denotes a total absence of protection and 1 denotes a situation in which it is very difficult for employers to lay off workers or hire new ones. I compare this indicator with the EPSI introduced in chapter 2. Other datasets provide indexes of employment regulations and their associated costs (Botero et al. 2004; OECD 2004: 117; Pagés 2004). None of them, however, have yearly information on a sufficient number of countries, making them inappropriate for pooled cross-sectional time series analysis.

A comparison between the EIU's "Restrictiveness of Labor Laws" measure and the EPSI reveals that most countries are similarly ranked in both datasets. Countries labeled "Pacesetters" in the SES database—Portugal, Spain, and Greece—have high EIU employment regulation scores. In the EIU dataset, Argentina, Greece, Korea, Portugal, and South Africa (for five years) have employment regulation scores of 2, while Bulgaria, Mexico, and Spain have scores of 3. Chile and the Philippines have low EPSIs and are thus included in the "Much-to-be-done" cluster. Similarly, the EIU gives them a score of 4 for most years. The average EIU scores for the remaining countries, which belong to the category of "Conventionals," is 3.2. A few discrepancies notwithstanding, the EIU and the SES databases substantively agree on the classification of a majority of countries.[7]

Turning to the second indicator, a comparison of the RSI and the "Extent of wage regulation" measure reveals less congruence. Most countries have EIU scores of 3 and 4. Yet four countries—Bulgaria, Portugal, South Africa, and Spain—are classified as "Pacesetters" in the SES database (ILO 2004: 272). Only South Africa and Ukraine (for the last five years in the series) have scores of 2. There is, however, an important difference between these measures. High regulation in the EIU dataset refers to high levels of government involvement in the collective bargaining process, enforcement of a strict minimum wage, and extension of collective agreements to third parties, which are among the other provisions that make wages more rigid. The RSI, the reader may recall from chapter 2, also taps into the rigidity/flexibility of the wage setting environment. The index, however, is not just a measure of the regulation of the wage setting process, it is also a measure of its centralization/coordination. Nevertheless, some similarities emerge when one compares the RSI and the "Extent of wage regulation" measure. South Africa, for example, is the only country with an EIU score of 2 for more than five consecutive years. In the SES database, it is also classified as a "Pacesetter" (ILO 2004: 249).

Another way to illustrate the suitability of the EIU wage regulation measure is by looking at cross-national differences in wage costs. The average monthly wage for an unskilled production worker in South Africa in 2002 was US$240, which was 45 percent higher than in Brazil, a country with a wage regulation score of 4. For the same year, the average monthly wage for a manager was US$1,850, twice as high as in Poland (which has a wage regulation score of 3), and three times as high as in Brazil (US$450).[8] In general, labor demand appears to be more responsive to labor cost changes in less developed countries (Heckman and Pagés 2004). Real wages in the developing world, particularly those in Latin America and Asia, tend to be far more flexible than generally assumed.[9]

Since the EIU indicators are available from 1994, the analysis conducted here begins in that year. To the extent that there are changes in wage regulation, they tend to be in the direction of less regulation. Employment regulation exhibits more variation over time. No country, however, exhibits the minimum or maximum value on either variable.

While the analysis is designed to avoid sample selection bias, I control for factors that are likely to differentiate countries systematically, such as their level of economic development or durability as a democratic regime. To be included in the analysis, a country had to have an overall Polity score equal to or greater than 6 for a particular year and should have begun its transition to democracy on or after 1974. Keeping with standard practice, observations belonging to countries that reverted to authoritarianism or partial democracy were not included.[10]

Finally, to account for region-specific patterns of labor mobilization, I consider introducing indicator variables for each of the regions. I opted not to include these indicators in the regression models since the within-country variance of each of these variables is 0, that is, these variables are completely time-invariant and this creates a problem in models with country indicator variables (or fixed effects). I now proceed to the analysis of labor market institutions and wage costs.

## Labor Market Institutions and Labor Costs

To illustrate the mechanisms linking labor market regulation to industrial conflict, I first analyze trends in wage costs (overall unit labor costs). Lower levels of labor market regulation, my analysis shows, decrease wage costs in new democracies. Since the dependent variable in this first part of the analysis is defined as the percentage change in the cost of producing one unit of output over the previous year with respect to the average monthly wage, I can ask whether factors that affect wage compensation are also responsible for cross-national differences in the frequency of labor protest. The following section provides a brief description of the variables used in the analysis. (See Appendix 3A for sources and definitions).

### Executive Partisanship

The partisanship of the chief executive, which can refer to the president or prime minister, captures the claim that left-wing governing institutions reduce strike activity while conservative governments amplify it.[11] The partisanship of the chief executive is coded categorically as Right, Center, Left, and Nonpartisan.[12] Following standard practice in models with categorical variables, the coefficients for Right, Center, and Left governments are interpreted with respect to the baseline category, Nonpartisan governments.

### Polarization

Polarization is a measure of the ideological distance between the executive and the legislature. In countries where the chief executive and her party have ties to organized labor but the president's party does not control the legislature, labor market reforms have not enjoyed broad support.[13] In addition, neo-corporatist concertation has proved unsuccessful if labor-based parties constitute the bulk of the parliamentary opposition.[14] In these situations, moderation on the part of the labor movement is not easily forthcoming. I expect the probability of industrial conflict then to increase with the degree of executive-legislative polarization, which varies from a low of 0 to a high of 4 (Keefer and Stasavage 2003).

### Potential Labor Power

PLP increases as the number of low-skilled workers decreases relative to skilled workers, and as surplus labor declines (Rudra 2002: 426). Ceteris paribus, a higher PLP is expected to result in wage moderation and a lower volume of strikes. Since Rudra's indicator is not available after 1997, I calculated PLP scores for all the countries and years covered in the analysis. The resulting PLP measure was then checked against Rudra's PLP indicator for those years and countries available, yielding a high correlation.

### Wage Deregulation

This variable, originally called "Extent of Wage Regulation" (see above), was renamed to more accurately capture the reality that, as its value increases, governments are progressively less involved and affect a smaller share of the economy. At a score of 5, there are no wage controls or enforced minimum wages; the latter are determined by market forces. A score of 3 marks a situation in which the government exerts some controls, including a strict minimum wage law. At 1, there are extensive wage controls and government influence is extensive. Higher levels of wage deregulation should be associated with decreases in wage costs and more participation in strikes.

### Employment Deregulation

I have also chosen to rename this variable to more accurately capture the idea that, as its value increases, governments and unions have less say in how employers utilize their workforce. Score 5 marks a situation in which there are no controls on hiring and firing workers, and score 1 marks the opposite. Since employment deregulation increases the reserve labor pool, higher levels should be associated with decreases in wage costs and less participation in strikes.

### Inflation

Inflation is expected to erode real wages and hence result in lower wage costs. Since inflation erodes the consumer purchasing power of daily necessities, it can be associated with more or less labor conflict depending on workers' ability to pursue collective action.

### Unemployment and GDP Growth

A tight labor market improves the status of unions as a labor price-setter by maximizing wage increases without sacrificing job security. Conversely, strikes are said to be more difficult in conditions of economic downturn and high unemployment, since unemployment weakens a union's ability to determine wages due to a rich pool of reserve labor (Korpi 1974: 1577).[15]

### Foreign Direct Investment (FDI)

Many Third Wave democracies depend crucially on trade and investment links with other countries. Consequently, they feature social pacts that combine wage restraint in exchange for some welfare programs and economic policies designed to control inflation and encourage investment (Przeworski 1991). Foreign direct investment, however, appears to increase the wage premium of skilled workers (Rama 2003: 164). Consequently, FDI may be associated with higher wages and lower labor conflict in industries benefitting from FDI, but not necessarily all industries.

### Polity Durability

The longer a country has been democratic, the longer its employer and worker organizations have had to learn the habits of institutionalized cooperation (Bresser Pereira et al. 1993). At the same time, democracy increases labor's share of the economic pie. Consequently, the earlier the transition to democracy, the lower I expect the number of strikes to be. Wage costs, however, should increase with each additional year a country has been democratic.

### Labor Productivity

A high level of development is associated with favorable job attributes such as high wages and short working hours. The association is mostly due to the fact that cross-country variations in manufacturing labor productivity and price levels account for more than 90 percent of the variation in manufacturing labor compensation (Flanagan

2006: 37–38). Consequently, it is important to control for the underlying level of wages in a country, which is primarily determined by the productivity of the workforce. That way we can assess the net effect of other variables on changes in wage levels from one year to the next. Labor productivity is calculated as Gross Domestic Product (GDP) per person employed.

### Trade Openness

Economic openness refers to the volume of imports and exports transacted in a given year as a share of GDP. This variable controls for the corollary that "corporatist institutions develop in small countries with strong national labor markets and highly open economies" (Western 1991: 283). Smaller nations have more circumscribed room for maneuver in the field of labor relations due to their location in the world economy (Katzenstein 1985). They are more vulnerable to international market trends, which in turn affects their macroeconomic performance. Since predictability and competitiveness are a must in countries with high levels of economic integration, I expect openness to be associated with wage and strike moderation.

### Labor Force

Finally, I control for the size of the labor force in each country since it is entirely possible that countries with larger number of workers have more strikes.

### Pooled Cross-sectional Time Series Analysis

For panel data, the most intuitive modeling approach is to assume the presence of country-specific sources of heterogeneity in the data. Two estimators, fixed effects and random effects, result in different parameterizations of these variables.[16] Fixed effects allow country indicator variables to be correlated with regressors. To the extent that they account exclusively for within-cluster effects, they provide estimates of *changes* in the levels of the independent variables (Plümper and Troeger 2005: 332–33). Fixed effects, however, cannot precisely estimate time-invariant or rarely changing explanatory variables because these variables are highly or perfectly correlated with the country level effect (Wooldridge 2002). The random-effects specification, on the other hand, assumes that country-specific effects are uncorrelated with regressors. This is clearly not satisfactory in many research situations involving "sticky" institutional variables.[17]

Until recently, scholars in comparative political economy had few readily available alternatives. A recent alternative, dubbed fixed-effects vector decomposition, gives unbiased estimates of the time-varying variables, but biased estimates of the time-invariant variables unless the time-invariant variables are uncorrelated with the country-specific effects (Plümper and Troeger 2007). In small samples, however, fixed-effects vector decomposition outperforms its competitors (Plümper and Troeger 2005: 27). The other benefit of using this method is that it allows researchers to interpret regression coefficients as reflecting differences in the effect of *levels* of the independent variables on the dependent variable. Since the dependent variable reflects *changes* in wage costs from one year to the next, this preliminary analysis illustrates then how changes in wage costs can be attributed to differences in levels of labor market regulation.

Before proceeding with the analysis, I calculated the ratio of between to within variance for all explanatory variables. I determined that employment deregulation, wage deregulation, polity durability, labor productivity, economic openness, and the size of the labor force should be treated as rarely changing variables.[18] To facilitate comparison, I also standardized all the variables except the binary indicators of government partisanship. This allows the reader to directly compare the magnitude of their effects. Table 3.1 reports results from three different regression specifications: fixed effects (FE), random effects (RE), and fixed-effects vector decomposition (FEVD).[19]

The coefficient of codetermination ($R^2$), which is 0.83 for the FE and the FEVD models, indicates that a great deal of variation in the dependent variable is accounted for. The FEVD estimates, moreover, reveal several advantages over pure fixed effects and random effects. Both wage and employment deregulation attain statistical significance. The large and negative coefficient for wage deregulation indicates this variable is the single largest contributor to changes in overall unit labor costs. Decreasing government regulation of the wage setting process by one standard deviation lowers overall unit labor costs by approximately 10 percentage points in a given year. The coefficient for employment deregulation indicates that higher levels of employment regulation raise wage costs slightly.

As expected, the correlation between left governments and employment and wage deregulation is negative (–0.13 and –0.04,

Table 3.1  Regression of Overall Unit Labor Costs in New Democracies, 1994–2003

| Independent variables | FE | RE | FEVD |
|---|---|---|---|
| Center government | 0.759 | 1.585 | 0.759 |
|  | (3.986) | (3.364) | (6.016) |
| Left government | −0.918 | 3.421 | −0.918 |
|  | (4.217) | (3.837) | (5.857) |
| Conservative government | 4.001 | 8.823 | 4.001 |
|  | (5.414) | (5.154)* | (6.364) |
| Polarization | −0.610 | 0.657 | −0.610 |
|  | (1.897) | (1.431) | (1.053) |
| Potential labor power | −3.548 | −1.539 | −3.548 |
|  | (1.730)* | (0.884)* | (1.091)*** |
| Wage deregulation | −8.722 | −8.643 | −10.184 |
|  | (5.569) | (4.312)** | (1.613)*** |
| Employment deregulation | −6.586 | −3.839 | −2.382 |
|  | (4.486) | (3.057) | (1.280)* |
| Growth in GDP | −1.529 | −2.237 | −1.529 |
|  | (1.355) | (1.310)* | (1.161) |
| Unemployment | −2.140 | −3.199 | −2.140 |
|  | (1.864) | (2.026) | (1.457) |
| Inflation | −9.941 | −7.531 | −9.941 |
|  | (1.874)*** | (0.980)*** | (1.113)*** |
| Foreign direct investment | 1.735 | 1.125 | 1.735 |
|  | (1.145) | (1.065) | (1.190) |
| Polity durability | 4.434 | 5.248 | 5.264 |
|  | (8.559) | (4.672) | (1.398)*** |
| Labor productivity | −2.833 | −5.038 | −6.067 |
|  | (10.494) | (5.249) | (1.722)*** |
| Openness | 0.894 | −3.786 | −8.393 |
|  | (2.592) | (2.662) | (1.525)*** |
| Labor force | 16.973 | −0.451 | −0.410 |
|  | (21.030) | (2.703) | (1.340) |
| Residuals |  |  | 1.000 |
|  |  |  | (0.069)*** |
| Constant | −1.162 | 12.280 | 17.555 |
|  | (11.481) | (4.660)*** | (5.765)*** |
| Observations | 139 | 139 | 139 |
| Number of countries | 19 | 19 | 19 |
| $R^2$ | 0.83 | 0.40 | 0.83 |

Notes: *$p<0.05$; **$p<0.01$; ***$p<0.001$.

respectively), whereas it is positive for conservative governments (0.13 and 0.10, respectively). Although signed in the expected direction, these correlations are not very large. Similarly, left governments are associated with wage moderation. Conservative governments, on the other hand, are associated with increases in wage costs. Only the random-effects coefficient for conservative governments, however, attains marginal significance. It appears then that while differences between left and conservative governments continue to shape the political economy of labor market regulation in new democracies, these differences are less consistent than the literature would lead us to expect. I will have more to say about partisan factors in the following chapter.

As hypothesized, labor power is significant and negatively signed in all three models. In addition, the variables polity durability and openness have attained high statistical significance. The coefficient on polity durability indicates that wage rates increase by approximately five percentage points for every additional year a country has been democratic. This result is consistent with the finding that democracy increases labor's share of national income.

The most revealing finding in this first stage of the analysis, however, is that labor productivity, which is a proxy for the level of development, is associated with wage moderation. There are two scenarios that would be consistent with this finding. The first is that corporatist institutions are better able to moderate wage costs in developed countries and thus that even when workers and/or unions demand higher compensation, corporatist institutions blunt these demands.

The second interpretation holds that more developed countries can afford slower wage growth precisely because wage levels are comparatively high in these countries. Due to pressures brought on by globalization, workers that receive high wages can be punished by firms, who can opt to exit the market in search of countries with lower wage costs (Wood 1994). Alternatively, investors can withhold capital from firms that allow their wage costs to reach levels that make their products uncompetitive. Without more analysis, however, it is impossible to tell which mechanism is at work.

If the first scenario is true, that is, if corporatist institutions work relatively well in more economically developed new democracies, we should expect labor productivity to be associated with less labor conflict as well. Alternatively, if productivity (as a proxy for economic development) is associated with more strikes in the second stage of the analysis, this would be an indication that more developed countries are under pressure to hold down their wage growth and workers in turn react by pressing for higher compensation. Since workers in these relatively more developed new democracies possess comparatively more resources, this would be an indication that corporatist institutions are not exactly providing the wage and strike moderation they tend to be associated with. I will have more to say about this in the second stage of the analysis.

One objection to the results reported in table 3.1 is that the predictors, in particular PLP and labor productivity, may not actually be explaining trends in wage costs, but rather changes in labor productivity as unit labor costs change from one year to the next. Since PLP captures the relative composition of the workforce, its reported effect could well reflect productivity differentials between high- and low-skilled workers. This interpretation, however, fails to take into consideration that the model controls for underlying levels of productivity in the economy. As previously mentioned, 90 percent of cross-country variation in manufacturing-labor compensation can be attributed to cross-national differences in productivity rates (Flanagan 2006: 37–38). This makes it possible to model other factors net of the economy's underlying rate of productivity.

If it were true, moreover, that inter sectoral differences in productivity are driving the results, the coefficient for the labor productivity variable would be positive, as workers in more developed countries generate comparatively higher increases in overall unit labor costs. Rudra's PLP variable would be associated with wage militancy (rather than moderation) as the numbers of skilled workers increase with respect to low-skilled and surplus workers. In line with the corporatist interpretation, however, PLP is associated with wage moderation, suggesting that the results are more indicative of the determinants of wages. This lends plausibility to the results, particularly in light of other variables that behave as expected.

Figure 3.1 plots the mean predicted change in overall unit labor costs versus the average wage regulation score for each country from 1994 to 2003. The graph shows that economically developed or more enduring democracies tend to experience more wage moderation. Since actual working conditions—wages, hours, and labor rights that workers experience—are highly correlated with the level of development (Flanagan 2006: 148), the graph strongly hints at the possibility that, as economic development increases, underlying levels of compensation increase and hence labor can afford more wage moderation. This interpretation is highly plausible since, net of the level of development, partisan variables, the labor market regulation variables, and PLP behave as expected.

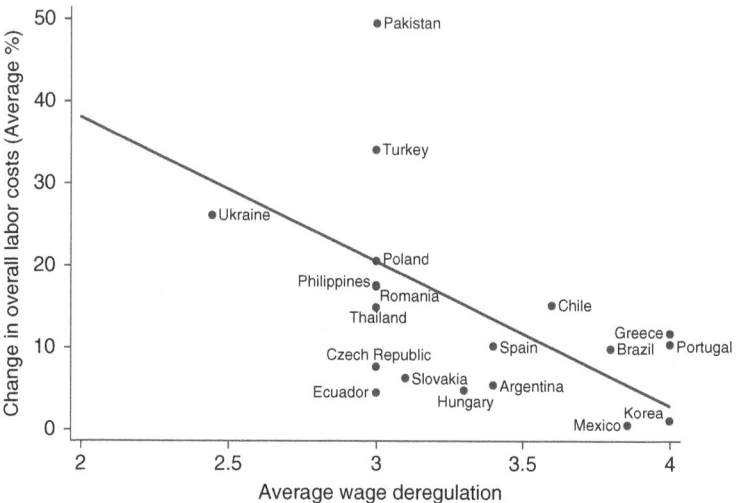

**Figure 3.1** Conditional Effect of Wage Deregulation on Overall Unit Labor Costs, 1994–2003

## Labor Market Regulation and Industrial Conflict

The dependent variables in this part of the analysis are the number of strikes and lockouts in a given country and year, and the number of workers involved in these events. As Flora, Kraus, and Pfenning (1987: 680) point out, the duration of strikes captures both the intensity of labor conflicts and the organizational capacity of workers to maintain solidarity. Unfortunately, days lost to strikes cannot be used due to the high number of missing observations this variable contains. Strikes sometimes involve other workers and employers indirectly. In some cases, the data excludes lockouts or workers indirectly involved, which would provide a complete picture of the extensiveness of conflict among capital owners and workers. Since this data is missing at random, however, it is not likely to bias the results systematically. Unless otherwise specified then, both dependent variables are event counts referring to the total labor force in a particular country and are taken from the ILO's LABORSTA Internet database.

I use the conditional negative binomial model for over-dispersed count-dependent variables (Hausman, Hall, and Griliches 1984). As with linear models, both fixed and random-effects specifications are available. To account for the unbalanced nature of the panel, the model conditions on the total number of observations per cross section. If both estimates agree on the significance of a variable, and if the coefficient is signed in the hypothesized direction, then the resulting coefficients can be interpreted as reflecting the effect of changes in the variable of interest within each country. The reader will note, however, that, unlike linear models, a correction to the fixed-effects estimator is not available for models of event counts. The results then contain a small amount of bias.[20] I report both sets of estimates in table 3.2.

As table 3.2 shows, both the number of strikes and lockouts and the number of workers involved in this form of collective action increase with wage deregulation. The effect of government involvement in the wage setting process turns up significant in all four models. Second, the coefficient on PLP is negative and significant for strikes, indicating that, as labor power increases, workers are in a better position to monitor their own behavior. Third, labor conflict decreases with employment flexibility, although this variable is not significant by conventional statistical standards. If one removes the variable openness, however, the effect of employment deregulation on the number of workers involved in strikes becomes statistically significant.

There are two reasons why openness to trade will be linked to lower strike participation, particularly in light of the fact that the variable is associated with wage moderation. First, economies that are highly exposed to international trade tend to offer significantly greater protections in the areas of employment, collective relations, and social security (Flanagan 2006: 151). One notable exception is the East Asian NICs, which are known for their minimum levels of decommodification despite their high levels of development and exposure to trade.[21] Second, trade competition provides incentives to manage the economy in a highly corporatist fashion, which has been shown to lead to strike moderation (Katzenstein 1985). Consistent with neocorporatist theories, then, the coefficient on openness is marginally associated with declines in strike participation by workers.

The coefficient for left-leaning executives indicates that left governments are associated with more labor moderation, but conservative governments are also associated with declines in strike activity, if not strike participation by workers. One has to be cautious in interpreting these coefficients, however, since collinearity between the partisan variables and the country indicator variables is likely to be

Table 3.2 Conditional Negative Binomial Models of Industrial Conflict in New Democracies, 1994–2003.

| | Strikes and Lockouts (Random Effects) | Strikes and Lockouts (Fixed Effects) | Workers Involved (Random Effects) | Workers Involved (Fixed Effects) |
|---|---|---|---|---|
| Center executive | −0.104 (0.404) | −0.361 (0.353) | 0.854 (0.531) | 0.642 (0.513) |
| Left executive | −0.757 (0.380)** | −0.812 (0.372)** | −0.161 (0.502) | −0.251 (0.488) |
| Conservative executive | −0.662 (0.404) | −0.726 (0.385)* | 0.008 (0.542) | −0.101 (0.525) |
| Polarization | 0.208 (0.073)*** | 0.195 (0.081)** | 0.090 (0.100) | 0.117 (0.104) |
| Potential labor power | −0.150 (0.054)*** | −0.125 (0.063)** | −0.005 (0.065) | −0.013 (0.069) |
| Wage deregulation | 0.179 (0.104)* | 0.279 (0.115)** | 0.257 (0.117)** | 0.302 (0.119)** |
| Employment deregulation | −0.014 (0.126) | −0.086 (0.122) | −0.175 (0.123) | −0.184 (0.135) |
| GDP growth | 0.047 (0.066) | 0.017 (0.063) | 0.119 (0.089) | 0.133 (0.089) |
| Unemployment | −0.001 (0.074) | −0.008 (0.083) | −0.122 (0.096) | −0.129 (0.099) |
| Inflation | −0.279 (0.122)** | −0.383 (0.137)*** | −0.172 (0.099)* | −0.168 (0.100)* |
| Foreign direct investment | −0.070 (0.093) | −0.077 (0.097) | 0.178 (0.103)* | 0.161 (0.108) |
| Polity durability | 0.021 (0.159) | −0.162 (0.195) | 0.029 (0.156) | −0.036 (0.173) |
| Labor productivity | 0.594 (0.223)*** | 0.548 (0.273)** | −0.030 (0.185) | −0.116 (0.197) |
| Openness | −0.136 (0.248) | 0.343 (0.236) | −0.366 (0.189)* | −0.281 (0.205) |
| Labor force | 0.456 (0.165)*** | 0.484 (0.193)** | 0.182 (0.160) | 0.154 (0.168) |
| Constant | 1.602 (0.404)*** | 1.811 (0.375)*** | 0.208 (0.500) | 0.355 (0.482) |
| Observations | 133 | 133 | 130 | 130 |
| Number of countries | 19 | 19 | 18 | 18 |

Notes: *$p<0.05$; **$p<0.01$; ***$p<0.001$.

present. The other variable that behaves according to theoretical expectations is labor force, which is associated with increases in the frequency of strikes, if not in the numbers of workers partaking in them. The magnitude of the coefficient confirms the expectation that workers in countries with more sizable cohorts find it easier to mobilize. This is particularly true of countries with large numbers of workers in skilled manufacturing. In their case, collective identities are easier to forge and mobilize in support of industrial action.

The most important effect these models reveal, however, is that the level of development (i.e., labor productivity) is significantly associated with more strike activity. The reader will recall that workers in economically developed new democracies also tend to enjoy substantial resources—a developed economy being the most important of these—but also protective labor market regulations and effective political incorporation. Since labor productivity is associated with wage moderation, it can only be concluded that corporatist institutions in these countries are not fulfilling the expected function of moderating wage costs *and* strike activity, particularly in light of other variables that behave as one would expect.

Whether workers strike in anticipation of slow wage growth, or whether their strikes register their dissatisfaction against collectively negotiated wages, the analysis reveals that corporatist institutions are not generating cross-class compromises in those countries that can best afford them. Labor market institutions there are moderating the overall wage growth, but only because outsiders (or workers without a permanent job contract) provide a buffer for increased militancy by insiders (or workers with a permanent contract and other benefits) (Alemán 2009). Outsiders enjoy more precarious wage and employment opportunities than insiders. Hence, employers can accommodate wage militancy by insiders by shifting wage and employment opportunities to outsiders.

The fact that labor productivity is significantly associated with the number of strikes but not the number of workers involved also indicates that strikes by insiders do not sometimes reflect the collective interests of the entire labor force. As the case study in chapter 5 demonstrates, Korean employers in recent years reacted to strikes by skilled manufacturing workers by shifting employment opportunities to workers with fixed-term and other temporary contracts, as these workers are paid lower wages and are generally not entitled to employment protection and other benefits that have to be funded through payroll taxes.

As a check on the robustness of the results, I also estimated models of strike activity using regional indicator variables. The two coefficients that are consistently significant are the one for Eastern Europe, which is negatively signed, and the coefficient for Western Europe, which is positively signed. This lends support to the arguments and evidence presented so far, namely, that labor movements have been radicalized in Western Europe and demobilized in Eastern Europe in recent years because the former enjoy political inclusion and protective regulations, whereas the latter are not meaningfully included in policymaking or afforded a great deal of protections. To the extent that these variables show regional clustering in patterns of labor mobilization, they are proxies then for path dependent phenomena that cannot be captured in a dynamic statistical model. However, since regional indicators are so highly correlated with other variables and swamp their effect when entered together, they were not included in the models.

## Conclusion

Industrial conflict in new democracies, this chapter has revealed, can be understood with reference to the degree of labor market flexibility prevalent in a particular country, the partisanship of the government, and the ability of workers to engage in policy negotiations with employers and the government. In addition, the analysis reveals that workers in countries that are more economically developed and with larger workforces are more militant than workers in less developed countries or countries with a smaller labor force. The finding that workers are most militant in countries where labor has been more effectively incorporated lends credence to the claim advanced in this book that the practice of subjecting economic outcomes to political negotiation has not been sufficiently institutionalized to create lasting class compromises in new democracies (Przeworski 1985; Buchanan 1995).

With respect to partisan accounts, both left and conservative governments are associated with reduced industrial conflict, left governments more so than their conservative counterparts. While partisan differences continue to manifest themselves in the political economy of labor market regulation in new democracies, these differences are less consistent than they were once in their established counterparts. Encompassing labor organizations, on the other hand, behave in expected ways since they both constrain wage growth and moderate strike activity.

Studies of labor politics see union incorporation as closing a channel for dissent. The evidence so far indicates, on the contrary, that workers in new democracies may stage strikes even as unions negotiate with employers and the government. To the extent that the benefits of social dialogue appear hypothetical and long-term whereas the costs are immediate and real, this is not altogether surprising. Asymmetries in costs dispose labor toward noncooperation while leaving employers relatively unconstrained in their options (Buchanan 1995). In this situation, it is worth asking, as chapter 4 does, whether higher levels of labor market regulation empower workers to come to agreements with employers and the government over wages and other benefits.

## Chapter 4

# Labor Market Regulation and Social Dialogue: A Qualitative Comparative Analysis

The previous chapter established a positive relationship between wage flexibility and industrial conflict. In this chapter, I examine how labor market regulations affect the other component of the industrial relations picture: the ability of labor to cooperate with employers and the government. To that end, I construct a database of social pacts—formal agreements over labor market outcomes concluded at the national level between representatives of organized labor, employers, and the government. Given the important role of social pacts in moderating labor conflict and maintaining a stable economy, this analysis highlights the detrimental effects of labor market flexibility on social cooperation.

Social pacts contain an implicit class-specific bias (Przeworski 1985; Brandl and Traxler 2005: 637). As has long been recognized, labor has no reason to agree to a pact in which wage moderation is the main objective of employers and/or governments. Even when a pact does not require an upfront concession by labor, the benefits may appear hypothetical and long-term whereas the costs are immediate and real (Buchanan 1995).Consequently, the question of why labor would agree to such pacts has long been of interest to political economists. With increased economic interdependence, moreover, pacts have broadened from issues of pay determination and macroeconomic policy to questions of labor market policy and social charges.

An analysis of the factors that explain social pacts complements then the analysis presented in chapter 3. To this end, I present a database of pacts among unions, employers, and government representatives in new democracies from 1994 to 2004. The database contributes to the project in two related ways. First, it represents the first systematic attempt to collect and analyze pact-making events in new democracies. As such, the hope is that collecting and analyzing these events will help anchor the political economy of labor incorporation in a firmer empirical footing.[1] Second, the database reveals that regulations that safeguard the employment and wage opportunities of workers are more conducive to social cooperation in new democracies.

A fundamental insight of the literature on industrial relations is that, while social dialogue can become routinized, social pacts are always in danger of being flouted due to economic fluctuations, domestic and international competition, and technological change, among others. In this situation, it can be shown that labor market regulations bind employers to particular levels of wage and employment provision. In the short term, more regulation increases wages and other benefits above prevailing market rates. Employers, however, may trade higher earnings in the short term for the social peace necessary to generate steady profits later. By increasing the collective action problem for unions, wage and employment flexibility render unions price takers in the labor market, allowing employers to ignore their demands. This flexibility, moreover, undermines labor's ability to cooperate with employers (and by extension the government).

To study the factors that contribute to social pacts, the chapter relies on qualitative comparative analysis (or QCA).[2] There is no limit to how many variables can be analyzed using this method. I limit myself, however, to the factors that have been highlighted as relevant to social cooperation: the role of government partisanship, the structure of the labor movement, and the level of regulation in the labor market. Although data for three of these factors has already been introduced, this chapter introduces a different indicator of union encompassiveness that more accurately reflects the use of this concept in research on emerging democracies. Using QCA, the chapter reveals that social cooperation is more frequently obtained in a regulated labor market. Left governments, on the other hand, are only associated with a small subset of pacts.

While the implications derived from this analysis are confirmed for each of the three types of pacts examined, I do not address the question of pact implementation. The structures of tripartite institutions, their operating rules, their relationship to the government and other political forces, and even their degree of institutionalization provide a dizzying range of variation in the group of new democracies (Ishikawa 2003: 30). Nevertheless, the analysis can be construed as implying that if a particular causal factor is associated with a pact in a given year and that causal factor does not change, it raises the probability that the agreement will last (Przeworski 1985).

## The Politics of Social Cooperation in New Democracies

Both tripartite institutions and labor market regulations share the purpose of containing the risks arising from the commodification of labor (Esping-Andersen 1990). The added advantage in the case of tripartism is that it can engender solidarity among the social actors. According to students of labor politics, social pacts are the most appropriate form of cooperation because they enable actors to concert their strategies across policy fields (Brandl and Traxler 2005: 637). These pacts can deliver higher employment, more wage moderation, and higher welfare obligations than are otherwise possible to attain (Ebbinghaus and Hassel 2000; Regini 2000; Rhodes 2001).

In agreeing to a pact, workers consent to deploy their labor in exchange for employers' promise to invest some share of their profits. Following Przeworski (1985), it can be argued that two factors affect the ability of workers to opt for such a compromise: the wages they expect in the future if the compromise holds, and the risk that the compromise will not hold. Because workers cannot be certain that the deal will hold, they tend to discount the future. Hence, their behavior depends on the likelihood that employers will observe the terms of compromise if one were to be concluded. Just as workers can withhold their labor and strike, employers can withhold their profits or invest them elsewhere. The degree of risk borne by employers depends in part on the rigidity of their wage bill and other commitments. If the wage bill can be reduced when times are bad, much of the risk is borne by workers.

It is important to examine then what factors increase the probability that both workers and employers will deploy their respective assets while deferring some wages and profits for future consumption. Since both employers and unions are vulnerable to the logic of competitive defection (Przeworski 1985: 182–97), resource mobilization theories have tended to emphasize the importance of monopoly representation of employer and worker organizations (Olson 1982;

Przeworski and Wallerstein 1982). Left partisan control over the government also factors in as a consideration (Siegel 2005: 109; Traxler 2003).

One of the earliest studies of the determinants of social cooperation in new democracies asked then whether the combination of labor's organizational strength, labor's presence in the cabinet, a small open economy, and full employment at the time of bargaining resulted in a social pact (Blake, 1996). Blake defined a social pact as the presence of a tripartite national wage agreement in a given country-year (Blake 1996: 41). A country could either experience a pact in a given year or not.

The study was limited to five countries—Argentina, Brazil, Chile, Spain, and Uruguay—and in each case it covered the first five years after the transition to democracy. More importantly, in 60 percent of the cases none, or only one, of the four conditions thought to lead to the conclusion of a social pact were present (Blake 1996: 42). Blake's most striking finding is that pacts occurred only in one nation, Spain, and only when they should not have occurred, that is, when none of the hypothesized facilitating conditions were present.

In recent years, theories of party union ties have provided an alternative explanation of social cooperation in new democracies. These theories see government-labor cooperation as a function of two variables; union competition, and partisan competition (Levitsky and Way 1998; Murillo 2000: 135–74; Murillo 2001; Robertson 2004: 253–72). There is a subtle difference in how these two variables are conceptually related, that is, whether union fragmentation implies that different confederations naturally seek alliances with competing political parties (Robertson 2004), or whether the relevant unit of analysis is the sectoral level within a single labor confederation (Murillo 2001: 11–12).[3] Nevertheless, when these two variables are combined, what emerges is a remarkably similar argument.

When one union organizes all workers and is affiliated with the governing party, partisan loyalty facilitates cooperation and union monopoly boosts the bargaining power of the union. This situation is characteristic of countries where unions are encompassing and closely integrated into left political parties. When different unions affiliated with the governing party compete, though there may be considerable grassroots unrest such as spontaneous protests and wildcat strikes, union centrals do not compete vigorously with one another to challenge the government.

Where industrial unions within a single federation are allied with competing leftist parties, the tendency is for unions to cooperate with their allies when they are in power and to be militant when their political opponents are in power. Finally, in countries where (left) partisan and union competition is intense, political coalitions between unions and political elites are fragile. This results in a very conflictual pattern of industrial relations.

Levitsky and Way (1998) similarly emphasize the importance of union centralization and links to party controlled resources in their examination of labor-backed adjustment in Poland and Argentina. The public sector is a sizable contributor to employment and consumption in many emerging and developing economies. Unions with ties to the government tend to be not only politically but also economically influential in many new democracies. While appealing, however, these studies base their conclusions on a small number of cases. Murillo uses three Latin American countries with similar corporatist traditions—Venezuela, Argentina, and Mexico; Robertson relies on three postcommunist cases (Poland, Bulgaria, and Russia), and Spain and Argentina.

Blake (1996) showed that the conditions thought to promote pacts rarely obtained in his cases and that pacts also rarely appeared amid such conditions, among them a leftist political apparatus in government with ties to a centralized labor organization. In other ways, however, Blake's analysis raises additional questions, some of which relate to his conceptualization and operationalization of social pacts and, more importantly, to the conditions that are thought to bring them about. First, pacts can take on many forms, including the national tripartite wage pacts Blake examined. Important as wages are as markers of labor market outcomes, social pacts can be more or less encompassing in terms of the functional areas covered, and more or less explicit in the guidelines they provide for implementation.

### Social Pacts in New Democracies

To explain the occurrence of pacts, I rely on fuzzy-set Qualitative Comparative Analysis (fs/QCA). QCA attempts to catalog the ways in which causal conditions or combinations of these conditions result in a particular outcome. While standard statistical techniques typically estimate mean causal effects in a population (King et al. 1994: 76–81), QCA is concerned with necessary and sufficient causation.

A necessary cause is one that, when taken away, fosters a different outcome. That is, the presence of the outcome necessarily implies the presence of the cause. The reverse, however, may not be true. A cause is sufficient when its presence necessarily implies the outcome. However, another cause may also be responsible for the same outcome. Thus the presence of the outcome does not imply the presence of the cause. Many causes are not simply necessary and/or sufficient, but must be combined with other causes to produce an outcome. These causes are known as INUS (Mackie 1965: 248)—a cause that is an insufficient but necessary part of a condition that is itself unnecessary but sufficient for the result.

Multivariate statistical models see causation probabilistically and may not completely account for a particular case. To embrace necessary and/or sufficient causation, on the other hand, is to assume causal determinism at the case level (Mahoney 2008). The key to reconciling the two is the recognition that, at the population level, causation occurs almost exclusively through INUS causes (Mahoney 2008: 423). If INUS causes are present, different combinations of variables can lead to a particular outcome (Ragin 2000). In fact, important INUS causes are "probabilistically necessary" and/or "probabilistically sufficient" at the population level.

In the context of the political economy of labor incorporation, for example, a hypothesis worth investigating is whether employment regulation is present in the different causal combinations associated with social pacts. In chapter 2 we saw a striking association between employment regulation and the rate of unionization in new democracies. If employment regulations render political incorporation meaningful, it is because they strengthen labor movements, and in so doing make them more politically influential. Another hypothesis worth investigating is whether left governments and/or encompassing labor federations are necessary for unions to forge pacts with employers and/or government representatives. If they are, they should be present in every condition (or combination of causes) found in the QCA. In the following section, I describe an original database of social pacts in new democracies that will be used to investigate these propositions.

### *A Database of Social Pacts*

QCA and its fuzzy-set variant (fs/QCA) conceive of causal conditions and outcomes as sets. A high degree of membership in a set is equivalent to presence of an attribute. This is denoted with uppercase letters. For example, membership in the "Employment regulation" set can be denoted as E, with W denoting membership in the "Wage regulation" set, L, membership in the "Left government" set, and P, membership in the "Labor power" set. Lower case letters denote the absence of the attribute (and hence nonmembership in the set). Appendix 4A describes how these sets were constructed and operationalized.

A model in which union-government alliances are thought to be sufficient for social pacts to materialize could be specified as follows:

$$LP \to PACT^4$$

On the other hand, if other conditions or combinations of conditions (X) also help bring about social pacts, a more complicated model would result:

$$LP + X \to PACT$$

A coding procedure should then be designed where various forms of social pacts (tripartite and bipartite wage pacts, agreements on social policy, government union-pacts, and so on) rank highest in their degree of membership in that set, with routine forms of collective bargaining ranking lowest.[5] At one end of the spectrum of membership in the set of pacts (PACT), social dialogue and tripartite policymaking result in or have the potential to forge a consensus over the formulation and implementation of socioeconomic policies (Siaroff 1999: 176); at the other end, labor market outcomes are the product of multiple and fragmented interactions, each representing few actors and/or small slices of the economy. Three kinds of pacts were coded and analyzed.

*Comprehensive pacts*: Tripartite agreements covering more than one functional area of socioeconomic policymaking. These pacts may or may not include a concrete agreement on wage levels, but the social partners signal their intention to cooperate on multiple issue areas. These agreements emphasize a range of issues such as promoting competitiveness, stable employment and social cohesion,[6] protecting and training the unemployed, guaranteeing safety in the work environment, improving social protection, health care, and education, and creating social insurance legislation.[7] While these agreements can be quite comprehensive in their scope, they tend to be sporadic and harder to judge in terms of implementation.

*Tripartite wage agreements*: Tripartite agreements covering wages. These pacts can occur even if not all union confederations sign the agreement. When one organization votes against a particular agreement but the national tripartite body approves it, the same rule applies.[8] Finally, when agreements cover the minimum wage or minimum wages are used as a benchmark for wages in the rest of the economy, this is also taken to mean that a national tripartite wage agreement has been signed.[9] The slightly lower score wage pacts receive denotes their more limited scope.

*Bilateral or single-issue pacts*: This category is reserved for three types of agreements: bilateral or trilateral agreements concerning the salaries paid to public-sector employees (e.g., Turkey 1997, 2001–2002), pacts between the government and politically influential unions (e.g. Argentina 1997, 2000), and pacts concerning an issue other than wages. In their degree of membership, these pacts are not as influential as tripartite national wage agreements or comprehensive pacts.

The database of social pacts in new democracies excludes routine labor legislation, because this legislation is often the product of a transitory period in which a serious attempt is made to consolidate democratic labor relations. In a similar vein, sectoral collective bargaining agreements were excluded on grounds that they have a lesser macroeconomic impact or are not regularly reported in the news media. These agreements can be seen as belonging to the set of "social pacts," but their effects are felt less strongly than their more encompassing counterparts. Their frequency and coverage for a specific country, moreover, is extremely variable. In their breath and scope, comprehensive labor market agreements, tripartite wage pacts, and other bilateral agreements send strong signals to domestic and international audiences about a country's political process and the quality of its industrial relations.

Finally, pacts reached with the sole purpose of ending a general strike were also excluded from the dataset. Some examples include agreements concluded in the 1990s in Bolivia and Honduras between the government and politically influential unions. By limiting the dataset only to the most conspicuous instances of compromise among the social actors, the analysis avoids the problem of endogeneity with outcomes that may themselves be a function of the causal conditions tested. All together, seventy-eight instances of consummated social pacts, most of them covering a twelve-month period, were recorded.

Cases where bargaining broke down or where it was not attempted were not included in the dataset since negative cases are not as uniformly covered in the press. Their inclusion would make it difficult to distinguish between genuinely negative cases and cases where bargaining and consultation did not take place. Their omission, however, does not bias the analysis since its objective is not to estimate independent, average statistical effects. Instead, the goal is to look for causal conditions that different kinds of pacts share.[10] Selecting on the dependent variable, a problem for statistical analysis, does not present a problem in QCA (Bennett and Elman, 2006: 462).

## Analysis of Causal Conditions

Of the four causal conditions tested, data on three of them is derived from the same sources used in chapter 3. Appendix 4B presents the list of cases (country and year) and their scores on the variables Pact (PACT), Employment regulation (E), Wage regulation (W), Left government (L), and Labor power (P).

Most regions of the world are represented in the data: 2 cases belong to Africa, 11 to Latin America, 55 are located in Europe and Eurasia, and 10 in Asia and the Middle East. From Appendix 4.B, it is also apparent that tripartite wage agreements dominate, with 36 cases (or 46.2 percent of the total), followed by comprehensive social pacts (20 cases, or 25.6 percent of the total). Bipartite agreements or single-issue tripartite agreements constitute 22 cases (or 28.2 percent of the total).

The results indicate four different paths to a social pact:

$$E + Wl + WP + wLp \to PACT^{11}$$

The first path is through more employment regulation (E); the second through more regulation of the wage-setting process in the presence of a conservative government (Wl); the third path through more regulation of the wage-setting process in the presence of a more encompassing labor organization (WP); and the final path combines low wage regulation with a left government and a fragmented trade union organization (wLp). The coverage of PACT by the four causal conditions is 0.82, which indicates that the four terms of the solution account for most instances of social pacts contained in the dataset.[12]

Employment regulation (E) alone explains approximately a fifth (22 percent) of all social pacts. With a raw coverage of .79, moreover, this condition is present in most cases of consummated pacts. If we focus only on configurations with at least three instances, then raw coverage increases to .98. No other causal condition or combination of conditions approaches this level of coverage. The last causal combination featuring the left government condition (wLp) provides evidence of political alliances between left governments and politically influential unions. In our population, these alliances tend to be found in countries with (more) fragmented union organizations. This last combination, however, is seen in only 8 cases. Similarly, an encompassing labor organization (P) is only present in the third combination (WP).

## Analysis by Pact

Separating the analysis by type of pact reveals that the causal conditions analyzed account for most instances of social cooperation. Accordingly, coverage for comprehensive pacts, tripartite wage pacts, and bilateral/single issue pacts is .70, .76, and .95, respectively. The left government condition (L) is present in each of the three types of pacts coded. Nevertheless, employment regulation is the condition most commonly associated with the different types of pacts. Looking at the first category of pacts, for example, the solution formula that emerges is

$Ep + WE + EL \rightarrow$ Comprehensive pact

In this case, all three components appear to delineate the importance of employment regulation (E). Employment regulation cannot be considered necessary for comprehensive pacts to occur since coverage for all solution formulas would have to approach 1. Nevertheless, employment regulation is by far the most relevant causal factor for comprehensive pacts. The third solution formula, for example, accounts for the largest number of cases in this category of pacts (11 out of 14). Turning our attention to the factors that account for tripartite wage agreements, the formula that emerges is

$E + WLP \rightarrow$ Tripartite wage agreement

This time employment regulation is present in 23 out of the 24 cases that display this type of pact. Finally, the solution formula that emerges for bilateral or single-issue pacts is

Wl + Ep + WE + wLp → Bilateral or single-issue pacts

The left government condition (L) appears only in one of the terms and not in combination with an encompassing labor organization (P). Although resource mobilization theories highlight the importance of encompassing labor organizations for social cooperation, this condition is not systematically associated with social pacts. Most likely, as chapter 2 revealed, employment regulation facilitates unionization, making labor movements more influential and rendering organizational encompassiveness superfluous. The last solution formula in the category of bilateral or single issue pacts, for example, represents 4 out of 17 cases that display this type of pact. In contrast, the first, second, and third solution formulas account for 6, 6, and 11 of the cases, respectively.

## Taking Stock

This chapter has analyzed the determinants of labor agreements in new democracies, many of which (approximately half) constitute tripartite wage pacts. While early attempts to institutionalize social dialogue in new democracies were not very successful (Blake 1994 1996; Bronstein 1995; Buchanan 1995), this chapter has demonstrated that new democracies have embraced the practice of national, peak level negotiations involving governments, employers, and labor organizations. In Eastern Europe in particular, "bargained exchange between organized interests and the state is both [*sic*] more frequent, extensive, and intensive than is normal for corporatism in relatively stable market economies" (Orenstein and Hale 2001: 281).

The analysis reveals that a great number of labor agreements are found in countries with comparatively high levels of employment protection, including some with right-of-center governments. Both the combined model and models examining each type of pact have revealed that employment regulation is the primary determinant of cooperation among unions, employers, and government representatives. The literature on labor politics tends to see these regulations as subordinate to the political strategies of left-leaning parties. Murillo (2005), among others, has argued that left governments use employment regulation to provide concentrated benefits to their unionized supporters. Only 11 of the 55 cases, however, showed an association between left governments and employment regulation. When a representative collection of cases is taken into account, moreover, alliances between left governments and encompassing labor federations are not present in any of the causal combinations. The analysis suggests then that the partisan explanation of social cooperation accounts for only a small part of the universe of labor market agreements in new democracies, and that the literature on labor politics and comparative political economy has focused on those factors that explain the least amount of variation.

The empirical analysis of labor agreements presented here suggests then that, as new democracies consolidate, they must address the tension "between rules that demand respect for market competition and policies that promote social solidarity" (ILO 2004: 335). The analysis presented in this chapter does not preclude the possibility that social pacts and strikes may occur simultaneously. It is important at this point to be explicit then about what claims I do not make and what questions this book does not address.

## Some Caveats

First, I do not claim that social dialogue is always good for workers. A recurring theme of the book is indeed how governments in many new democracies have contradicted the spirit, if not the letter, of tripartite statutes when they set out to use negotiations to advance goals that contradict those historically associated with regularized consultation, bargaining, and negotiation. Second, I do not claim that social pacts are sufficient to dampen labor protest. While this interpretation is consistent with a treatment of labor politics in established democracies, it is not a realistic expectation in institutionally unconsolidated democracies or countries where industrial relations remain in flux.

In that sense, while the results in chapters 3 and 4 can be interpreted to mean that labor market flexibility uniformly increases labor conflict, it is important to compare levels of conflict at any particular time to trends as they reveal themselves over time. A few strikes in a given year in a country that consistently registers few strikes are not evidence of a radicalized labor movement. Likewise, even though this chapter has revealed that protective regulations increase cooperation, several tripartite agreements concluded in a given country are not definitive proof of harmonious industrial relations. It is important to know which countries had a priori more labor market regulations and hence can benefit from the effects of these regulations on social cooperation.

All of this is to say that deductive or inductive research strategies complement each other in this study. Take the relationship between social pacts and strikes: we would expect pacts to dampen strikes, but strikes may also reveal important information about the preferences of workers that is otherwise difficult to elicit when pact making is not well institutionalized. Indeed, the evidence presented in this study reveals that to the extent strikes and social pacts are a function of labor's ability to bargain with employers and the government, we should expect some degree of pact making and strikes in some countries and little of *both* in others.

Finally, the question of when precisely concertation is demanded by the government is one I do not address.[13] Implicit in the literature is the assumption that social dialogue is a functional necessity of modern capitalist societies, an assumption that I to some extent share. In demanding social dialogue, the government may be responding to a struggling economy, the need to increase economic competitiveness, the recommendation of an Intergovernmental Organization such as the International Monetary Fund (IMF), the desire to revise the labor code, or all the above. Whatever the immediate catalyst, the government in most cases perceives a need to seek cooperation from business and labor organizations in managing the economy. Given space constraints, however, I limit myself in this chapter to documenting how widespread the phenomenon of tripartism has been in new democracies.

Whether the interests of unions and employers are equally served by labor agreements merits closer attention. To that end, I conclude this chapter by foreshadowing the case studies featured in chapters 5 and 6.

### Case Selection

The purpose of the case studies in chapters 5 and 6 is to investigate the causal processes that give rise to the empirical regularities observed in the previous two chapters. Since neither a purely deductive nor a purely inductive approach is completely satisfactory in studies dealing with observational data, comparative researchers have formulated strategies to gain analytical leverage from historical observations. The comparative strategy I adopt tries to find cases located "off-the-line" from the regression slope in figure 2.4. That is, these are cases that are not located in the two quadrants where most observations that establish the relationship between employment protection and voice representation tend to be located. This amounts to finding countries where either political representation or employment protection is insufficiently provided. I will therefore attempt to compare a country located in the upper left quadrant of figure 2.3 with another country located in the lower right hand quadrant of this diagram. This amounts to a comparison of a country with a more inclusionary but flexible labor market regime to a country featuring a more exclusionary but protective labor market regime.

First, in order to trace the impact of employment protection, I decided to compare one country with substantial regulation of the employment relationship to another country with very flexible employment regulations. Consequently, I adopt the strategy of comparing a "Pacesetter" or "Pragmatist" country and one in the "Much-to-be-done" category. Of the countries in table 2.1, Chile and Moldova have low outcome EPSIs and are thus located in the upper left quadrant of figure 2.3. While Chile is a member of the "Much-to-be-done" cluster, Moldova is in the cluster of "Conventionals." Chile (together with Thailand) is also located in the lower left side of figure 2.5, indicating the very low commitment on the part of the government to both voice representation and employment security. Consequently, I will use Chile as one of the cases for in-depth comparison.

Having selected on the level of employment regulation, I then searched for cases with (relatively) high employment protection but low voice representation. Out of all the countries located in the lower right quadrant of figure 2.3, Korea and Mexico have the lowest voice representation outcome scores. Korea actually belongs to the cluster of "Pragmatists," while Mexico is located in the "Conventionals" cluster. Nevertheless, both exhibit some of the lowest RSI outcome scores in the group of new democracies.

Countries labeled "Conventional" have higher scores on the input dimension relative to "Pragmatists." The reader may recall that input indicators assess the formal commitment of the state to representation security, leaving aside the question of whether this commitment is actually effective. Their scores on the outcome dimension, however, are actually lower than those of "Pragmatists." As a result, labor unions and workers in countries located in the "Conventionals" category are probably stronger politically than in the market. Conversely, the state is not as committed to representation security in countries labeled "Pragmatists." Since these countries have higher scores on the outcome dimension, one can infer that workers in these countries are stronger in the market than in the political arena.

Since Korea exemplifies exclusionary corporatism better than Mexico, I choose Korea for a comparison with Chile. These two countries, it turns out, share a number of crucial similarities and differences that make them good candidates for within-case analysis. Both are open and economically thriving Newly Industrialized Countries (NICs) with relatively small public sectors. Both experienced similarly repressive and exclusionary bureaucratic authoritarian regimes. In addition, both have had to contend with persistent authoritarian legacies, most conspicuous among them being the labor codes that severely check the strength of labor unions. In both countries, dynamic export-oriented conglomerates have advocated adherence to market forms of labor control, making social dialogue a difficult undertaking. Finally, in both cases labor unions gained strength with democratization.

There are other cases where labor, after enduring repressive military regimes, was in a position to gain in strength with democratization. As chapter 1 noted, four countries (Chile, Korea, Philippines, and Spain) registered net increases in trade union membership from 1988 to 1997. As the working class gains in numbers, more workers can be organized into unions. This in turn empowers workers at the bargaining table. In pairing Korea with Chile, however, I try to maximize variation on the dependent variable (Geddes 2003; King et al. 1994). As it turns out, the Chile-Korea pair provides substantial variation on one measure of the dependent variable, the number of workers involved in strikes and lockouts as a share of the labor force.[14] This allows us to test the possibility, alluded to earlier, that employment regulation may provide resources to workers to stage strikes.

Finally, Chile and South Korea also provide an interesting contrast in the extent of labor mobilization during the transition to democracy and the crucial question of ties between left governments and trade unions. While South Korea experienced a workers' uprising during its transition to democracy (Koo 2001), Chile experienced little labor mobilization, the exception among Southern Cone countries in Latin America (Bronstein 1995). Following the restoration of democracy in Chile, Chilean public-sector unions continued to be excluded from the labor legislation until 1994, and thereafter were forbidden to strike. Consequently, Chile is a good test of the efficacy of social concertation in the presence of a center-left government. Conversely, by considering how social concertation operates under a conservative cabinet, we can avoid deterministic conclusions about partisan effects in the political arena. The Korean experiment with concertation involves an additional test of rigor, since it took place in a climate of economic crisis in which, in exchange for small improvements in labor's political and organizational status, Korean union leaders agreed to laws that had a serious effect on wages and employment.

In conclusion, the Korea-Chile comparison allows us to control for a number of causal factors that are likely to provide resources to workers, such as the level of economic development, while examining factors that are likely to affect the ability of workers to pursue their interests, in particular the strictness of employment protection. In the Chilean case, employment and wage flexibility are likely to result in plenty of grievances, but *lower* collective resources and consequently reduced levels of labor protest. If any significant level of protest and labor-government or labor-management conflict is seen in a case as unlikely as Chile, it is more likely that the scope conditions of the theory are correctly specified. In the Korean case, on the other hand, employment protection should provide more resources for unions and workers to stage strikes, but the level of conflict should also be influenced by the low level of voice representation unions enjoy.

## Chapter 5

# Protest and Social Dialogue in South Korea, 1987–2007

This chapter looks at the development of democratic and inclusive labor relations in a country in which workers already enjoyed some degree of employment security. The Republic of Korea exhibits a long tradition of exclusionary corporatism in the field of labor relations (McNamara 1999; Wade 1990: 27). Owing to the country's division since World War II and the Korean War, Korea has single-mindedly pursued national security and economic development. Since the 1960s, the state has stimulated the growth of conglomerates owned and managed by a small number of families (Kwon and O'Donnell 2001). At the same time, it has actively cooperated with big business to control wages and suppress union rights.

> In the number of hours worked; in the risks to which they were exposed in the workplace; in the number of fatal injuries they incurred; in the arbitrary and capricious manner in which they were treated (especially women); in the physical repression to which they were subjected by their bosses and the state; and in the gross limitations on their rights and freedoms as both workers and citizens, before the 1980s the Korean working classes suffered under labor relations regimes that have few equals in terms of their authoritarian nature.[1]

Labor has gained materially from democratic politics and is more meaningfully incorporated in the political system and policymaking than it has ever been. The core union membership in heavy industrial sectors, where most workers continue to receive high wages and job security, has especially benefited from a more democratic system of labor relations in the context of an open economy. Since the early

1990s, the government has embarked on successive experiments with corporatist policymaking.

In recent years, however, the Korean government has also relaxed labor regulations. That is, as the industrial relations regime has become more democratic and inclusive, labor market regulations have become more flexible. Not only has labor market flexibility increased apace, but this has resulted in higher unemployment, more labor market segmentation, and greater labor turnover. Consequently, as labor, employers, and the state forge new social pacts, labor conflict has also increased.

## Background

Despite South Korea's democratic transition, the realm of labor relations is plagued with legacies from the bureaucratic authoritarian period (1961–1987). After the Korean War, the country adopted a policy of compressed development based on a state-led, manufacturing intensive economic model centered on family conglomerates known as *chaebol*. Cheap labor was an integral part of this development strategy. Through the Economic Planning Board, the government dictated the annual rate of wage increases companies were allowed to pay their workers. Companies that agreed to higher rates could face a reduction or withdrawal of bank credit (Eder 1997: 13).

Prior to the inauguration of the Sixth Republic in 1987, organized labor was politically repressed and organizationally weak (Buchanan and Nicholls 2004: 63). The national level union center, the Federation of Korean Trade Unions (FKTU), was a puppet organization with little more than paper status. Created as an official organ of Rhee Syngman's ruling party (1948–1960), reorganized and overseen by the Korean Central Intelligence Agency (KCIA) under Park Chung Hee (1961–1979) in 1963, it was placed under further restrictions by the revamped National Security Commission (the successor to the KCIA) under Chun Doo Hwan's Fifth Republic (1980–1987). Under the authoritarian labor relations system, only one union was allowed per firm, firms' unions did not have to associate themselves with the FKTU, unionists involved in strikes had no legal protection from dismissal and arrests, and unions were not allowed to participate in political activities (Song 1999: 4–5).

The Fifth Republic in 1981 instituted a labor regime even more regressive than the one already in place. The new labor code banned interference by industrial federations and the FKTU in labor-management affairs. Church groups were the original targets of this "third party" clause in the 1970s, but the clause was extended to include any entity jurisdictionally above or beyond the firm. In addition to beefing up the KCIA, Chun Doo Hwan had the Anticommunist and National Security Laws combined and a special agency to deal with labor established. The FKTU was reorganized into sixteen federations, 107 local branches closed and the chairmen of twelve industrial federations were replaced (Kwon and O'Donnell 2001: 31). In the first half of the 1980s, more than 2,000 labor leaders were imprisoned, and others friendlier to the Chun regime put in their place (Song 2000: 2).

At the same time, however, the development model inaugurated in the 1970s based on heavy and chemical industries placed a large premium on skilled workers, whom firms had to retain by extending benefits. Thus a combination of government policy and labor market conditions served to strengthen employment protection to workers even as the labor regime became more authoritarian. Firms established a seniority-based system for promotion, while the government made firing workers very difficult and exercised the right to impose wage curbs and binding arbitration in the case of disputes. Employers could only dismiss workers for "justifiable" reasons, and the South Korean courts interpreted "justifiable" narrowly (Lee 2002).

The state-sponsored move toward capital-intensive industrialization shifted the composition of the workforce in the 1980s from predominantly unskilled female workers in textiles to skilled male workers in petrochemicals, automobiles, shipbuilding, and steel manufacturing. Ironically, as economic growth outpaced social ills such as inequality and repression, workers began to turn away from the state and company paternalism characteristic of Korea's exclusionary corporatism (Kwon and O'Donnell 2001: 16). Choi Jang Jip (1993: 20) speaks of the contradiction between the democratic ideals proclaimed by the state and its authoritarian practice as the first political cleavage in South Korean politics. In the arena of industrial relations, many saw the continuing domination of the Korean economy by the *chaebol* and the confinement of union activities to welfare and safety in the workplace as a strong contributor to the emergence of a pro-democracy protest movement.[2]

Beginning in 1986, the labor movement made its grievances heard through dozens of wildcat strikes and national demonstrations in favor of direct presidential elections. When the ruling Democratic Justice Party ignored its own promises and anointed Roh Tae Woo as the designated successor, the country exploded in the worst wave of street demonstrations ever seen. As police mobilization reached a record level, Roh Tae Woo announced on June 29, 1987 the government's acceptance of the opposition demands that included, among others, a revision of the constitution to allow direct presidential elections, human rights guarantees, lifting of press restrictions, encouragement of local and university autonomy, and promotion of political parties. Roh's June declaration ended South Korea's political crisis, paving the way for a peaceful transition to democracy.[3]

## The "Great Workers Struggle" and Militant Unionism

When compared with countries that did not have an exclusionary form of corporatism, a recurring theme in South Korea after 1987 is the struggle to organize unions that are independent of state administration, allowing the labor movement to capitalize on its numeric strength while pressing for political goals. In the first five years of South Korea's Sixth Republic, workers took advantage of a more democratic labor code and organized into unions not affiliated with the officially sanctioned FKTU. Meanwhile, with the opening of the political opportunity structure, wage militancy and industrial conflict exploded. In the face of workers' ability to obtain wage increases, the government came to see repression as ineffective and began to lean in the direction of national social dialogue.

In his June 29 declaration, the president-elect, Roh Tae Woo, conceded that the economic boom he inherited had not filtered down to workers. What politicians did not anticipate, however, is how challenging the expansion of political opportunities would be for South Korea's labor regime. On July 5, only a week after the surprise announcement, workers in strategic export zones began to set up unions. These unions claimed the right to collective wage negotiations, sometimes with support from the industrial federation, but mostly on an independent basis.

As part of its negotiations with the opposition, the government announced its intention to reform the labor code. Opposition party negotiators initially asked for deep reforms to the labor regime. The ruling DJP, however, prevailed in favor of limited revisions. On November 28, 1987, ruling party and opposition negotiators agreed to a minimum wage law—the country's first.[4] They also announced a package of labor reforms that abolished compulsory arbitration and made it easier to declare strikes. The changed Trade Union Act simplified the organizing process,[5] gave union members greater control over the selection of their leaders,[6] and limited administrative powers over internal union affairs.[7] Most significant was the green light given to independent industrial federations.

In what has come to be known as the Great Workers Struggle, 1.3 million workers in 3,300 firms engaged in fierce attacks against employers and managers (Vogel and Lindauer 1997). There were 3,749 labor disputes in 1987; in contrast, the average number of disputes in the previous six years had been 171. The struggle itself, a kind of class war, gave rise to new democratic unions independent of the government and also a new union leadership (Silver 2003: 62). The new leaders adopted a militant posture even if it meant breaking the law.[8] This new militancy represented a sharp contrast to the conciliatory and subordinate attitudes of the FKTU. As demonstrated in figure 5.1, it was also unprecedented in its ferocity.

Since militancy often triggers the emergence of unionization, almost 8,000 new unions were created in the two years after 1987, the rate of unionization rising from 15 to 23 percent (Song 2000: 6). Horizontal unionization was matched by vertical expansion. Five

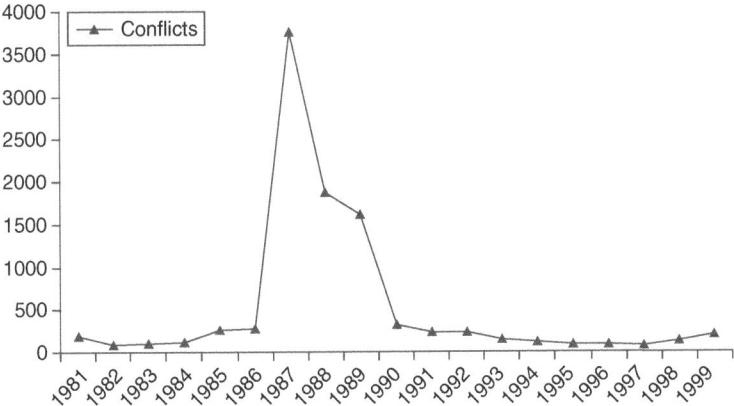

Figure 5.1 Labor Disputes, 1975–2001
Source: Laborsta Internet. http://laborsta.ilo.org/.

industrial federations were established by splitting existing federations and unionizing previously unorganized white-collar employers. White-collar unions, unimaginable in the past, adopted a progressive and somewhat radical orientation.

Looked at from a labor perspective, however, the amended labor code retained the authoritarian character of the industrial relations system. While the right to strike was explicitly recognized, no strike could be conducted without legal authorization from the applicable government agencies. More insidious still, the Trade Union Act upheld the three "nos" in Korean industrial relations: no third-party mediation in disputes (including trade union mediation), no labor participation in politics through collaboration with or financial contributions to a political party, and no more than one union per jurisdiction (Mo 1996: 301; Im 1999: 82). This meant, for example, that there could be only one federation representing enterprise (firm) unions in the same industry.

The new labor code clashed with the avowed aspiration on the part of workers to create a democratic union movement able to promote the political interests of the working class. This is manifested in changes in the character and tactics of labor collective action in the years following the inauguration of the Sixth Republic. There were 1,173 labor disputes in 1988 and 1,678 from January to October of 1989. While the number of disputes stayed fairly high, collective action became more political in orientation and tactics more disruptive. In 1987, 70.1 percent of all labor disputes had been over wages. In 1988, 51.6 percent of the disputes were over pay, followed by 47.6 percent in 1989. As for the right to bargain collectively, the numbers were 16.9 in 1988 and 25.5 in 1989. The average duration of a dispute, moreover, increased to 17.8 days in 1989 from 10 days in the previous year. Most significant is that 69 percent of these disputes were deemed illegal under the newly conceived labor laws.[9]

The South Korean government initially took a hands-off approach to the unrest. Employers, on the other hand, did everything they could to resist workers, for example, through bad faith collective bargaining, the use of thugs to break up strikes, and the registration of fictitious or "yellow" unions. Labor militancy was particularly acute at Hyundai, the site of the first labor troubles in the summer of 1987. In December 1988, workers at the Hyundai shipyard in Ulsan began a yearly ritual of crippling strikes that resulted in massive military-style operations by law and order agencies (Kwon and O'Donnell

2001: 117). In April 1989, a wave of solidarity strikes lasting 109 days shut down plants in the nation's largest conglomerates (Eder 1997: 25).

As the 1980s ended, strikes had raised workers' real wages by 45 percent since 1987. Labor militancy posed a serious threat to South Korea's export led economy. Consequently, the government signaled a change in policy from declared noninvolvement to active repression. In 1989, for example, the government frustrated an attempt to unionize public servants and teachers.[10] Regional and trade union leaders became the target of accusations of violating the labor code and the National Security Act. Violence-prone workers found themselves under increased pressure from the courts, police, and public opinion as the government pledged rigorous enforcement of labor laws and no annual wage increases beyond 10 percent.

It is in this context that the government first proposed in 1989 the formation of a National Wage Council where the FKTU and the Korean Employers' Federation (KEF) would jointly negotiate national wage increases. The FKTU, however, rejected this proposal on grounds that the government would use the body to curb wage increases. Instead, the FKTU suggested the establishment of a National Economic and Social Council (NESC) that would exclude discussion of wage guidelines from its agenda. The NESC, the first bipartite institution of social dialogue in Korea, was formed in April 1990.

The NESC, however, quickly lost its relevance because the government was not included and, more importantly, labor's rank and file remained cool about its activities in a country with no prior experience with social concertation. Amidst an economic downturn, moreover, the government responded by intervening again in labor relations at the firm level. In 1991, the government enforced a wage control policy to alleviate rising labor costs and deteriorating corporate competitiveness, both caused by spiraling wages (Lee and Lee 2002: 6). Second, the government used its veto to oppose demands from the opposition for further democratization in labor-capital relations (Mo 1996: 298).

Finally, the government engineered a merger among the three conservative parties in the legislature. The supermajority Democratic Liberal Party (DLP), modeled on the LDP in Japan, superseded the DJP, Kim Young Sam's Reunification Democratic Party (RDP), and Kim Jong Pil's New Democratic Republican Party (NDRP). The purpose of the three-way merger—which took place on January 12, 1990, the same day the Korea Trade Union Congress (KTUC) was launched—was to realign the conservative camp (Kyoon 2000: 493).[11] This "parliamentary coup" deprived labor unions of the possibility to form an effective political alliance with the opposition (Tae 2002: 9). It, however, did not slow the unionization momentum.

Independent trade unionists organized into the KTUC, consisting mainly of unions in the manufacturing sector, and the Korea Congress of Independent Industrial Trade Union Federations (KCIIF), formed by white-collar workers. The efforts to consolidate unity and solidarity led to the successful 1990 national workers' rally demonstrating the united force of manufacturing, office, and professional workers and the first call for a general strike.

Due to the peculiar legacy of authoritarian labor relations then, the Korean legal structure for labor relations in the late 1980s represented an odd mixture of antiunion laws and surprisingly pro-labor measures concerning job security (Koo 2002: 68). Key measures required companies to seek court approval for layoffs, to refrain from laying off striking workers, to pay the salaries of full-time union officials, and to accept arbitration in certain economic sectors.

As described in this section, the protections that the workers enjoyed served an important role in allowing them to organize and demand higher wages. As of 1989, however, pluralism still prevailed in Korea's industrial relations. This institutional feature greatly limited the strategic capacity of Korean labor in dealing with comprehensive issues (except for wages). Under the company-based union system, the FKTU lacked the exclusive capacity to represent workers as a whole and pursue a solidarity strategy. In this situation, the government's attempt to initiate social dialogue quickly stalled.

## Kim Young Sam's Globalization and a "New Labor Policy"

In late 1992, ruling party candidate Kim Young Sam became the first civilian elected to the presidency in thirty-two years. Following his inauguration, the Kim Young Sam government proclaimed the principle of autonomy in labor-management relations and carried out a series of unprecedented political and socioeconomic reforms. Kim favored the modernization of Korean industrial relations through the incorporation of interest groups into the policymaking process.[12]

This was manifested in the government's "New Labor Policy," which departed from previous practice in calling for more autonomy in labor-capital relations.

The government's "New Labor Policy" was designed to go along with a five-year plan for a new economy. The Kim government therefore pursued a policy based on social consensus between labor and management. This included greater involvement of workers in corporate decision-making and in policymaking, the revision of labor-related laws, the introduction of an active labor manpower policy, the introduction of an unemployment insurance system, and the activation of dialogue between labor, management, and the state. With this new labor policy, the government would strive to overcome the ineffectiveness of labor control by providing the necessary institutional and administrative support for the autonomous interplay of labor-capital relations.

In early 1993, representatives of the KTUC pledged to cooperate with the government's reform policies and to refrain from mass mobilization. The government got the KEF and the FKTU to cap wage increases at a 5 percent annual rate of growth. The president himself recommended centralized wage bargaining as part of the compromise. Subsequently, on April 1, 1993, the KEF and FKTU agreed, for the first time in Korean history, to limit wage gains to between 4.7 and 8.9 percent. The FKTU-KEF agreements were used as guidelines for wage negotiations at the firm level (Lee and Lee 2002: 7).

In addition, in October 1993, the government, the FKTU, and the KEF adopted a trilateral pact, in which they agreed to forge new cooperative industrial relations in order to restore the sagging national economy. This "Joint Agreement for the Development of the National Economy and Labor-Management Relations" declared an era of new cooperation in which the three parties would consult on wage, employment, welfare, tax, and price issues and the government would implement relevant policies according to the agreement.

In 1994, the FKTU asked the government to participate in wage negotiations, justifiably arguing that the wage guideline was meaningful only when the government kept consumer prices under control. As a result, the government established, on February 28, a working counsel that consisted of two representatives each from labor, business, and the government. The working counsel agreed to set the wage increase rates for private sector workers in 1994 from 5.0 to

8.9 percent and to undertake policy consideration in the areas of dismissals, unemployment compensations, and elimination of illegal labor practices.

The social pacts in 1993–1994 were typical examples of concertation at the macro level (Im 1999: 85). These pacts, moreover, were promoted by a conservative government in a country with no labor-leaning parties represented in parliament. They were a positive start to national level tripartite coordination. The state and employers seemed to believe that, despite labor's organizational and political weakness, national level tripartite negotiations would help stabilize industrial relations and increase national competitiveness.

The new system, however, bore little resemblance to a West European version of macro-corporatist tripartite bargaining. While strong in numbers, workers lacked the ability to organize multiple firm-level unions, to create their own labor centrals, and to affiliate with political parties. Negotiations on issues such as employment, work conditions, working hours, and technology continued to be conducted in a decentralized manner (Im 1999: 85). With the KTUC excluded, the chance was slim that pacts would actually be implemented.

The government-labor relationship began to sour when the government insisted on efforts to freeze wages despite an 8 percent increase in GNP in 1993. This led to a growing distrust within FKTU's ranks, causing some affiliates to switch sides, a move that seriously undermined FKTU's organizational base. Neither the two collective bargaining agreements nor the "Joint Agreement" of 1993 was much fulfilled, except for the unemployment insurance provisions. Its political rhetoric notwithstanding, the Kim Young Sam regime regarded the advent of strong labor as a threat to economic development. Hence, the FKTU was not in a strong position to bargain with the government or the KEF.

Pressures induced by these developments precipitated a second national mobilization to create an alternative union central. In June 1993, the Korean Council of Trade Union Representatives (KCTU) brought together leaders of all "democratic" trade unions into a single national body comprising approximately 400,000 workers in some 1,145 unions (Kwon and O'Donnell 2001: 34). These unions had opposed the FKTU in wage bargaining. This paralleled an FKTU announcement in July 1994 that it would not participate in the previously agreed upon wage pact. The FKTU had insisted that the outlawed KTUC be allowed to join social pacts. KCTU put forward a plan that called, among others, for a concerted campaign demanding revisions of labor-related laws, the creation of a "National Democratic Labor Center Preparatory Committee," and its formal launch in the spring of 1995.

The Conference had as its backdrop a drawn-out stalemate at Hyundai. In response, the government abandoned the principle of nonintervention in industrial disputes and mobilized the law and order agencies. This development appeared to undermine the call for labor peace that Kim Young Sam had made following his election. After losing the by-elections of June 1994, a setback attributed in the general press to the growth of labor unrest, president Kim Young Sam took a hard line against the unions. The Ministry of Labor (MOLA) begun to investigate dissident labor unions, a throwback to the labor politics of authoritarian regimes. The government utilized the provision of third-party intervention—which it had pledged to repeal—as an instrument to imprison a large number of labor union leaders.

In the summer of 1994, almost 100,000 workers walked off their jobs—in the subway systems of Pusan and Seoul, Korean National Rail, Hyundai Heavy, Kia Motor, Daewoo Automakers, and Kumho Tire—many of them associated with the KCTU. These strikes combined economic demands with the fight for independent trade unions. Not since the "Great Workers' Struggle" in the summer of 1987 had there been such an impressive show of force by workers.

By November 13, 1994, the Preparatory Committee for the Korean Confederation of Trade Unions (KCTU) had been created. Its main task was to prepare and facilitate the reorganization of individual unions into various industrial federations. This led to a nationwide struggle in 1995 against a new wage curb policy driven by government and employers. As a show of strength, a national workers' rally was organized by representatives of over a thousand individual unions. On November 11, 1995, KCTU was officially established, although it would be four more years until the Ministry of Labor would deem it a legal organization.

As the mid-1990s drew to a close, another attempt at social concertation had proved unsuccessful in a country lacking the experience, trust, and goodwill necessary to sustain national level corporatist policymaking. The pattern of wage growth since 1987 showed some redistribution of income to workers through rapid wage increases. This increase in relative income spoke to the change in industrial relations brought about by democratization. Although the social partners followed up with a comprehensive agreement and two tripartite wage pacts designed to bring wage costs under control, the analysis presented in chapter 4 demonstrates that comprehensive labor agreements are not typically forged by conservative governments. With respect to the two tripartite wage pacts signed in 1993 and 1994, the analysis also illustrated that these pacts tend to occur in the presence of high employment regulation. The latter makes it easier to organize white-collar and blue-collar laborers in unions that can speak for the interests of both. In Korea's case, however, one important labor group (the KCTU) was excluded from the negotiations, spelling trouble for the ability of the social partners to implement these pacts. As resource mobilization theories discussed in chapter 2 also make clear, the presence of more than one labor federation undermines workers' ability to speak with one voice.

Finally, left governments sometimes favor policies that compensate workers for the short-term losses they incur. In the early 1990s, however, Korea ranked below other late developing countries in its level of welfare provision (Im 1999: 86). Rather than being provided by the state, welfare programs were funded and provided by individual firms. This market dependent welfare system increased the inequality in socioeconomic security between workers in large firms and those in small and medium-sized enterprises.

### Revision of the Labor Laws and the First General Strike

Beginning in the mid-1990s, collective bargaining established itself at the firm level in accordance with the prevalent firm-based union structure.[13] Although the bargaining structure was basically decentralized, the influence of labor federations on firm-level bargaining became noteworthy. As a result, labor unions increasingly began to adhere to legal procedures for solving disputes, including the legal requirements for providing prior notice and allowing for a cooling-off period before actually initiating a strike (Lee and Lee 2002: 9). The two federations, that is, the FKTU and the KCTU, would suggest nationwide proposals for wage increases and other contractual changes (e.g., the reduction of working hours) at the beginning of each year. These proposals often served as an influential guideline to firm-level unions. In response to these proposals, the Korea Employers

Federation (KEF) would offer its own bargaining guidelines to firms.

Consequently, in the mid-1990s trade unions began to emphasize unions' right to participate in management, social reforms, and revisions to the labor code.[14] Since 1993 the International Labor Organization had called on the Kim Young Sam government to make Korean labor laws consistent with the principle of freedom of association. The ILO had been particularly critical of the controversial clauses that banned multiple unions, third-party intervention in collective bargaining, union political activities, and restricted labor rights for government employees and teachers. Most importantly, international pressures intensified in 1996 as Korea entered into membership negotiations with the OECD.[15] The latter urged the Korean government to bring its labor-related laws up to international standards. In response, the government notified the OECD of its intention to establish a presidential commission on industrial relations reform.

Korea's decision to seek OECD membership did not encounter severe resistance from employers or politicians. After all, the OECD membership agenda provided significant momentum for financial reform, capital account liberalization, and trade openness. From a primary concern with promoting economic competitiveness, however, the business community begun to raise its voice in favor of reforming the outdated legal framework for labor relations. Business leaders criticized existing labor laws as denying the employer the right to utilize manpower in a flexible way (Koo 2000: 237). This became a common response of Korean firms to the growing international competition.

First, employers argued, the existing labor relations system was incompatible with the structure of the changing labor market. Fundamentally, legal and institutional arrangements were based on the framework molded by the strong developmental state. Yet Korea's industrial structure had undergone great changes since the mid-1980s. In addition to the increase in white-collar workers, the number of atypical workers had considerably grown. The labor-related laws did not appropriately respond to these changing forms of employment.

The Kim Young Sam government, however, entertained two conflicting objectives: one argued for a decisive shift toward a market-neutral and structurally flexible labor market. This would involve challenging two pillars of Korea's political economy: a fragmented system of company unionism based on lifetime employment and seniority, and a bureaucratically driven financial order supplying subsidized bank loans to large firms.[16] The second objective concerned the creation of a normatively "just" labor market. This would involve abolishing legal clauses checking unions' activities, thereby giving rise to a relationship based on genuine participation and cooperation. This model envisioned productivity coalitions and a shift to a union-friendly mind-set on the part of employers.

President Kim Young Sam was determined to honor his earlier pledge to enter the OECD by December 1996. Consequently, in May of that year he established a Tripartite Presidential Commission on Industrial Relations Reform (PCIRR).[17] This presidential advisory Council was composed of more than twenty representatives drawn from the government, academia, unions, and employers' associations.[18] The participation of the KCTU constituted a landmark event in Korea's industrial relations. The PCIRR represented an experiment in political exchange, allowing unions to play a part in policy formulation and implementation.

On July 16, 1996, the PCIRR agreed on the basic principles that would guide the reform of labor laws and institutions.[19] Despite a strong mandate for change, however, reforms predictably ran into difficulties. The representatives of business associations opposed any tampering with Korea's system of "three prohibitions." In particular, they strongly objected to a proposed plurality of labor unions in the workplace for fear of having to negotiate with more than one union during collective bargaining. To protect the right to strike, past labor-related laws strictly banned employers from replacing striking employees with outside temporary workers. Employers, however, called for an immediate implementation of a "no work, no pay" principle, beginning with nonpayment of wages for full-time union staffers and ending with the creation of the "three systems"—the freedom to make hiring and firing decisions, to establish contracts, and to allocate working hours.

Leaders of both the conservative FKTU and the progressive KCTU defended Korea's traditional system of lifetime employment and seniority while calling for an immediate lifting of the three prohibitions. The KCTU representatives in particular argued that the ban on multiple unionism undermined the freedom of association of workers and was inconsistent with international practice. Furthermore, they asked for the right of government employees and teachers to unionize and the end of restrictions on collective bargaining for certain strategic sectors such as the defense industry.

Despite ten rounds of public forums and thirty committee meetings, the PCIRR failed to agree on a single proposal for legislation. This stalemate was followed by KCTU's withdrawal on October 1 and the PCIRR' failure to submit a bill to the president. Although the government initially judged that clauses providing the key demands by both sides should be drafted into a law, differences promptly emerged between the economic ministries, on the one hand, and Ministry of Labor (MOLA) on the other.

On December 3, the government hurried to finalize its revision of the existing labor-related laws. The bill drafted allowed multiple nationwide unions. This meant that the KCTU would be legally recognized in 1997. However, on the question of plural unions at the workplace, a grace period was inserted into the bill postponing their introduction until 2002. This was the most contentious issue pitting labor and management representatives, who feared that competition for workers' loyalty would lead the KFTU and KCTU to outbid each other in their demands. The technocratic compromise also struck down provisions banning ties between unions and third parties. Only national union centrals, however, qualified as third parties (in this case the KFTU and the KCTU). Finally, whereas firms and business associations could continue their political donations, unions were prevented from donating funds to political parties or supporting particular candidates.[20]

On the economic side, new provisions made it much easier for employers to fire workers in cases of "administrative emergencies." Provisions that extended working hours into the evening without paying overtime would allow employers to reduce labor costs. A measure particularly intended to weaken unions' influence in collective bargaining allowed employers to bring in substitute workers and seek temporary workers to fill in key positions, thus effectively reducing the number of permanent employees who had to be given fringe benefits and bonuses. To make matters worse, strikers could be replaced immediately under the new government-drafted bill (the law required companies to pay workers during strikes). The new bill, however, rendered union demands for payment as well as company offers of payment illegal. Under the newly stipulated "no work, no pay" principle, once unions decided upon strikes to pressure management, striking workers and their families would also have to endure wage losses.

Finally, the government-drafted bill required unions to pay for their full-time officials. It had been a long-standing practice for companies to pay wages to full-time union leaders. Management often deemed the practice necessary to win cooperation during bargaining. But employers now opposed the payments since multiple unions were expected to increase their financial burdens. Some labor unions at large firms could afford the changes, but smaller unions were predicted to undergo severe financial difficulties. Although the government draft proposed to lift the ceiling on union membership fees, unions would be forced to depend exclusively on their individual members.[21] Finally, teachers would be allowed to form their unions in 1999, but collective action by public employees continued to be proscribed.

In sum, the technocratic "compromise" reached by the Kim Young Sam government accommodated almost all the demands made by the business community, while giving only minor concessions to labor. They weakened the bargaining powers of organized workers in the labor market and continued to curb democratic rights in the political arena. Prime Minister Lee Soo Sung admitted that the bills fell short of fully satisfying both labor and management. But in his view they represented the best possible solution to a system plagued with high costs and low efficiency.[22]

Sensing defeat, the KCTU and the FKTU issued a joint call for a general strike.[23] To block passage of the government drafted bills in the ongoing regular session of the National Assembly, they agreed on a coordinated campaign against political parties and candidates lining up in favor of the bills. The business community, anticipating the possibility of a phased struggle and further labor-friendly revisions, staged a last minute public relations blitz to make the case that reforms where a matter of national survival. The bills were finally submitted to the National Assembly on December 10, 1996.

The opposition parties proceeded to boycott the session, staging a sit in on the Assembly floor.[24] This forced the ruling New Korea Party to bundle the labor-related laws and a bill concerning the Agency for National Security Planning and call the Assembly into a special session. Despite criticism from opposition parties, who made clear the bill stood no chance, the ruling party rammed the bills through at predawn on December 26 without the presence of opposition legislators.[25]

The labor laws railroaded by the New Korea Party (NKP) were more pro-business and antilabor than the bill proposed by the executive in several respects. While the bill submitted by the executive approved the existence of multiple umbrella union groups in 1997, the NKP version contained a three-year moratorium.[26] Second, absent layoff-related regulations in previous labor laws, employers had depended on case by case court rulings to proceed with layoffs. The bill drafted by the executive addressed this complaint by establishing a company's reasonable cause when threatened with bankruptcy. The NKP-railroaded bill expanded the scope of admissible causes so loosely as to allow firms to identify any situation as an emergency.[27] Finally, the NKP-railroaded bill granted school teachers a consultative role, but it stipulated that the latter could not form unions with full labor rights.

These surreptitious changes, the work of ruling party hawks, caught the opposition by surprise. Shocked by the NKP's railroading of the labor-related laws, the KCTU and the FKTU initiated wildcat strikes.[28] President Kim Young Sam's call for strict enforcement of the law prompted calls for an indefinite nationwide struggle.[29] The KCTU in particular, reacting against the postponement of plural nationwide union bodies until 2000, issued a call for an all-out strike.

Strikes in early January 1997 spread from manufacturing industries to white-collar industries such as state-run research centers and financial institutions.[30] Thousands of broadcasting and hospital unions joined the snowballing strikes. Violent protests erupted in Seoul and other large cities, where blue-collar and white-collar workers once again joined hands.[31] The KCTU claimed that some 220,000 strikers, including unionists at broadcasting stations and general hospitals, had joined the antigovernment strikes, and threatened that subway and telecommunication workers might also take part soon.[32]

Following a monthlong mobilization, the KCTU, which had led the massive walkouts, announced that it would limit strikes to one day per week (Wednesday).[33] This gave the president and opposition leaders breathing room to hold a summit meeting, which laid the groundwork for useful inter party negotiations in the National Assembly. The opposition National Congress for New Politics (NCNP) and United Liberal Democrats (ULD) then drafted a new bill scrapping automatic layoffs, allowing multiple firm unions after a five-year moratorium, and granting immediate legal recognition to the KCTU, among others. In comparison to the labor bills railroaded by the NKP, the opposition's draft was more protective of the rights and interests of workers. It opposed legalizing a flexible working hours' system. Meanwhile, business groups called on the NKP to stick to the initial labor laws.

The ruling and opposition parties engaged in heated negotiations of the labor bills. In what amounted to a shift in strategy, both the KCTU in the FKTU began to insist that wage payments during strikes be fully guaranteed by employers. With the deadline for implementation looming, the ruling and opposition parties narrowed their differences on controversial issues, working out a package almost identical to the basic framework of the original government-proposed bills. On March 10, 1997, the National Assembly passed a new Labor Standards Act, finalizing the first major revision of the labor laws since the democratic reforms of 1987.[34] Albeit minor and not directly the result of the monthlong strike, the revisions proved a significant triumph for organized labor. At the center of the concessions was the immediate recognition of multiple federations of labor unions. For the FKTU, this meant that it had to try to dispose of its image as loyal to the government, even though its current leadership had already engaged in efforts to distance itself from the government.[35]

The new Labor Standards Act delayed the introduction of the controversial "automatic layoffs" for two years. It also introduced the "no work, no pay" principle, freeing employers from the obligation to pay workers during walkouts. It also held employers to a maximum of fifty-six hours per month per worker, provided the maximum daily shift did not exceed twelve hours. Although restricted to the same line of business, employers were allowed to mobilize "alternative" staff, thus paving the way for business to continue operations even in case of a walkout. In a political compromise between the rival parties that left much room for disputes between labor and management, payment for full-time union staffers was phased out after five years, that is, it was retained until 2002. Workplaces subject to a virtual ban on collective action included railways, public utilities, and medical institutions. Finally, the new labor laws failed to specify if teachers and public servants would be allowed to unionize.

During the tense negotiations, the ruling NKP leaned on the side of management, while the opposition showed some sympathy to the rights of workers ahead of the forthcoming presidential election. However, it was apparent that the opposition parties made more concessions than vice versa. As a result, the two national union organizations actively opposed the revised labor laws, threatening to launch a new round of strikes in May. The business community likewise expressed considerable disappointment over the amendments. In their view, the revision was based more on political considerations than economic realities. Compared to other countries, the FKI and the KEF noted, the Labor Standards Act fell far short of ensuring flexibility in the labor market, and ran counter to their original intent of strengthening the country's industrial competitiveness. According to them, the compromise version should have at least precluded the payment of wages for permanent union staff should the multiple union system be adopted.

To sum up, since reforms of industrial relations involved the reshuffling of economic privileges, labor support was essential. In a globalized economy, the *chaebol* could tame unions with threats of capital flight and unemployment. To avoid a backlash, however, employers and policy-makers had to create ways for unions to voice their demands. The product of these efforts was a labor code that suffered from internal contradictions with respect to the balance between political representation and labor market regulation. While the reforms lifted some prohibitions that stood in the way of more meaningful labor participation in politics, they did not go far enough in democratizing industrial relations at the firm level. In addition, while the labor market became more flexible, the reforms did little to compensate labor for this increased flexibility.

## The IMF Crisis and Kim Dae Jung's "Democratic Market Economy"

On December 3, 1997, the IMF and the Korean government announced an emergency $57 billion rescue loan in response to the financial crisis then affecting the country. The dawning of the IMF stewardship regime coincided with a historical political transition in which Kim Dae Jung became the first opposition party candidate to be elected president since the founding of the Republic in 1948. Kim Dae Jung had campaigned on the theme of a "democratic market economy" balancing efficiency through the market with participation through political institutions. Having been elected with working-class support, he was the first politician to form a political coalition with labor.[36]

The economic collapse, however, created an urgent sense of national crisis that permeated all Korean institutions (Koo 2001: 202). Recognizing that the deal between the IMF and the outgoing Kim Young Sam government would provoke fierce resistance from both the *chaebols* and the unions, Kim Dae Jung established the first permanent Tripartite Commission in January 1998. The Commission (*Nosajeong Wiwonhwe*) was created as a presidential advisory body and its members included eleven senior figures from the government, the main political parties, the KCTU, the FKTU, and business.

The IMF demanded reform of Korea's labor market on the grounds that its rigidity was an obstacle for corporations seeking to enter it through mergers and acquisitions. It urged the Korean government to pass legislation in order to facilitate redeployment of labor and, in particular, to ease restrictions over redundancies. The IMF rescue package consisted of two components: short-term macroeconomic measures designed to cope with the foreign exchange crisis, and microeconomic reforms designed to correct structural deficiencies in the Korean economy. The combination of monetary and fiscal austerity on the one hand and microeconomic changes on the other went well beyond standard IMF programs.[37] Accordingly, fair burden-sharing emerged as a central concern for both the government and the social partners.[38]

On January 15, 1998, more than a month before his official inauguration, Kim Dae Jung forged a landmark five-point accord with the *chaebols* to expedite structural adjustment, ensure transparency in management, and restrain illegitimate labor practices. In return, unions were asked to approve layoffs and redundancy legislation—including the use of fixed-term contracts and dispatched workers. Partly in response to IMF demands, the government and employers demanded that labor accept the abandonment of the two-year moratorium on redundancy dismissals. The KCTU and the FKTU blamed the crisis on big business and threatened a general strike if the government and employers went ahead with the reforms.

Unions, however, were also aware of the need to restore international credibility and attract foreign investment. On February 6, 1998, they agreed to the most encompassing social pact in Korea's history, the "Tripartite Accord on Overcoming the Economic Crisis." This accord featured ninety agreements on different aspects of labor market and social policy reform. Most notable was the revision of the Labor Standards Act and its subsequent passage in an extraordinary session of the National Assembly.[39] The Act paved the way for redundancy dismissals, corporate mergers and acquisitions, and a new dispatch workers system (Yang 2006: 222).

In exchange for the concessions labor made, management agreed to exhaust all other options before resorting to layoffs—such as cuts in salaries and working hours, retraining, and unpaid leave. Furthermore, employers agreed to notify the Ministry of Labor (MOLA) and consult the company union sixty days in advance. Finally, management was obliged to rehire dismissed workers within two years if opportunities permitted. In return, unions were promised the introduction of an unemployment insurance fund, collective bargaining rights for public-sector workers, legal recognition of the KCTU,[40] and amendments to the law to permit union political activities before June (allowing unionists to run in the upcoming local elections). In return for legalized layoffs, the new labor laws provided a package of measures to extend financial assistance to the unemployed, including the creation of a 6 trillion won job security fund. Since trade unions had already engaged in pervasive concession bargaining entailing pay freezes and reductions in welfare allowances, wage restraint was not a critical component of this pact (Lee and Lee 2002: 12).

The social pact provoked an immediate crisis within the KCTU. At the eighth national congress of the organization on February 9, just three days after the signing of the historic pact, the social pact was rejected, and the KCTU leadership was voted out and replaced by hardliners from the Hyundai Heavy Industries union. The KCTU then withdrew from the negotiations.[41] Accordingly, in the first half of 1998 the *chaebol* were confronted by a wave of strikes against mass layoffs. The KCTU organized a symbolic protest action on May Day, followed by a brief general strike in July.[42] The FKTU also joined forces with the KCTU to stage large protest rallies in Seoul.[43]

The government launched the second round of tripartite talks on July 3, 1998.[44] Tripartite Commission II introduced consultative committees to oversee the restructuring of the economy and the development of guidelines to avoid unfair labor practices. These included four subcommissions, namely, the Economic Reform Sub commission, the Employment and Unemployment Measures Sub commission, the Labor Management Relations Sub commission, and the Social Security Sub commission. In addition, three special commissions were created: the Special Commission for Tackling Unfair Labor Practices, the Special Commission for Restructuring the Public Sector, and the Special Commission for Improving the Financial Industry.

Following on his pledge to restructure South Korea's economy, President Kim Dae Jung personally presided over the liquidation or merger of three of the top five *chaebols*—Hyundai, Samsung, Daewoo, LG, and SK. Layoffs resulting from these "Big Deals" (or the swapping of unprofitable business subsidiaries among top conglomerates) ultimately quadrupled the precrisis unemployment rate, from 2 to 8 percent. In 1998 these five firms alone slashed 80,000 jobs from their 600,000-strong workforce. In protest, both the KFTU and KCTU pulled out of the Tripartite Commission on February 24, 1999, the latter never to return.[45]

The KCTU demanded the government scrap its legalized layoffs as precondition for its returning to the bargaining table. In an effort to normalize the Commission, the government legislated a special law to transform the advisory panel into a standing organization. On May 3, 1999, the ruling Millennium Democratic Party unilaterally railroaded the Tripartite Commission Act and the Teachers' Labor Union Act through the National Assembly.[46] This was followed by a personal appeal in June 1999 from President Kim Dae Jung to the two labor representatives and the beginning in July 1999 of a Ministry of Labor (MOLA) special investigation into illegitimate labor practices.

With these legislative strokes, the government finally delivered on its promise to legalize the outlawed KCTU and allow teachers to form their own unions. In other ways, however, it faced a complicated balancing act in light of the economic crisis and the subsequent wave of corporate restructuring. Although employment recovered rapidly through 1999, the government continued its efforts to rationalize the industrial and financial sectors. Its decision to split and sell off Daewoo in 1999 led to the largest corporate bankruptcy in world history. In addition, five banks were shut down in 1999 alone.

The government-led economic restructuring resulted in profound changes to the labor market. The proportion of permanent workers in the economy declined, to be replaced by temporary workers. The traditionally well-paid manufacturing and construction sectors suffered downward pressures on real wages as a result of unemployment and the growth of low-paid service sector jobs. The number of labor disputes, which had fallen below 100 during the previous three years (1995–1997), increased rapidly from 129 in 1998 to 250 in 2000. Consequently, the unemployment rate quickly emerged as a contentious issue between unions, the government, and employers. Unemployment soared from half a million to nearly two million in the year following the crisis (Song 2002: 226). The public-sector workforce was cut by 19 percent between 1998 and 2000. Overall wage growth declined in 1998 by 2.7 percent. But as the Korean economy recovered from the crisis in the second half of 1999, labor unions demanded renegotiations, which resulted in more than a 7 percent rate of increase in 2000 (Lee and Lee 2002: 11). Labor disputes during this period erupted in large firms as unions opposed management's employment adjustment plans (e.g., Hyundai Motor Co).

Amending the labor code to provide payment to full-time union representatives also emerged as an issue of considerable disagreement. After all, unions in small and medium-sized enterprises (SMEs) could hardly afford a full-time union staff. The problem surfaced after a secret government-labor agreement on May 25, 1999 scrapping a clause from the current labor law banning salaries by employers to full-time union workers from 2002. The agreement was made in order to dissuade labor from leaving the Tripartite Committee. The secret accord, however, angered employer representatives, who claimed the abolition of the clause was a violation of the principle of "no work, no pay."

The government hastily called for a system to limit the number of full-time unionists, inserting a new proposal stipulating that an employer has an obligation to pay wages to full-time unionists. In an effort to placate employers, the government also drafted a clause vowing a crackdown on labor disputes, citing the issue of payment to full-time unionists. But labor and business showed great dissatisfaction over the government's arbitration efforts. The FKTU rejected the proposal on grounds that it restricted workers' rights to negotiate and go on strike.

Although the government tried to reconvene the Tripartite Commission in September 1999,[47] the KCTU refused to participate. Commission III drew up several major agreements, the most important being an amendment to the Political Fund Law allowing union contributions to political parties (November 1999).[48] Nevertheless, the FKTU, which had made a policy alliance with the ruling party, pulled out in December in protest at the government's refusal to amend the law on full-time union representatives. As South Korea recovered from the Asian financial crisis then, fair burden-sharing exposed the contradictions in Korea's protective but exclusionary labor market regime. The government strove for a compromise that would deregulate certain protections while giving labor more political representation. My theory predicts, however, that absent more meaningful political representation, the Tripartite Commission would fail to forge common ground on a number of important questions since, in order for workers to engage in positive sum bargaining with employers, they have to wield extensive power over public policymaking. It is in this context that another example of a failed political exchange, the struggle for a five-day workweek, first arose.

### Flexibility and the Struggle for a Five-Day Workweek[49]

Trade unions first proposed shortening legal working hours from the prevailing forty-four to forty just after the mass layoffs were approved in 1998. The IMF crisis had led to more employment insecurity, a sharp increase in irregular employees, and worsening income inequality (Koo 2001: 201; Lee and Lee 2002). A shorter workweek, unions claimed, would encourage job sharing because management would have to hire part-time or temporary employees to fill the extra hours. At the same time, unions clamored for fair burden-sharing, claiming workers had borne the brunt of South Korea's economic crisis while employers had profited from their collusive ties to the government. In the eyes of the union leadership, a shorter workweek would mean more leisure, constituting the basis for improved national competitiveness through increased productivity.

The Tripartite Committee had agreed to consider a shorter workweek in 1998 when it was first established. One year later, the Committee decided to draw up a law. In October 1999, the more progressive of the two umbrella unions, the KCTU, submitted a parliamentary request to revise the law on legal working hours. Despite the government's resolve to reduce the working burden for workers, employers resolutely opposed its introduction. The KEF pointed to a holiday system unique to South Korea whereby in addition to Sundays and seventeen national holidays, male workers could take one day off each month and female workers an additional day off. For working more than a year, they were also automatically given an annual ten days off. This meant a minimum thirty-nine days of leave for male workers who had been employed for a year, and much more for those who worked longer. Finally, a worker was entitled to be paid in cash at the end of the year if she did not take these days off.[50]

In 1999, however, the International Labor Organization released a study ranking South Korea seventh among seventy five countries in the number of working hours per week. A survey conducted by the Organization for Economic Cooperation and Development (OECD) in 2000 also revealed that Koreans worked the longest hours among the twenty nine members of the Organization. In response to the news, the Tripartite Committee agreed in April 2000 to set up a special committee to shorten legal working hours to forty-four per week. Sharp differences, however, separated labor and business.

Employers were strongly opposed, claiming that shortening the work week would only raise wage costs. The employers' side attributed South Korea's long hours to the gap between legal and actual working hours, highlighting the fact that overtime was attractive to workers as it can add up to 50 percent of regular pay. This led to a widespread tendency to use existing workers rather than part-time or temporary employees. In addition, most workers preferred to get paid at the end of the year to using available days off. As a result, employers insisted on abolishing the monthly one-day holidays, drastically lowering the period of annual leave, and cutting overtime pay.

Small and mid-sized companies were also opposed to the introduction of the five-day workweek, claiming it would substantially weaken their competitiveness. In June 2000, however, the Korean Employers' Federation (KEF) accepted the five-day work week on condition that the traditional one day off per month for employees and the one day paid health leave provided to women be abolished. In addition, a cut in overtime pay to 25 percent from the prevailing 50 percent and a twenty-day limit on annual leave were among the demands made by employers.

Labor rejected the KEF's proposal, since this violated its goal of creating more jobs via the reduction of actual working hours without pay reductions. The progressive KCTU called the KEF's conditional acceptance a ploy to revise the law in management's favor.[51] To show how serious workers were about shortening working hours, the umbrella KCTU threatened a national strike for May 31, 2000. Its more moderate counterpart, the FKTU, also warned of a massive walkout on June 1 if the government did not take action toward changing working hours.

Nevertheless, the Tripartite Commission announced an agreement on October 24, 2000 that reduced the amount of legal weekly hours from forty-four to forty hours and introduced a five-day workweek. The three parties also agreed to seek revision of the Labor Standards Act by the end of the year to implement the work hours agreed upon by the three parties. To cut the weekly hours as scheduled, they decided to trim the aggregate annual working hours per worker to 2,000 from the prevailing 2,497, according to the type of business and their size. The government also agreed to expand training and leisure facilities to comply with the plan.

The agreement, however, did not automatically lead to changes, since the social partners failed to agree on ways to implement it. The agreement called for the introduction of the forty-hour workweek on a gradual basis, but it did not specify a time frame for implementation. Labor called for its immediate implementation at the start of 2001, while employers insisted on a considerable grace period. In response, the FKTU pulled out of the tripartite commission to protest its decision to gradually introduce the five-day workweek.

Workers' dreams of a five-day workweek took a step closer to reality when President Kim Dae Jung instructed the government in July 2001 to positively consider its implementation. Labor Minister Kim Ho Jin indicated the government's goal was to submit the bill on a shorter working week to parliament within the year and implement it in phases after a one-year grace period, meaning 2003 at the earliest. If the Tripartite Commission failed to reach a compromise on implementation, he warned, the government would draw up the bill on its own. When the Commission failed to resolve the deadlock over the shorter workweek issue, the more moderate FKTU negotiators ended its participation.

Following FKTU's withdrawal on November 13, 2001, the labor component of the Commission ended negotiations over the introduction of the five-day workweek, accusing the government of attempting to block introduction of the shorter work schedule. The FKTU also threatened to call a general strike in alliance with the KCTU. Critics of the government and the Tripartite Commission noted the latter had already agreed on the shorter workweek in October 2000, but the final, formal accord signed more than a year later was actually a compromise package intended to bridge irreconcilable positions between labor and management. The Commission also failed to reconcile government and union disagreements over allowing civil servants the right to bargain collectively and protecting the rights of temporary workers. Talks about a union for public employees had been at a standstill for almost a year after a draft allowed civil servants to assemble and discuss labor issues but not engage in collective bargaining.

In February 2002, moreover, the Tripartite Committee decided to put off implementation of two policies that were slated to go into effect in 2002: a ban on the payment of salaries to union staff who work full time and approval for multiple unions in a work place. In response, the KCTU filed a complaint against the Tripartite Committee with the International Labor Organization, charging that the committee's five-year suspension of approval for multiple unions at a work site infringed upon labor's right to organize. This created considerable anger among labor circles, which continued their campaigns of strikes and protests against the government-led restructuring programs and its unsatisfactory mediation efforts.

In the summer of 2002, the Tripartite Commission attempted once more to find agreement on the introduction of the five-day workweek after two years of discussion. The government proposed adopting the shorter workweek at medium and large companies by July 2006, limiting annual paid leave to twenty-five days, and guaranteeing no pay cuts for workers. Union representatives, however, strongly opposed leaving smaller companies out of the implementation timetable and not compensating workers for unused paid vacation days. Employers for their part claimed the terms in the revisions were too vague and made it sound as if there will be no pay cut, even in stipends and for unpaid holidays. With the failure to reach an agreement satisfactory to all sides, the government launched a partial introduction of the shortened workweek at its agencies.

The Tripartite Commission also failed to agree on the legalization of the civil servants' union and on pension reforms. By 2002, the FKI, a *chaebol* interest group, had gone as far as calling for the dismantlement of the Tripartite Labor Commission. Included in a bundle of policy suggestions, the lobbying group suggested the next government should put the decentralization of unions high on its labor agenda by scrapping the right to collective agreements with management and allowing individuals to negotiate their own workplace agreements. In addition, an FKI think tank called for lifting downsizing limits in a bid to force increased flexibility into the labor market.

The struggle for a five-day workweek provides an opportunity then to reflect on the challenges of institutionalizing political exchanges, particularly in a country in which employment is practically the only safety net afforded to workers. Korean unions, as we have seen, were not inclined to accept demands that would leave employment opportunities intact for the majority of workers but almost certainly result in lower nominal compensation. Absent a more comprehensive social safety net, unions had little incentive to accept a reduction in available benefits. These questions would continue to dominate the reform agenda of Kim Dae Jung's successor.

### Roh Moo-Hyun and the Future of Social Dialogue

Foreign investment, mergers, and acquisitions of troubled companies had resulted in more unstable working conditions, something the government had attempted to fight by strengthening the social safety net for the underprivileged. Before 1998, unemployment insurance had been limited to firms with more than thirty employees. As a result of the financial crisis, the program had rapidly expanded: from firms with ten or more employees (January 1998), to firms with more than five workers (March 1998), to all firms (October 1998), to temporary, part-time, and day workers in July 1999.[52] Only 26 percent of atypical workers in 2003, however, were covered by unemployment insurance (Yang 2006: 223). Without government financial inducements, both small business owners and atypical workers remained reluctant to abide by social security laws.

With collective dismissals de facto impossible, labor market flexibility was being achieved through the expansion of atypical work. Employers who wanted to use fixed-term contracts faced no restrictions in firms with fewer than five employees. Also, large firms were allowed to make fixed-term contracts of up to one year without a specific task. Not surprisingly, the share of atypical workers rose from 45.6 percent in 1997 to 56.6 percent in 2002 (Yang 2006: 222).

It is in this context that Millennium Democratic Party candidate Roh Moo Hyun succeeded Kim Dae Jung to the presidency on December 19, 2002. Roh enjoyed widespread union support, and consequently served notice that he would continue to work toward a more equal distribution of income and a more participatory government. In the area of labor relations, Roh declared that Korea would pursue a win-win strategy benefiting both workers and businesses as a whole.

In one of the fist moves pursued by the new government, President Roh organized a Labor-Management Relations Development Committee composed of eleven labor experts from the government and the academic circles. Soon after his election, however, the Korean economy entered an economic slowdown and the government began to give more emphasis to achieving a $20,000 per capita income and attracting foreign investment. Among a series of measures the government announced, companies were permitted to sue striking workers to recoup revenue losses generated by strike action. The government's moves sparked a wave of protests in the summer of 2003. Arrests and use of repressive legislation by the Roh government led to a return to the methods of suicide by union leaders in protest at government's perceived pro-*chaebol* policy (Bramble and Ollett 2007: 583).

A half-day labor strike, spearheaded by the powerful Korean Confederation of Trade Unions (KCTU), brought many South Korean factories to a grinding halt on November 6, 2003. About 40,000 employees of the Hyundai Motor joined the strikes, designed to put pressure on the government to retract new laws diminishing union power. Then on November 12, 2003, sections of South Korean industry ground to a halt again as tens of thousands of workers in the automobile, metals, textiles, chemicals, transportation, and electricity sectors participated in a KCTU-led nationwide strike against government's perceived antilabor policies. As of November 2003, state-run firms had filed for damages amounting to W40bn (US$34.1m) against union leaders at forty workplaces, and brought charges against 132 strikers.

In December 2003, the Labor-Management Relations Development Committee recommended labor-management councils at the industrial and regional level with the goal of laying the foundations for competitive industrial relations. The committee report called for the creation of regional consultative bodies sponsored by local governments as social dialogue channels. Wage increases in large companies with stable employment had emerged as a concern for both employers and the government, particularly since these companies enjoyed exceptional export revenues and a monopolistic market position at home. A government spokesman also hinted that the government was seriously considering adopting the Dutch model of industrial relations in which unions trade wage moderation for participation in management decisions.

In a significant departure from the politics of confrontation, however, labor unions, business leaders, and the government finalized the "Social Convention on Job Creation" on February 10, 2004, the first comprehensive accord since 1998. The pact came amid mounting concerns about rising unemployment due to a slow economy and a lack of job market flexibility. According to government statistics, overall unemployment stood at 3.6 percent at the end of 2003, but unemployment among young adults between the ages of fifteen and twenty-nine stood at 8.6 percent. Experts attributed the high unemployment rate among the age group to companies' reluctance to hire them, out of fear that they would be unable to implement layoffs if needed because of strong regulations and labor resistance.

In order to create jobs and improve wages for irregular workers and employees working in small or medium-sized companies, labor unions agreed to minimize pay increases for large companies that offered relatively high wages. Companies agreed to consult with labor unions to minimize layoffs and make efforts to rehire laid-off workers. In return, the government agreed to cap annual inflation at 3 percent or less, remove restrictions limiting corporate activities, and provide financial and tax assistance for creating jobs. The agreement, however, was not approved by the powerful KCTU, which played a leading role in most of 2003's major strike action. By the end of June, there had been 330 work stoppages, more than the number for the same period in the previous year. A particular test for the government was the strike by subway workers, because the dispute involved public workers negotiating with the government.

On September 11, 2006, unions, management, and the government reached an agreement on a new labor reform bill, but shelved some controversial proposals for a later date. At the recommendation of the International Labor Organization, the social partners agreed to abolish the government's authority to force arbitration in labor strikes in fields directly linked to the national economy and public livelihood, such as railroads, hospitals, airlines, sewage systems, and blood supply services. Instead, the agreement designates sectors where walkouts are prohibited and allows employers to hire alternative workers in times of strikes. In return, the government and employers agreed to put off paying salaries to full-time union staffers and allowing multiple unions at the same company until December 2009. Most recently, a new law introduced limitations on the duration of fixed-term contracts and mandated equal pay for equal work. The law went into effect in large workplaces in July 2007 and will be phased into smaller workplaces over the next two years.

In September 2006, however, the Swiss-based International Institute for Management Development (IMD) ranked Korea last of the sixty-one evaluated countries in the quality of its industrial relations.[53] Korea has held this rank for four consecutive years since 2003, the year Roh Moo Hyun took office. It is certainly true that Korea's industrial relations climate has improved in the last twenty years. Between 1987 and 1998, more than 50 percent of the strikes staged in Korea were illegal, while the proportion dropped to around 30 percent after 1991, and fell as low as 10 percent during 1995–1996 (Lee 2004: 57–58). Nevertheless, strikes and labor disputes increased in the aftermath of the IMF crisis, reaching 462 in 2004 before dropping to 287 in 2005.

## Conclusion: South Korea at a Cross Roads

Korean labor relations stand at a crossroads. How then do we evaluate the country's experience with tripartite social dialogue? The word "contradictory" readily captures the sense that democratization and labor market deregulation have achieved conflicting political and economic objectives. On the one hand, labor has gained materially from democratic politics and is more meaningfully incorporated in the political system and policymaking than it has ever been. The core union membership in heavy industrial sectors, where most workers continue to receive high wages and job security, has especially benefitted from a more democratic system of labor relations in the context of an open economy.

On the other hand, not only has labor market flexibility increased apace, but this has resulted in higher unemployment, more labor market segmentation, and greater labor turnover. In 2006, about 37 percent of Korea's salaried employees were operating on a fixed-term contract—10 percentage points higher than in 2002 and two and a half times the OECD average. Approximately 30 percent of all new jobs created in the service sector in the past decade were self-employed, with most workers not choosing to be self-employed but being forced into it for lack of permanent jobs. The self-employed accounted for 34 percent of the total workforce in 2004, placing Korea fourth after Turkey, Greece, and Mexico among OECD countries, and at more than twice the OECD average of 17 percent. Since the mid-1990s, furthermore, Korea's income disparities have experienced the highest increase among major countries in the Asia Pacific region.

Labor, it must be emphasized, did not accede to increased labor market flexibility willingly, but only because union leaders believed it was the only alternative to the more severe labor market conditions that might result from corporate failures. Reflecting the need to increase their influence, labor unions have aggressively pursued reforms that would increase their voice representation. High on the agenda is a move toward industry-wide unions grouping together workers in specific fields (Baccaro and Lee 2003: 3). Labor circles also launched the Democratic Labor Party and fielded candidates in the April 2000 general elections. The DLP, the first labor party in Korea's history, gained ten National Assembly seats in the 2004 parliamentary elections. Unemployment compensation, the expansion of social security, reform of the *chaebol* and public corporations, and political reforms are at the forefront of the agenda in a country in need of a very different labor market paradigm.

More fundamentally, the complex nature of the questions facing the social partners has created a growing sense of mistrust among them. This heightened level of distrust explains why, after initially declining in the early 1990s, labor conflict is on the rise again in South Korea and why the country witnessed its first general strike in 1998. The problem, however, is not solved with simply more pacts between labor and business. It is very much also tied to the very different views labor and capital hold about the future of South Korean capitalism. Business favors an American style labor market with maximal flexibility (Baccaro and Lee 2003: 2), while labor prefers a comprehensive social contract. This stalemate is not altogether surprising in light of the fact that it took several decades of conflict (from the end of the nineteenth century to the mid-twentieth century) for many advanced industrialized countries to finally achieve industrial relations models that fit their circumstances.

Korean workers benefit from an increasingly more developed economy and a concentration of the labor force in sectors (e.g., heavy industrial manufacturing) that lower the costs of collective mobilization. The next chapter investigates the relationship between political inclusion, labor market regulation, and social cooperation in democratic Chile, a country that experienced a very different pattern of economic and political reforms in recent decades. If Korea underwent democratization, then political inclusion, and finally labor market flexibilization, Chile exhibits a very different sequence: political incorporation followed by exclusion, labor market flexibilization, and democratization of labor relations. Relations between unions, employers, and the state in Chile have grown as acrimonious as in Korea. Because Chilean workers enjoy fewer resources than their Korean counterparts, however, they have been less effective in pressing their demands.

## Chapter 6

# Protest and Social Dialogue in Democratic Chile, 1988–2006

Advocates of labor market reforms argue that East Asian economic success has largely resulted from a significant degree of labor market flexibility. This compares to the experience of many Latin American nations, which continue to rely on fairly protective labor market regulations.[1] If ratification of International Labor Organization (ILO) conventions is one measure of a government's willingness to regulate labor markets, we would have to conclude that South Korea, having ratified only twenty conventions, has a much more flexible labor market than Chile, which has ratified fifty-nine.[2] Yet when compared to Chile, involuntary labor mobility in Korea has been quite low, around 9 percent throughout the 1990s. Chile, on the other hand, is characterized by a high degree of employment and wage flexibility, as demonstrated by its extraordinary level of involuntary labor mobility.

Chile's democratic government has been praised for its efforts to correct the country's severe social inequalities, strengthen social welfare, and maintain a stable macroeconomic environment. Per capita income has increased at an annual rate of 4.1 percent since 1990—the first year of democratic politics—compared with just 1.1 percent a year in Latin America. Nevertheless, after more than a decade of strong economic recovery, Chilean labor has grown increasingly hostile toward both the *Concertación*-led government and business.

To understand this paradox, we need to examine the roots of the "Chilean economic miracle" and the vicious "bourgeois counterrevolution" that produced this miracle (Pollack 1999: 53). As such, neoliberal democracy in Chile came at the expense of labor's economic and political standing and resulted in a legacy of profound socioeconomic disparities. An average executive salary runs at 160 times the monthly minimum wage, earning Chile the distinction of being one of the seven countries with the most unequal distribution in the world.[3] Even with GDP growth of 6 percent in 2005, about 30 percent of Chile's workers are in the informal sector (ILO 2004: 141).

This chapter provides then a second critical test of my theory relating political inclusion and labor market regulation to the quality of industrial relations. It does so in a country governed by a supposedly labor-friendly center-left government. My analysis begins with the neoliberal reforms instituted by the military regime, which produced a highly flexible labor market in the period before democratization. The chapter then explores labor relations in the context of reforms to the labor code in the early 1990s, the politics of social concertation during the 1990s, and another round of reforms in 2001. The 2003 general strike illustrates the challenges facing the social partners in Chile as they struggle to find a middle ground between flexibility and protection.

### The Military's "Seven Modernizations"

How Chile became one of the most flexible economies in the world is directly linked to the policies pursued by the military regime of Augusto Pinochet (1973–1990). In the arena of industrial relations, the military's fundamental goal was the commodification and depoliticization of labor after a period of extensive state intervention in the economy, class polarization, and rampant inflation.

The team of technocrats and administrators installed by the military junta and known as Chicago-Boys believed that statist clientelism had plunged the country into political and economic chaos during Salvador Allende's socialist government (1970–1973). Initially, the military outlawed the main labor federation *Central Unitaria de Trabajadores* (CUT); voided all existing contracts; eliminated minimum wage regulations; suspended all agreements regarding salaries, benefits, and other forms of remuneration, as well as automatic adjustments to pensions to compensate for inflation; and suspended all collective bargaining and conciliation mechanisms. Finally, it abolished industrial courts and labor judges[4] and gave itself special powers of intervention and designation with regard to union leadership (Buchanan and Nicholls 2003).

After a period of vacillation and disagreement within the Junta about how to institutionalize a new labor relations regime, the military adopted a series of decree-laws, executive orders, and constitutional edicts that came to be known as the Labor Code. The 1979 *Plan Laboral* outlined the legal framework governing capital-labor relations. The laws were designed to prevent coherent strategic planning above the firm level. As such, they outlawed labor confederations and collective bargaining, except in the case of firm-level negotiations concerning wages and working conditions. By allowing contracts to be signed by nonunionized "groups" of workers and individual workers within firms, moreover, the military regime enabled employers to pursue a divide and conquer strategy vis-à-vis workers. All worker participation in management decision-making schemes was forbidden. Salaries negotiated by collective agreement did not have to be transferred to unorganized workers.

Strike legislation set a maximum strike period of sixty days, after which it was considered that strikers had unilaterally ended their employment. It also allowed employers to hire replacement workers during a strike as well as permit strikers to return and negotiate individual contracts after thirty days. Certain clauses allowed for individual and mass dismissals without cause or without more than the minimal severance pay and removed the right of union officials to carry out union activities. The combination of political repression, economic depression, and legislation proved effective in stimulating a form of labor market Darwinism and reducing the ability of workers to defend their rights. As such, the promulgation of the Labor Plan in 1979 functionally linked the dictatorship's repressive labor policies to its extreme market-oriented development model.

Presaging the deep shock therapy programs that many countries would call upon in the 1980s and 1990s, the Chilean military presided over one of the most radical neoliberal transformations a country had ever experienced.[5] Ffrench-Davis (2002) notes that the executors of the economic model enjoyed exceptional autonomy in the design, implementation, and adjustment of policies. This package of reforms encompassing the areas of industrial relations, social security, health care provision, education, municipal control, agriculture, and the judiciary has come to be known as the "Seven Modernizations." Market neutrality, in its most abstract and technocratic formulation, would provide the most efficient way to organize the economy and guide social relations. No longer would people look to the state for the supply of services or, worse yet, clientelistic rents. Instead, the private sector would assume the role of the major motor of change. While reforms in various realms of administration and social policy proceeded gradually, the economy was subjected to two massive waves of structural reforms, the first starting in 1975 and the second after the economic collapse of 1982. These reforms eliminated most safety nets for workers and had enormous consequences for their ability to organize, which remained illegal until 1979. In the area of social security, state-managed pension and social security programs were eliminated in 1979 and the insurance industry privatized. Private pension fund management companies (the *Administradoras de Fondos Provisionales*) began to operate in 1981. By 1980 most health care services had been privatized, leaving the poor dependent on the whims of the market.[6] Ffrench-Davis (2002) notes that by 1989 total public expenditures in education, health, and housing had fallen 12 percent per capita compared to 1970. Cumulative cuts in health funding totaled 60 percent between 1973 and 1988. The two pillars of reforms in social policy, deregulation and privatization, were also applied in education.

In sum, two decades of profound neoliberal reforms produced dramatic effects in an economy long subjected to state intervention (Edwards and Edwards 2002: 35). Most domestic consumer industries folded, whether they had been nationalized or not. Industrial production remained 8.3 per cent below 1972 rates in 1986. Manufacturing as a percentage of the GNP dropped from 25 to 21 percent between 1970 and 1981. Unemployment more than tripled the historic rate, with industrial employment registering the sharpest declines.

Real wages fell more than 20 percent during the first two years after the coup and remained relatively stagnant for the next decade. By 1989, average earnings were 8 percent below their 1970 level, unemployment was double pre-coup figures, union density rates were half that of the Allende years, and almost half the population (44 percent) lived below the poverty line in a region already known as the most unequal in the world (Barrett 2001).

> In other words, over nearly two decades average wages, rather than increasing as is natural, fell, and something similar happened with pensions. The minimum wage declined by a similar percentage over the period, and its coverage narrowed considerably. (Ffrench-Davis 2002: 188)

Not only did the military dictatorship of Augusto Pinochet preside over the atomization and demobilization of the working class, its policies also resulted in the rise of a new class of capitalists with a stake in the extreme form of neoliberalism the country has become known for. Linked to the financial markets, exports, and high technology, it matured into the natural base of support for the military regime and its legacy, the political right. After 1990, the right cemented its powerful political position through electoral overrepresentation.[7] This became possible due to the authoritarian enclaves written into the 1980 constitution, particularly the presence of nine designated senators and one senator for life.[8] Not until the summer of 2005 did the Chilean Congress enact a law restoring full electoral and civilian accountability and eliminating the ten nonelected senators from its ranks.[9]

## Protest and Opposition to the Military Regime, 1973–1990

Despite its distinction as one of the most stable democracies in the Western Hemisphere, Pinochet's market authoritarianism left a deep imprint on Chile's democratic institutions, the most important among them the reduced status of the left nationwide. The military regime targeted the parties of the left as responsible for the political polarization and breakdown of the constitutional process during the Unidad Popular period (1970–1973). Under the Pinochet regime, political parties, leftist movements, interest representation, and state guidance of economic affairs became defined as enemies of Chile (Haagh and Bravo 2004: 169). Instead of socialism by democratic means, supporters of President Salvador Allende and the Unidad Popular government witnessed the creation of a new class of capitalists tied to a radical vision of neoliberal economics.[10]

Pinochet sought to provide a legal foundation for his regime through decree-laws, the Constitutional Acts of 1976, the 1978 plebiscite, the 1980 constitution and plebiscite, and the 1988 plebiscite. The 1988 plebiscite in particular would have allowed Pinochet to stay in office for another term. By making it clear to the regime that there was no alternative to a timely return to democracy, however, political protest played a large role in the eventual process of re-democratization.[11]

The labor movement under the newly formed CNT played a central role in launching a massive protest movement, considering the institutional restrictions imposed on workers by the Labor Plan, increasingly severe unemployment resulting from the economic crisis of the early 1980s (which averaged 26 percent in the years 1982–1985), and the passage of new labor legislation that further weakened job security. Labor opposition to the regime began to appear in various forms from 1979 to 1982, culminating in a general strike organized by the newly formed National Workers Command (CNT) in 1986 (Oxhorn 1995). The state of siege of late 1984 and early 1985, however, forced moderate organizations within the coalition confronting the regime to pursue their goals according to the regime's own rules (Angell 1991; Oxhorn 1994, 1995).

Indeed, confronted by the military's overwhelming strength and willingness to resort to ever greater doses of violence to defend the regime's 1980 Constitution and its transition procedures, nearly the entire opposition (with the major exception of the Communist Party) gradually concluded it had no choice but to focus on the October 1988 plebiscite on General Augusto Pinochet's continuation as president as the only means to defeat the regime.

### Democratic Transition and the Origins of Social Concertation

In several respects, the electoral strategy proved more successful than even its strongest proponents had imagined (Barrett 2001: 579). The democratic forces that opposed General Pinochet's bid to a second eight-year term united and formed the *Concertación de Partidos por la Democracia*, a conglomerate that included seventeen political parties and groups. A similar number of parties and political groups supported General Pinochet in his plebiscite bid. The still illegal Socialist and Communist Parties found themselves excluded by a clause in the Constitution that banned "Marxist" groups from taking part in the plebiscite.

Using the military's own procedures, the *Concertación* defeated Pinochet's bid to expand his tenure by another term. The parties existing before 1973 became the most successful in obtaining votes. Christian Democrats (PDC) led the *Concertación* and obtained more votes than any other political party, followed by Socialist Party factions. Shortly after the 1989 elections, the groups that formed the Socialist Party merged into the newly officially registered *Partido Socialista* (PS).[12] With the official unification of all socialist groups, the *Concertación* effectively became a coalition with two major members, PDC and PS.

The 1989 elections also consolidated the *Concertación* as the only viable alternative to the conservative vote. The Communists, despite their strong presence in labor and student organizations, were unwilling or unable to join the government, yielding the center-left political spectrum to the *Concertación*.[13] This reduced the number of political conglomerates to three: the RN (Renovación Nacional)-UDI (Unión Demócrata Independiente) alliance with about 35 percent of the electorate in the right; the PCD-PS *Concertación* with more than 55 percent of the vote in the center-left; and the Communist Party in the extreme left. The remaining parties disappeared after the 1989 elections.

Despite its victory in the 1989 elections, however, the *Concertación* was unable to challenge the legitimacy of the 1980 Constitution or to modify the regime's skewed electoral institutions. The regime, for example, insisted on retaining its "binomial" electoral system[14] and nine designated senators, which gave the right a majority in the Senate. But perhaps more importantly, by forcing the opposition to abandon a social mobilization strategy and to adhere to its transition procedures and timetable, the Pinochet regime was able to carry out a second phase of structural transformations, consolidating its transformative project. Chief among them were a second wave of privatizations and an expansion of the privatized social security system. These measures facilitated the emergence of a business community more structurally powerful and dynamic than ever and firmly committed to the regime's economic model (Barrett 2001: 580).

As part of the political pacts forged by the anti-Pinochet coalition, agreements were made among the opposition political parties and the CUT as well as business sectors grouped in the *Confederación de la Industria y Comercio* (CIC). Whoever won the national election, it was agreed, would revise the labor code to make it more democratic (Buchanan and Nicholls 2003: 76). The newly formed *Central Unitaria de Trabajadores* (CUT) was expected to refrain from strikes so as not to provoke a backlash from the military.

Although *Concertación*'s program was favorable to labor, it made only general statements regarding labor market and social policy. In fact, it stated explicitly that its proposals were only basic criteria open to debate. Furthermore, it made clear that the final form labor reforms would take would be decided by a new Congress. In any case,

*Concertación* politicians preferred that problems in labor-capital relations be dealt with via direct negotiations between labor and business, with minimal intervention by the state. Throughout the 1980s, however, business leaders were reluctant to enter into discussions with organized labor, much less entertain the possibility of changes in the labor code. As Barrett (2001: 583–584) emphasizes, there were three principal reasons for this. One was their profound distrust of the CNT—renamed the *Central Unitaria de Trabajadores* (or CUT) in 1988. Employers viewed the unions as communist, the enemy of private property and an instrument of the Allende government. The second was their fear that by engaging in a dialogue with the CNT/CUT, they would not only validate it as labor's principal representative, but also open the door to bargaining beyond the level of the firm. Finally, and closely related to this previous point, they were fully aware that the flexibility that the Labor Plan afforded them had played a key role in the economic expansion of the 1980s.

The *Concertación*, for its part, began to argue that changes in the labor code were not an effective means of strengthening the labor movement. If the latter sought to improve its position vis-à-vis business, it would have to achieve it as an autonomous social force rather than by relying on the state. Labor policy was therefore to be guided by the principle of "social autonomy" and based on the understanding that in both public and private companies, labor relations should be defined by workers and management, independently of the state. The role of state intervention in labor-capital relations, in other words, was to enforce compliance with the rules of the game.

### The Framework Accord and Labor Relations, 1990–1994

In January 1990, three months before the inauguration of Chile's new democratic regime, the CUT, the Confederación de Producción y Comercio (CPC), and the government signed a preliminary accord on social dialogue and industrial relations. This led to the establishment of joint committees on various aspects of labor relations and social and economic questions involving the Ministers of Finance, Economy, Labor, and Social Security. The committee's preparatory work paved the way for the adoption of a Framework Accord named "Chile: A Historic Opportunity" in April 1990.

The Accord laid down the principle of development with equity and the autonomous roles of employers' and workers' organizations.

It was intended to facilitate, not replace, direct dialogue among the actors. Independent or joint initiatives were targeted in relation to economic growth and development, education and training, health care, housing, wages and pensions, increased productivity, technological change, employment generation, public sector management, and welfare for the poorest. It envisaged permanent forms of information exchange and consultation, together with the development of employers' and workers' organizations.

Initially, it appeared that there was considerable reason for optimism. The accord contained agreements confirming property rights, the central role of private enterprise, the market and an open economy, and the importance of free, representative, and autonomous labor and business organizations. In addition, it stipulated that the minimum wage and minimum pensions would be increased, that a pact over labor reforms would be sought, that increased social spending would be financed by a tax reform, and that the three parties would maintain a permanent dialogue.

The government's first objective had been to get representatives of workers and employer organizations to agree on the foundations of economic, social, and institutional development. The agreement, however, was the result of a process of mutual understanding rather than a complete convergence of views on the task of economic and social development. Establishing the rules in which the question of labor relations could be discussed required deep changes in both parties' attitudes, if not aspirations. The CUT in particular was asked to recognize the roll of private enterprise and of economic growth and to consider the exigencies of an open and competitive economy.

Throughout the negotiation of these agreements, bargaining was an arduous process where the government would propose draft agreements of reform legislation and submit them for their consideration to the parties. On the basis of this, debates in bipartite sessions (the government with each party separately) and in tripartite sessions would ensue. The process would be led by the Ministry of the Labor, which proposed alternatives whenever the parties disagreed. The Federation of Chilean Industry (SOFOFA) made repeated demands for concessions from the CUT. Even after all of its demands were incorporated and the CUT was still willing to sign, SOFOFA rejected the Framework Accord. At that point, however, the other branches of the CPC, seeing the Accord as a historic victory for business, declared that they would all sign separately and leave the SOFOFA isolated.[15]

The final agreement was crucial to maintain the disposition to engage in tripartite dialog and see the process through parliamentary deliberation. In fact, the signing of the Framework Accord, coming only one month after the new government assumed office, marked the high point in business-labor relations under the *Concertación* (González 1998: 102).

Three more agreements were subsequently concluded, but they had a more instrumental character than the first. The first concerned wages, especially their recovery with respect to the overall economy. An agreement indexing the minimum wage to expected inflation and average productivity allowed the government to identify a precise criterion concordant with the objectives of growth and stability. Finally, the government agreed to seek legislative approval for revisions to the labor code that would abolish some of the more repressive measures contained in the authoritarian framework of labor relations.

The preparation of these agreements established a procedure that became ideal: there was always a "technical" first stage in which advisors to the parties participated. There the fundamental bases in the agreements were established, to be followed by a phase of tripartite negotiation in which technical criteria, if necessary, were adjusted by political exigencies. Sectoral agreements were reached using the same objectives and methodology. The most important ones concerned four in the public sector on readjustment of remunerations, working conditions, and promotions. In addition, tripartite agreements in the port industry and bipartite accords in the coal industry were signed.

Negotiating an agreement over labor reforms proved far more difficult and quickly led to an impasse between the CPC and the CUT. Faced with this impasse, the Aylwin administration was forced to take the initiative and, inevitably, to take sides. It negotiated separately with the CUT and the CPC with the ostensible purpose of maintaining a neutral position, but it leaned heavily in favor of the latter. Indeed, with the CUT and the CPC unable to reach an agreement, the government presented its own set of legislative proposals, which were a watered down version of its 1989 Program. The 1991 legislative reforms allowed industry-wide collective bargaining.[16] With respect to labor confederations, they were given legal status for the second time in Chilean history (the first time occurring in 1971).[17] The new labor laws thus introduced some measures to strengthen the process of unionization, but preserved the atomizing thrust of the legislation and the emphasis on a narrow definition of collective bargaining.

The ruling *Concertación* coalition was composed of parliamentarians who were inclined to follow the wishes of the CUT, sometimes going beyond what the executive judged reasonable and prudent. Accordingly, one of the government's first decisions was to send important proposals to the Senate, where the government did not have a majority, so as to make them undergo the most difficult test. The Senate would reveal the real margin of possibilities the reforms had. Although the legislature was defined as the place where main decisions should be made, the government wished to avoid a scenario in which the first parliamentary transaction of a bill became a forum for the insertion of more radical changes in the lower chamber, the Chamber of Deputies.

The process took place in two phases, tripartite concertation and political negotiations, which were concentrated in parliament. In effect, if a proposal floated in parliament became contentious, the government would call for consultations between CUT and CPC representatives. This resonated with government's view of the social partners as the forum for analysis, endorsement, and testing of the diverse alternatives that arose in the course of parliamentary negotiation. An important aspect of the processes of negotiation was the conviction of the government that reform in sensible matters had to be attentive to the distrust and prejudices of all actors.

The 1991 reform was expected to facilitate the use of collective negotiations. The government pointed to improvements in the material conditions of workers, a growth of unionization, and the low level of labor conflict as proof that its policies had succeeded in reconciling growth, stability, and equity. The majority of the business leadership, however, saw in the reforms a tool to weaken the CUT. Similarly, the CUT began to see the overall thrust of the reforms as designed to preserve the fundamental features of the Labor Plan, introducing largely cosmetic changes that helped to further institutionalize the profound power imbalance in capital-labor relations and the subordination of labor policy to the demands of the economic model (Barrett 2001: 564).

Regarding the minimum wage, which became the subject of yearly tripartite negotiations, the Aylwin administration faced a number of strikes in the public sector. They successively affected the *Corporación del Cobre* (Codelco), Railroads of the State, the Docking Company

(*Empresa Portuaria*), university professors, and health workers. In almost all cases, strikes were caused by demands for higher compensation together with the opposition of the workers to privatization proposals, real or feared (Chile's state-owned port and railroad companies) that threatened their employment stability and the power of their unions, as well as modernizing attempts that jeopardized the job security they legally or de facto enjoyed.

All these situations were solved without creating (via excessive concessions) a precedent of excessive militancy by workers in the public sector. This ensured the political cohesion of the government and the parties of the *Concertación* in the treatment of such conflicts. Partial exception to this rule were the special indemnifications granted to employees in the railroad company when parts of the company were privatized and incorporated. Similar was the case of Enacar, when the loss of economic viability and liquidation threatened substantial reductions in personnel. Only in agriculture, industry, commerce, and finance, however, was there a net increase in the number of workers involved in strikes. The CUT saw in the relatively low turnouts and the short duration of these disputes a sign of the strike's lack of effectiveness. The flexible regulations contained in the labor code made it extremely difficult for unions to organize and sustain strike activity, since they hindered workers' ability to act collectively.

Consequently, nearing the end of President Aylwin's tenure (1990–1994), the CUT began to call for new reforms. This call threatened to reopen the debate on the rules of the game in labor relations, eroding one of the explicit objectives of social concertation favored by the government. Indeed, the significance that business attached to this issue cannot be overstated, as it touched upon what many employers regarded as their most fundamental prerogative, the power to determine the destiny of their firms (Barrett 2001: 587). This sentiment was well illustrated by their frequent characterization of the strike as a profound threat to property rights. This attitude no doubt helps to explain business's increasingly noncooperative and intransigent posture toward labor, symbolized by the CPC's decision to withdraw from the annual tripartite negotiations over the minimum wage in 1993 (Barrett 2001: 588).

As a result of this turn of events, there was growing pressure within the CUT to distance itself from the government and to abandon its defensive posture in favor of a more aggressive, confrontational one. CUT's Christian Democratic President, Manuel Bustos, began to denounce the government publicly (Barrett 2001: 590).

In 1994 the government launched the yearly tripartite meetings of the technical commission on wages, but employer representatives boycotted them, prompting CUT representatives to withdraw their signature. This action by employers, the first of its kind since the signing of the Framework Accord, led CUT to suspend its ties to the government and call for a "Day of National Dignity."[18] On May 20, CUT declared its intention to call for mobilizations by June if workers' demands were not met through dialogue (Frías 1995: 67). Major strikes in health, education, and coal mining were accompanied by growing calls within the *Concertación* caucus in Parliament for more labor reforms.[19] The government responded by creating the Productive Development Forum—an annual tripartite commission devoted to developmental issues. CUT, however, severed relations with the administration in November, angered by the government's slow response and its "neoliberal-business" profile (Barrett 2001).

As Chile emerged from its first four years under democracy, it is evident that its record was decidedly mixed. The country experienced various social pacts and labor-related agreements. Some of these agreements, as the analysis in chapter 4 revealed, are possible in the presence of a left-leaning government and a unitary labor confederation. Nevertheless, Chile lacked a characteristic associated with the ability of the social partners to forge comprehensive pacts and tripartite labor agreements: regulations that safeguard the employment opportunities of workers. The Chilean case shows then why employers have no reason to cooperate with unions and government representatives: they enjoy overwhelming advantages in the market. In addition, an examination of labor relations during this period reveals that although workers hold legitimate grievances, labor unions are constrained in their ability to mobilize workers and launch industrial action.

## Labor Relations during The Frei Administration

In March 1994, the legislature amended the Labor Code to grant civil employees the right to unionize.[20] Nevertheless, public servants remained subordinate to Article 19 of the 1980 Constitution, which forbade strikes in economic sectors deemed essential to national security or well-being (Buchanan and Nicholls 2003: 76). On January 11, 1995, President Frei signed a bill on collective negotiation and unionization into law. Its main purpose was to guarantee and extend the right of unionization, making it effective, to reinforce workers' access to collective negotiation, and to extend it to all legally constituted unions. Seeking to combat its pro-business image, it submitted a new package of labor reforms to Congress.

As a result, relations between CUT representatives and the government improved, with CUT returning to the tripartite commission. Over the course of the year, however, relations became progressively strained as CUT representatives publicized their demands and met with parliamentarians to elicit their support. The CUT's organizational weakness and its fear of undermining a still fragile process of transition only served to deepen the internal political divisions that had plagued it throughout the 1980s (Barrett 2001: 588). Socialist and Communist Party militants criticized the union leadership attached to the PDC.[21]

CUT representatives continued to denounce firm abuses, antiunion practices, and dismissals after negotiations and the constitution of unions.[22] But the CPC no longer felt compelled to pursue a dialogue with the CUT. Instead, business demonstrated an increasingly antiunion posture, as evidenced by the large number of dismissals that followed wage negotiations and strikes and by its refusal to participate in a tripartite commission to evaluate labor reforms, among the most important of them being changes to the labor code that would facilitate unionization and the negotiation of collective agreements.

As revealed by a 1994 government investigation, collective negotiations above the firm level were practically nonexistent, accounting for two out of a total of 2,779 cases in 1992 and twelve out of 1,083 in 1993. It was also revealed that Article 161 of the Labor Code allowing layoffs in case of a business emergency was being used by employers to terminate contracts in the period immediately proceeding the formation of a union (Frías 1995: 68). This, coupled with drops in union affiliation and reductions in the number of workers belonging to unions (50 on average), had increased the number of nonaffiliated workers involved in wage negotiations.[23]

As a result, CUT demanded the creation of an unemployment insurance program (Frías 1995: 66). In March of 1995, it sent a document to *Concertación* parliamentarians requesting the elimination of the quorum to approve and to accept strikes, the elimination of the terms to vote and to make the strike effective, and the imposition of a minimum floor for negotiations based on the previous contract.

The document also demanded that intercompany unions negotiate with the companies where they are affiliated, and that companies negotiate with all their employers, not just with groups of them. The majority of employers voiced persistent and generalized rejection, using all the means of communication they controlled. They rejected intercompany negotiations and the ban on replacing striking workers, reiterating their opposition to making productivity, quality, and efficiency objects of negotiation. In their view, wages could be tied to productivity only on a case by case basis. For that reason, they tenaciously opposed intercompany collective negotiations and tripartism as a venue for collective decision-making. For industrialists, the state had to remain outside the ambit of negotiations.

The reforms' immediate rejection by the rightist majority in the Senate, business' virulent campaign attacking the CUT, and the government's less than energetic efforts to see the reforms passed led the CUT to resume its confrontational approach, which included another break with the administration in December 1995 (Barrett 2001: 591). The government's reply was as usual technocratic, arguing that given the distribution of legislative votes, a broader national consensus was necessary to go forward with additional reforms. For that, a space had to be created where the parties could hammer out the technical aspects of their proposals so that the government could persuade the necessary number of legislators. If it was revealed that certain laws legitimated unjust practices or were not enforced, the government maintained, the need for reforms would be self evident.

As Barrett (2001: 591–592) documents, there was talk of creating a parallel labor federation. Moreover, the Communists scored major victories in a series of federation elections, particularly in the public sector. The most dramatic example of rank-and-file dissatisfaction was the PC's victory in the Teachers Association, the largest of the CUT's federations and a traditional PDC stronghold. The surge in support for the PC helped set the stage for a dramatic CUT election in April 1996, in which the CUT's Socialist vice president, Arturo Martínez, defied his own party by brokering a deal with the PC, helping to elect fellow Socialist Roberto Alarcón as president and a Communist as vice president and thus signaling the collapse of the *Concertación* coalition within the labor movement.[24]

These leadership struggles paralleled strikes in the public sector, particularly among health workers.[25] The trend continued in 1996, with a focus on better wages.[26] SOFOFA's president, Pedro Lizana, accused the government of yielding to illegal pressures when a general mobilization in the public sector ended with the Frei government giving in to teachers' wage demands.[27] At the same time, dock workers used strikes and demonstrations to protest against the privatization of their facilities. This followed the creation of a docking workers' confederation with 50,000 members and the announcement of mobilizations in favor of changes to the labor code.

But perhaps the most dramatic mobilization of the year took place at the Lota coal mines, where workers staged the longest protest since the return to democracy in 1990, at least in the public sector.[28] The strike began on May 17 with the dismissal of ninety-seven workers, lasted more than forty days, and included a takeover of the Ministries of Finance and Economy by two dozen miners.[29] In June, an agreement was reached after the government threatened to close the entire mine, which would result in the loss of 1,800 jobs.[30] The agreement had been rejected on three occasions by the Lota assembly of workers, who argued for restitution of the 97 dismissed and rejected government claims that the mine operated at a loss.

In the mid-1990s, moreover, labor market flexibility increased without any commensurate rise in compensatory public programs. As late as 1995, over 65 percent of unions remained at the shop-level, as did the number of collective contracts (Buchanan and Nicholls 2003: 82). Between 1992 and 1997, moreover, the percent of workers covered by collective bargaining decreased from 15.1 to 10.9. For the first time since the beginning of the transition in 1989, this indicator fell below its initial level (11.6 percent). Nevertheless, the average number of workers per strike remained in the hundreds, albeit average days per strike decreased somewhat from the 1990–1994 period.

In the opinion of certain academics and politicians, the low index of labor conflicts was proof that the labor code was working properly.[31] In fact, there was a growing realization among trade unionists that the labor code did not guarantee an expansion in bargaining coverage. Consequently, while business groups or conglomerates could coordinate their policies, maintaining complete control over information in their firms, workers were dispersed in various groups, many of them temporary. This gave employers the ability to defer increases in wage and nonwage benefits. Due to the presence of a drop in collective bargaining, on the other hand, workers were experiencing reductions in benefits obtained through collective contracts.

The Frei administration did not lose sight of demands from CUT for further revisions of the labor code. For three years, however, the government could not get the legislature to consider its initiatives. In September 1997, a political accord between the leader of the Senate's labor commission—designated Senator William Thayer—and Labor Minister Jorge Arrate resulted in committee approval of President Frei's reform initiatives. The government's proposals would have given workers the right to bargain collectively across company lines and end the ability of employers to hire replacement workers fifteen days into a strike. They would have strengthened the bargaining clout of contract workers, like construction laborers, who did not work full time for a company. The proposal, however, continued to allow negotiations between employers and unaffiliated workers, something the CUT opposed as a government concession to the right.

The private sector, meanwhile, remained tenaciously against the proposed reforms. Faced with a revolt by some senators within his own Christian Democratic party over the measure, President Eduardo Frei pledged that he would selectively veto certain provisions of the bill. Reassured by the promise, the Christian Democratic dissidents toed the party line when the package came up for vote. But senators from the right-wing opposition also presented a united front, resulting in a 23–23 deadlocked vote (under the Chilean constitution, a tie vote is equivalent to a defeat).

In public, the Frei administration blamed the right for the defeat of its reform initiatives.[32] A month before the 1999 presidential election, the Frei government tried once more by submitting a bill to Congress, whose "urgency" status forced deputies to immediately debate on it despite business opposition. The bill would have required industry-wide collective bargaining, denied companies the right to replace striking employees, and given temporary workers greater leverage in negotiations with their employers. Opponents blasted the bill, claiming it would drive up labor costs, discourage investment, and lock in unemployment at levels near the current rate of 11 percent. They also criticized the government's decision to force fast-track consideration of the project, which had languished in parliament for five years, two weeks before the vote.

Despite its avowed intentions then, the Frei administration could not avoid the impression that it had done little to promote the interests of workers. Labor market flexibility, as we have seen, increased apace during the second half of the decade with no corresponding rise in the ability of workers to contest their situation. By the end of the decade, it was clear that labor reform would have to wait another day. In a symbolic gesture aimed at appeasing its electoral constituency, the government issued Decree 227, which promulgated and ratified ILO conventions 87 (freedom to unionize); 98 (right to bargain collectively); 105 (prohibiting forced labor); and 138 (enforcing a minimum working age).[33] Although these actions did not automatically bring Chilean law into compliance with ILO statutes, the government signaled its intention to apply relevant international conventions on labor rights. In addition, Law 19,637 increased social security payments to laid off workers, while Decree-Laws 39 (June 17, 1999) and 1 (January 20, 2000) regulated Law 19,234 governing dismissals for political reasons (Buchanan and Nicholls 2003: 76).

### The Lagos Presidency and The 2001 Reforms

The 1999 presidential elections pitted the *Concertación*'s socialist candidate, Ricardo Lagos, against the center-right RN-UDI coalition candidate Joaquin Lavín. Both men broadly supported Chile's market-oriented economic system, but on the labor issue they held deep philosophical differences. Whereas Mr. Lagos favored spreading the benefits of economic growth, Mr. Lavín argued for deepening neoliberal reforms. Lavín's goal was to restore economic growth, which had slowed in the midst of a recession.

Lagos ran on the promise of overhauling labor legislation and bolstering the bargaining powers of unionized workers, who made up 10 percent of the work force, bringing local legislation in line with International Labor Organization conventions ratified by Chile in January 1999. He also called for the creation of a permanent tripartite "Social Dialogue Council" that would replace the Productive Development Forum launched in 1994 but quickly rendered ineffective. Lagos won the presidency by only 2 percent of the vote in the second round.

Thanks in part to *Concertación*'s new majority in the Senate, several significant changes in the Labor Code were made since 2000 that expanded statutory union rights. Decree 649 promulgated on April 26, 2000 ratified ILO conventions 131 on minimum wages, 135 on worker protection, and 140 on study leave for unionized workers. For the first time in its history, this brought Chile into agreement with the most important ILO standards (Buchanan and Nicholls 2003: 77).

Despite his government's pro-labor stance, however, Lagos was wary of provoking a backlash from business and decided to involve employer organizations once more in the process of drafting new labor legislation.

In March 2000, talks began on labor reform. The negotiations aimed to find common ground on key points of reform among labor, business, and government representatives. On September 14, Labor Minister Ricardo Solari, a Socialist Party veteran, unveiled a reform package to be sent to Congress within the year covering a number of issues addressed in the talks. The more controversial reforms would be postponed. Two key points considered nonnegotiable by business and excluded from the bill banned the replacement of workers during a strike and extended collective bargaining to the intercompany level. Under the proposal sent to Congress, replacement workers and part-time employees would receive protection for the first time, and companies and their unions, if they so desired, could form a pact to reduce the monthly work schedule to 180 hours from the current 192. Also, the bill proposed a reduction in the number of workers needed to form a union, which varies depending on the size of the firm.

With unemployment the worst in a decade, employers argued that investor uncertainty about changes to the labor market was hindering economic recovery.[34] Thus, with business opposition and support of the new Socialist president, a *Concertación*-controlled Congress passed another round of reforms in September 2001. The new law marked a break with the 1979 Labor Code, imposing restrictions on laying off workers, making statutory arrangements on the distribution of working hours less flexible, facilitating the formation of labor unions and strengthening their position in collective negotiations, increasing the number of labor inspectors and fees assessed for violations of the law, and injecting a regular flow of financial resources into the CUT through compulsory deductions from workers' salaries.[35]

A new unemployment insurance scheme also went into effect in May 2002. Under a law promulgated in May 2001, payroll costs went up by an additional 2.4 percent. Employers were required to pay 2.2 percent of monthly wages into each worker's unemployment insurance account, of which 0.6 percentage points is deducted from the worker's wage. Employers were also asked to deposit an additional 0.8 percent of wages into a solidarity fund designed to finance unemployment benefits for workers with insufficient insurance coverage. The law granted unemployment benefits to insured workers who had completed a minimum of twelve monthly contributions to their accounts. Another law approved by Congress in January 2002 cut the number of working hours from forty-eight per week to forty-five from 2005. Commemorating Labor Day in 2002, President Lagos pointed to the government's policies as a success and claimed that in his first two years in office the government had significantly advanced workers' rights.[36] CUT President Martínez, however, used a workers' march through central Santiago to criticize the government's economic model. Martínez asked the government to increase the minimum wage, claiming that if it continued to be pegged to inflation, the Lagos administration would end up with higher poverty levels than the Pinochet regime. With the level of animosity high among the social partners, tripartite talks continued to stall.[37]

On August 21, 2002, about 5,000 Chileans marched in Santiago again to protest the country's high unemployment rate and proposals to lower the minimum wage. Employers had been pressing the government to legalize alternative forms of labor contracts, such as shorter or more flexible work schedules. The private sector also argued it would ease unemployment. In particular, labor leaders were reacting to a report by the IMF recommending more labor market flexibility and moderate or zero increases in the minimum wage in 2002 as a way to combat high unemployment and an economic slowdown. With a unionization rate of 12 percent, however, worker's ability to fight conditions in the labor market remained limited.

On August 14, 2003, the 640,000-strong CUT staged a general strike to protest Chile's neoliberal economic model, low minimum wages, and persistent unemployment. The strike, the first since 1986 when Pinochet was in power, was also the first since the transition to democracy in 1990. Labor leaders wanted to draw attention to Chile's low minimum wage of $165 a month and the gap in earnings between the rich and the poor. With many workers remaining on their jobs, however, a nationwide paralysis, which the strike leaders had vowed, did not materialize. The strike created a profound split between CUT, dominated by Socialists and Communists, and the left-of-center coalition headed by President Lagos. In fact, in September of 2005, the CUT took the extraordinary step of announcing an independent and autonomous position from the government even as the *Concertación* coalition prepared to elect its Socialist candidate, Michelle Bachelet, as president.[38]

## Conclusion

The Chilean case demonstrates then the essential role meaningful political inclusion and protective labor market regulations play in fostering cooperation between labor and capital. Since 1990, the government undertook a series of modest reforms that democratized labor relations and decommodified the labor market. These include increasing the amount of severance pay and social security compensation, allowing public employees to bargain collectively, and prosecuting labor violations. The *Concertación*'s 2001 labor reforms seem to indicate a growing recognition on its part of the need to strengthen labor. Its commitment to an economic model that places a high priority on labor market flexibility as a key component of international competitiveness, however, only means that the current government will make little progress in addressing labor's grievances. Even if the *Concertación* were to succeed in introducing legislative reforms, this would very likely result in serious opposition from business.

The 2003 general strike serves then as a powerful metaphor for the theory laid out in this book. Leaders of the CUT umbrella union wanted workers to show their frustration with the lack of compliance with labor laws, low wages, and low voice representation. Similar calls for a general strike in 2004 and 2005 and the government's retraction of its intention to legislate on temporary work highlight the reality that conflict among unions, employers, and the government has increased in Chile in the years following its democratic transition. After the initial excitement surrounding the framework accords (1990–1993), there have been no new tripartite agreements. The labor movement, moreover, has taken the very public step of severing its alliance with the *Concertación* government, and in particular the Socialist Party.

The 2003 general strike, however, has revealed another side to a deregulated labor market. As figure 6.1 demonstrates, the number of workers involved in strikes in Chile as a percentage of the labor force has been declining since the transition to democracy in 1990. The first four years of democratic politics saw not only the highest levels of industrial conflict, but also the only instances of pacts among labor, employers, and the government. No new social pacts have been agreed to since 1994, but the share of the labor force involved in strikes has also declined even as the relationship between labor, employers, and the government deteriorates.

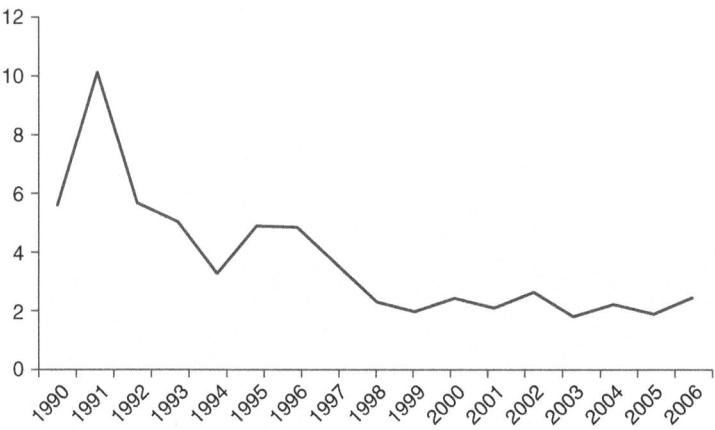

**Figure 6.1** Percent of the Labor Force Involved in Strikes in Chile
*Source*: Laborsta Internet. http://laborsta.ilo.org/.

In the absence of a concerted effort by the government to improve the lot of workers and increase their bargaining power in both the labor market and the political arena, trade unions have little power to bargain on their behalf for higher wages and better working conditions. Thus, to the extent that Chilean workers possess fewer resources than their Korean counterparts, we can explain not only why they have benefitted less from democratization, but also why they have been less successful in pushing for reforms.

# Conclusion: Participation, Flexibility, and the Future of the Third Wave

Corporatism and democracy have been treated as poor bedfellows in much of the developing world. The literature on labor politics has tended to dismiss the importance of concerted policymaking among governments, trade unions, and employer representatives in new democracies. In the excitement surrounding democratic transitions, initial examples of corporatism were quickly eclipsed by studies that argued governments in new democracies pursued a number of strategies toward labor unions, many of them detrimental to meaningful union incorporation and participation in policymaking.

For many new democracies, co-opting labor in the context of profound and painful adjustment processes seemed to be the catalyst for the first examples of tripartite politics. In the 1980s and early 1990s, economic adjustment and the transition to democracy dominated labor politics in Latin America, Southern Europe, and Eastern Europe. Governments relied on social pacts to control wage costs, reduce inflation, and court foreign direct investment. In recent years, however, many governments seem to have realized that social dialogue is eventually ineffective simply as a tool to control labor. For this and many other reasons, this book has argued, the idea that the politics of consultation and negotiation are inherently in the long-term national interest of their societies is a view many governments now share.

The experience of the past decade shows that if the purpose of including labor in policymaking may have been initially to co-opt unions or demobilize workers during periods of economic retrenchment, this no longer seems to be the primary objective of many governments in new or Third Wave democracies. This book has demonstrated that social dialogue has finally arrived in the emerging democracies of Latin America, Eastern Europe, and East Asia. Tripartite dialogue on wages and other labor market outcomes, the sine qua non of corporatism, is alive and well outside Western Europe. This dialogue, moreover, is not limited to wages or incomes policy. On the contrary, it has expanded to include a diverse agenda of topics and issues of concern to employers, workers, and government representatives.

More importantly, the transformation in government attitudes toward social dialogue has rendered the debate about government partisanship less relevant. Taking stock of the phenomenon over the previous two decades, this book has shown that governments of all political stripes—conservative and leftist alike—have promoted the benefits of labor incorporation in policymaking. The pragmatic willingness many governments have shown in favor of dialogue and consensus, moreover, has been more important to the success of tripartite agreements than their partisan orientation or previous patterns of interaction with relevant trade unions.

At the same time, the study has illustrated the profound irony that tripartism in the late twentieth and early twenty-first centuries has in many cases served goals that are in contradiction with those social dialogue has traditionally been associated with, namely, to provide labor with higher wage and other nonwage benefits. Corporatism in the traditional sense prioritized high wages, more employment protection, and welfare benefits. As a result, scholars long ago concluded that it is vulnerable to defection by capitalists, unless of course the state is able to keep capitalists in the game (Schmitter 1985).

Employers in new democracies were often favored by trade liberalization, privatization, and financial deregulation. The strengthening of business actors has diminished union's relative power in society (Cook 2007). With the spread of globalization and the emphasis on economic competitiveness, many governments have concluded that if workers are going to receive higher benefits than the labor market would accord, this should at the very least be the outcome of a framework of institutionalized dialogue and cooperation. The problem is then that labor market flexibility is the price employers demand for their continued participation in tripartite councils and other forms of social concertation.

The corporatist literature, however, does not explore how interest groups learn to cooperate with one another. This literature has been concerned mostly with variation in macroeconomic performance among countries where labor market institutions, policies, and actors have been stable over several decades. The problem many new democracies face, and one that this book has systematically documented, is that the institutional basis for dialogue and cooperation are not well developed. Strategically or not, many governments have used tripartite policymaking as a way to promote economic competitiveness, in particular the flexibility of the labor market. The results, however, have not been favorable to unions and workers in many countries.

The objective of this study has been to investigate how workers have responded to these challenges—varying levels of voice representation and labor market regulation. The question has been systematically tackled through a combination of methodologies. In the end, I hypothesized, the extent of labor conflict with governments and employers would differ across countries. In countries with a history of political incorporation and protective labor market regulations, the analysis revealed a comparatively higher level of strikes. In countries where labor was weak to begin with, on the other hand, my expectation was that workers would have lost the ability to press for regulatory and policy changes that would increase their bargaining power vis-à-vis employers and the state.

One way to assess these claims is to return to the EIU Market Indicators and Forecasts database. One particular indicator assesses the quality of industrial relations in each country. The variable is coded from 1 to 5, with 1 indicating high levels of industrial conflict and 5 the opposite. This information can be linked to figure 2.3 displaying the position of all countries in a two dimensional space defined by the presence of effective voice representation and employment regulation. Consequently, figure C.1 plots this measure for the countries and years available.

Figure C.1 reveals three clusters of countries with respect to the quality of their industrial relations. The first cluster is composed of countries with low levels of industrial conflict: Czech Republic, Hungary, Russia, Slovakia, Taiwan, Thailand, and Ukraine. With the exception of Taiwan, which is not included in the Socio-Economic Security (SES) database, these are all countries located in the lower left quadrant of figure 2.3. That is, these countries all lack effective voice representation and labor market regulation. A second cluster of countries with conflictual industrial relations can be detected in figure C.1. They are Argentina, Ecuador, Greece, Korea, Peru, South Africa, and Spain. Peru has lapsed into autocracy in recent years and

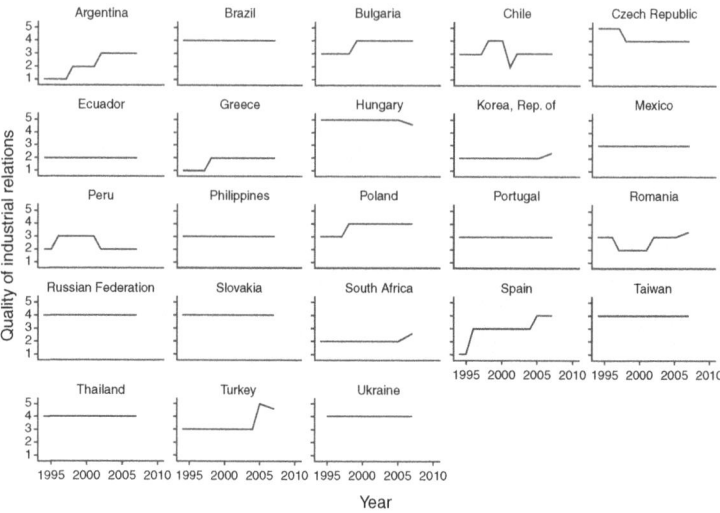

**Figure C.1** Quality of Industrial Relations by Country
*Source*: EIU Market Indicators and Forecasts.

Ecuador has been a highly unstable polity. Korea and Argentina have much lower levels of effective voice representation than their level of employment security would predict.

Greece, South Africa, and Spain are located in the upper right quadrant of figure 2.3. That is, workers in these countries enjoy the highest levels of voice representation and labor market regulation. These are the countries in which we would expect workers to be militant when economic reforms affect their material interests. But these are also countries in which social pacts and other labor market agreements would be easier to forge. Consequently, we would not expect the quality of industrial relations in these countries to be uniformly bad, and according to Figure 7.1, the quality of industrial relations has indeed been improving in recent years in Greece and Spain.

The final cluster of countries has middling levels of industrial conflict: Brazil, Bulgaria, Chile, Mexico, the Philippines, Poland, Portugal, and Turkey. Brazil, Bulgaria, and Chile are located near the center of figure 2.3. Mexico, the Philippines, and Portugal are not well predicted by their location in figure 2.3. Based on its low voice representation, Mexico should have experienced higher levels of industrial conflict, while the Philippines should have experienced lower levels based on its lack of regulations and effective representation.[1]

There are obviously many variables missing from figure C.1, including pacts and the moderating effect they could exert in some countries. Social pacts, which chapter 4 showed are linked to higher levels of employment regulation, have the potential to moderate labor movements in the second and third clusters of figure C.1. It is not a coincidence then that my theory predicts countries located in the lower left quadrant of figure 2.3 the best. These are countries that do not experience much industrial strife. While the evidence presented in figure C.1 is not conclusive, it does suggest that when workers possess resources such as employment protection and a developed economy, they can use industrial action to press for more economic and political gains. This is true even if voice representation is low or not too effective, as the Argentine and Korean cases demonstrate.

My theory also explains why patterns of conflict seem to be region specific. That is, regional experts have found patterns of labor and popular mobilization particular to Eastern Europe and Latin America that are puzzling if not difficult to explain within existing accounts (Greskovits 1998; Kurtz 2004). Whereas labor movements in Eastern Europe have been especially quiescent, particularly with respect to Western Europe (Crowley 2004), the evidence with respect to Latin America is more mixed (Kurtz 2004; Arce and Bellinger 2007).

Deteriorating labor market conditions and the liberalization of labor legislation in Eastern Europe have given employers extensive opportunities to reduce labor costs and strengthen labor discipline (Borisov and Clarke 2006: 628). There has been a widespread transition in the region to the use of short-term individual labor contracts, often anticipating changes in labor legislation that legitimate the practice. As a result, whether one speaks of tripartite agreements, collective bargaining, or labor legislation, trade unions in Eastern Europe have had little or no discernible impact on wages and working conditions. The theory and evidence I present account well for these findings, since, as already alluded to in figure 2.3, Eastern Europe's new democracies afford their workers modest levels of incorporation and very flexible labor market regulations, particularly when compared to their counterparts in Western Europe. I now proceed to highlight my more specific findings.

## Summary of Detailed Findings

Compared to established democracies, I showed that the partisan composition of the government does not have a consistent effect on labor compensation or the ability of workers to cooperate with employers and the government in new democracies. While left parties are significantly associated with strike moderation, they have no significant effect on wage compensation. Neither encompassing labor organizations nor left parties, moreover, are significantly associated with the ability of labor to strike compromises with employers. The only variable that is significantly associated with the ability of labor to strike compromises with employers and the government in new democracies is the level of employment protection. As a result, my findings downplay the importance of partisan factors to the political economy of labor incorporation in new or Third Wave democracies.

Second, in a situation of profound asymmetry, I argued that regulation of the wage setting process is essential to guarantee unions a level playing field with employers. Wages provide workers with the most tangible reward for their labor and constitute the most important link in the worker-employer relationship. There may be a number of reasons why governments intervene in the wage-setting process, but, among the most important ones, economic competitiveness and macroeconomic stability feature prominently. The study has revealed that contrary to the varieties of societal corporatism that prevailed in Western Europe until the early 1980s, workers—particularly in the more developed new democracies—respond with more militancy when wages rise at a sluggish or moderate pace.

Wage militancy in some countries is a function of already existing low wages. Wrenching economic and political changes have depressed real wages in most of the developing world. In Latin America, for example, the wage (or labor) share of total income declined by 13 percentage points from 1993 to 2002, the fastest of any region in the world (ILO 2008: 6).[2] More surprising, however, was the finding that wage moderation tended to increase with the level of economic development. As a result, I hypothesized that higher regulation of the wage-setting process would increase wages and reduce industrial conflict. Conversely, lower levels of regulation would reduce compensation and hence lead to more protest. These hypotheses were tested on a sample of new democracies, including those that have featured wage and other pacts in recent years.

## CONCLUSION

Third, the study revealed that while low regulation of the wage-setting process by the government was linked to more labor militancy and industrial conflict, employment regulation had more complicated effects on industrial relations. First, employment protection increased labor's ability to cooperate with employers and the government. Employment flexibility, I argued, gave employers no reason to strike pacts with unions over wages and other policies. Employment flexibility, however, also decreased the ability of workers to organize and demand higher benefits.

The links between employment security, effective voice representation, and industrial relations were examined through two critically chosen case studies, South Korea and Chile. These case studies lie outside of the region that has experienced the clearest growth in social dialogue—Eastern Europe—and as such guard against the possibility that the results obtained are driven by the process of European integration. Prior to democratization, Chile and South Korea were characterized by very different labor movement trajectories; nevertheless, they both faced daunting challenges in reforming and reorienting their labor market institutions in the 1990s.

Until the late 1990s, South Korea maintained political bans on independent unionism, a legacy of an authoritarian system of labor control that combined employment protection and real wage increases for workers with the political demobilization of organized labor (Pempel and Tsunekawa 1979; Deyo 1989). During the 1990s, however, the South Korean government attempted various social pacts designed to incorporate part of the labor movement into policymaking (Tae 2002). At the same time, it sought to continue prohibitions on multiple unions in the workplace.

Chile, on the other hand, exemplifies a pattern of labor incorporation in the democratic political arena, combined with very flexible labor market policies (Heckman and Pagés-Serra 2000: 114; Pagés 2004: 69–70). Collective bargaining covered approximately 12 percent of the workforce in the 1990s, a problem compounded by low unionization rates, which have averaged between 10 and 20 percent of the workforce. Chilean workers have not been as successful as Korean workers in pressing employers and the government for more material and political benefits. The difference can be attributed to the higher levels of employment protection in South Korea.

The case studies also demonstrated that labor movements in both countries are too well organized to be simply price takers in the market, but also too weakly organized to produce a comprehensive social contract. The South Korean case illustrates then how workers respond to the deregulation of employment contracts when the government attempts to give employers the freedom to make decisions on hiring and firing, to establish contracts, and to allocate working hours in exchange for greater political freedoms for unions. The Chilean case, coming from the opposite end of the regulatory spectrum, illustrates how conflict has increased in Chile in spite of changes in the regulation of temporary contracts and new freedoms to organize and bargain that have resulted from recent reforms to the labor code.

To conclude, an in-depth look at industrial relations in democratic Chile and South Korea has revealed how workers respond to insufficient levels of labor market regulation or voice representation. As the theory laid out in this book suggests, labor market regulation and political representation result in some decommodification of labor market outcomes. This relationship, however, begs the question of how countries are supposed to react in response to market pressures that intensify competition, free movement of goods and capital, and punish countries for maintaining generous welfare states.

The answer comes in the form of "competitive corporatism," a term used by scholars of established democracies to describe the harmonious combination of flexibility and security, or "flexicurity," practiced in continental European welfare states (Rhodes 2001). Scholars have also referred to the phenomenon as "competitive macroconcertation" (Siegel 2005) or "supply side corporatism" (Traxler 2003: 13). The role of the government in these arrangements is to construct and fund comprehensive social safety nets for workers ousted from the labor market, in the form of compensations or active labor market programs. These programs enhance the skills of the work force and its (re)employability, allowing labor to acquiesce to flexible labor market reforms.

Not all countries, however, are in a position to implement, let alone benefit, from competitive corporatism. It is here that we return to encompassing trade union associations, since these associations tend to be associated with public policies that demand a long-term outlook and the ability to overcome the problem of collective action over repeated interactions. Powerful national trade unions would be the only ones with the incentives and power to install a universalistic social welfare system that enhances solidarity among workers and thereby increases the political power of the working class

(Yang 2006: 213–15). Union leaders free from firm- or sector-specific interests are likely to pursue long-term economic interests as opposed to narrow sectoral ones.

If union movements lack institutional means for comprehensive negotiations of distributional issues, however, collective action problems are most likely to be prominent and pervasive. This situation is most prevalent in countries with low or ineffective levels of labor market regulation. Under such conditions, as chapter 3 emphasized, major distributional struggles will tend to be particularistic and temporally shortsighted and are likely to favor wage maximization. Likewise, in response to neoliberal pressure for labor market flexibility, individual unions would prioritize job security over flexibility, since losing a job means losing one's economic livelihood, as the Korean and Chilean cases attest.

## Policy Implications

In institutionally consolidated capitalist democracies the character of labor demands—militant versus moderate—is well defined. In Third Wave societies, however, especially when nondemocratic labor systems have been the norm, basic demands for wages, security, and/or recognition can be considered unduly militant (Buchanan 1995: 72). This is especially the case when labor federations play a dual role—as economic and political agents.[3] This dual nature is most evident in anti–status quo centrals like the Korean Confederation of Trade Unions (KCTU) or the Central Unitaria de Trabajadores (CUT), which consider the overall political role they play to be more important than their economic function. To a large degree then, we can expect protest to be more important in defining the balance of power between labor and capital in countries with intermediate levels of voice representation and labor market regulation.

Beginning in the mid-1980s, economic efficiency and competitiveness rather than social peace became the paramount goal of policy-makers around the world. Economic changes brought on by three major trends—trade liberalization, financial liberalization, and privatization—led governments, employers, and workers to search for new socioeconomic formulas that more readily accommodate flexibility in the production process and in labor organization. Two ways governments have responded, as discussed in this book, have been to facilitate the process of hiring and firing labor and to decentralize collective bargaining (Traxler 1995: 3). The first reduces the costs of labor and makes it easier for employers to adapt to the changing level of employment. The latter tends to bring wages in line with economic conditions and levels of productivity prevailing at the firm level. The main challenge is how to achieve this flexibility without severely reducing worker protection.

Decentralizing wage negotiations has been accompanied by a rise in wage flexibility, linking remunerations to enterprise competitiveness. The process of decentralization, however, has not played out to the same extent throughout the world. While several countries—notably, the United Kingdom, New Zealand, and Chile—have in fact made the firm the only level of wage bargaining (Tokman 2002: 178), the move away from centralized forms of collective bargaining that affected established democracies in the 1980s was reversed in the 1990s (Hassle 2006: 84). In many new democracies, however, national negotiation has been replaced by negotiation by sector, and negotiation by sector is being replaced or supplemented by negotiation at the firm level.

More generally, there has been a change in how labor is regulated, which, in fact, has redefined the relations between the government, markets, and labor unions. According to Tokman (2002: 178–79), this move is known as the passage from heteronomy to autonomy. Heteronomy—which was common under Keynesian macroeconomic coordination and import substitution industrialization (ISI)—refers to a process where the state defines, sanctions, implements, and monitors labor regulations. The move toward social autonomy is meant to enhance the capacity of social partners to respond to economic challenges. In new democracies, however, more autonomy sometimes glosses over the prevailing imbalance of power between labor and management. Ironically then, government and employers are placing added burdens on unions even as they undercut unions' ability to play meaningful roles. In so doing, they may be trading long-term objectives for short-term goals.

There is a need then to strengthen unions and to improve their capacity to represent their members and intervene or participate in decision-making on economic and social matters. In recent years, a number of new democracies have reestablished the right of workers to associate freely and bargain collectively.[4] Strengthening worker protection has drawn governments of all political stripes into labor matters. Nevertheless, state intervention can result, as it unfortunately has in many Third Wave democracies, in subordination of social actors to government and employer objectives.

**Final Observations**

In both Chile and South Korea, the labor regime has become significantly more democratic, primarily because labor unions fought fierce struggles and defended their right to represent the interests of their constituents in a new political environment. The strategies adopted by unions to represent workers' interests in these new scenarios include lessons learned from dealing face-to-face with representatives of government and business. Most importantly, they focus more on rank-and-file needs, are aware of the need to keep the labor force competitive at a global level, and recognize the need to consider employers' and government's demands.

In both countries, moreover, organized labor has become better organized and more autonomous. This would seem to indicate that both tigers, at least in the arena of labor relations, are becoming more "normal." In closing, however, an anonymous Korean striker reminds us that *whereas in the United States and Europe workers bargain first, then strike, in some new democracies workers start with strikes and then perhaps bargain.* At least in this sense, new democracies remain far from anything resembling convergence or consolidation along the lines of their established counterparts.

In registering this profound difference, the goal is not to advocate pessimism. Rather, it is to note that the behavior of labor movements in new democracies is heavily conditioned by factors that have proved more durable and resistant to change than many recent transformations would seem to suggest. These legacies have conditioned trade union strategies and ideological frameworks. Consequently, recent changes in the structure and operation of interest representation systems do not guarantee the success of political inclusion and representation. Consolidation, a process more than an outcome, implies that labor movements may cooperate with governments and employers at times, and may turn militant if the price of cooperation turns out to be too high, as the Chilean and Korean labor movements demonstrate.

# Appendixes

**Appendix 3A**  Data Sources and Definitions

| Variables | Description | Sources |
|---|---|---|
| *Dependent variables* | | |
| Overall unit labor costs | Percentage change in the cost of producing one unit of output over the previous year, in local currency, with respect to the average monthly wage | Economist Intelligence Unit (EIU) Market Indicators and Forecasts[1] |
| Strikes and lockouts | Count of all strikes and lockouts | LABORSTA Internet[2] |
| Workers involved | Count of all workers involved in strikes | LABORSTA Internet |
| *Independent variables* | | |
| Executive partisanship | Partisanship of chief executive's party. Right; Center; Left; Non-partisan | Database of Political Institutions[3] |
| Polarization | Maximum polarization between the executive party and the four principle parties of the legislature. (0) if elections are not competitive or the chief executive's party has an absolute majority in the legislature. Otherwise the maximum difference between the chief executive's party's value and the values of the three largest government parties and the largest opposition party | Database of Political Institutions |
| Durability | Indicator of polity durability based on the number of years since the last (3-point or greater) regime transition | Polity IV dataset[4] |
| Potential labor power | (Ratio of the numbers employed in skill-intensive manufacturing industries relative to numbers employed in low-skill manufacturing industries) * (1 divided by the number of surplus laborers in the economy) | Industrial Statistics Database. CD-Rom. |

Continued

**Appendix 3A** Continued

| Variables | Description | Sources |
|---|---|---|
| | Surplus laborers is calculated as the total working-age population (between 15 and 65) minus the total labor force minus students enrolled in secondary and tertiary education. This total is taken as a percentage of the economically active population | World Development Indicators UNSTATS[5] |
| Wage deregulation | (1) Very low: government determines wage structure. (2) Low: extensive wage controls; government influence extensive. (3) Moderate: some controls including strict minimum wage law. (4) High: wages determined mainly by supply and demand; some minimum wage regulations for specific sectors. (5) Very High: wages determined by supply and demand; no wage regulation; no minimum wage law or law not enforced | Economist Intelligence Unit Market Indicators and Forecasts |
| Employment deregulation | Strictness of employment protection: (1) Very low; (2) Low; (3) Moderate; (4) High; (5) Very high | EIU Market Indicators and Forecasts |
| Inflation | Annual consumer price index (1995=100) | World Development Indicators (WDI)[6] |
| Growth in GDP per capita | Annual percent | WDI |
| Unemployment | Percent of the labor force unemployed | WDI |
| Foreign direct investment | Net incoming foreign direct investment as a percentage of GDP in constant terms | WDI |
| Labor productivity | Gross domestic product (GDP) at purchasing power parity (PPP) in US$ per person employed | Economist Intelligence Unit Market Indicators and Forecasts |
| Openness | Imports plus exports divided by GDP, expressed in real terms | Penn World Table[7] |
| Labor force | Size of the labor force, in total number of workers | World Development Indicators |

## Appendix 4A: Procedures Used for Assigning Fuzzy Set Membership Scores to Causal Conditions

To create a database of social pacts, I selected the following keywords from the secondary literature: "social dialogue," "social concertation," "tripartite concertation," "wage agreement," "national wage agreement," "social pact," "wage pact," "incomes pact," and "unions," and "pact." Once again, I included only countries with a polity score equal to or greater than six.[9] I then searched the Factiva news service for articles pertaining to the topic. Because data for the causal conditions tested is available only since 1994, cases that predate this year were discarded. When a wage agreement or pact covered more than a twelve-month period, only one observation was recorded in the dataset.[10]

While QCA only allows binary variables, its fuzzy-set variant (fs/QCA) makes it possible to examine continuous and interval-scale variables. Fs/QCA begins with the calibration of causal conditions into sets. To carry out analytical operations with fuzzy-sets, some cases have to be considered more "in the set" than others. Cases with a score between 0.5 and 1 are typically considered "more in the set" than out, whereas cases with a score between 0 and 0.5 are considered "more out of the set" than in. Score 0.5 constitutes the crossover point where maximum ambiguity exists regarding whether a case is more "in" or more "out" of a set.

Following the principles of fuzzy set analysis, the following scores were assigned to the outcome PACT:

1.0 for comprehensive pacts
0.8 for tripartite wage agreements
0.6 for bilateral or single-issue pacts

For the independent variables, the range of values observed should be considered and corresponding measures calibrated. For Wage and Employment regulation, the variables used are the same ones introduced in chapter 3 (derived from the EIU Market Indicators and Forecasts). For these variables, 2, 3, and 4 are the only values observed. Since their averages are respectively 2.8 and 3.38, the following scores were assigned to both the Employment and the Wage regulation (W and E) sets:

Score .9 corresponds to a value of 2 in the original variable. In our population of cases, 2 denotes a high level of regulation, or cases that are "rather regulated."

Score .6 reflects a value of 3 in the original variable. This corresponds to a moderate level of regulation. Score .3 reflects a value of 4 for the original variable. In our population, it corresponds to a low level of regulation.

To test for the presence of alliances between influential political parties and unions, a measure of government partisanship was created. Once again, I rely on the partisanship of the chief executive as coded in the Database of Political Institutions (Beck et al. 2001). The variable receives the following values: Right (R); Left (L); Center (C); and Not applicable (0). In assigning set theoretic scores, countries with conservative chief executives receive a fuzzy score of 0, those with left executives a score of 1, and those with centrist and non partisan executives a score of .5.[11]

With respect to the construction of a labor power measure (P), I collected information on the relevant number of national confederations or trade union centers for each country. In many countries, more than two union centers exist but only one or two effectively organize most of the active labor force. To remain as faithful to the literature as possible, the degree of conflict between competing union centrals was also assessed using the secondary literature.[12] Countries with one peak trade union confederation received a fuzzy score of 1, indicating that these cases are as close as possible to the idea of an encompassing trade union organization.[13]

Countries where two peak federations compete for workers' allegiance received a fuzzy score of .7 if their relationship can be construed as competitive, and a score of .4 if their relationship can be characterized as conflictual. In most countries with two trade union centers, the existence of dual organizations is itself a cause for fierce inter-confederal rivalries (Bulgaria, Korea, Poland, Portugal, and Spain). The score of .4 indicates then that these cases are far from representing "cohesive labor organizations." Finally, countries with three or more national trade union centers (Hungary, the Philippines, and Romania) were assigned a fuzzy score of .1. This score indicates that these labor movements are almost certainly fragmented. The following table provides a list of the most relevant union confederations by country, followed by summary measures of union membership represented by these confederations (1993–2003).

| Country | Abbreviation | 1993 | 1998 | 2003 | % change |
|---|---|---|---|---|---|
| Argentina | CGT | | | | |
| Bulgaria | CITUB | 65.10% | 78.10% | 75.70% | 10.6 |
| | CL Podkrepa | 22.80% | 19.90% | 21.10% | -1.7 |
| Chile | CUT | | | | |
| Czech Republic | CMKOS | 50% | | | |
| Greece | GSEE | 67.30% | 63.40% | 66.00% | -1.3 |
| | ADEDY | 32.70% | 36.60% | 34.00% | 1.3 |
| | ASZSZ | | | 16.00% | |
| Hungary | LIGA | | | 10.70% | |
| | ÉSZT | | | 9.10% | |
| | MOSZ | | | 6.00% | |
| Korea | KCTU | | 418,000[8] | | |
| | FKTU | | 901,000 | | |
| Mexico | CTM | | 5.5 million | | |
| | FAT | | + 2 million | | |
| | CGT | | ~600,000 | | |
| Philippines | KMU | | | | |
| | TUCP | | | | |
| Poland | OPZZ | 67.70% | 61.00% | 42.10% | -25.6 |
| | NSZZ | 30.10% | 36.60% | 41.10% | 11 |
| | Solidarność | | | | |
| | FZZ | | | 16.80% | |
| Portugal | CGTP | | | 56.00% | |
| | UGT | | | 34.30% | |
| Romania | Meridian | 1.20% | 14.50% | 34.10% | 32.9 |
| | Cartel Alfa | 36.10% | 35.50% | 22.70% | -13.4 |
| | CNSLR | 38.60% | 27.60% | 18.10% | -20.5 |
| | CSDR | 19.60% | 21.00% | 14.80% | -4.8 |
| | BNS | | | 9.60% | |
| Russia | FNPR | 75–98% | | | |
| Slovakia | KOZ SR | 99.40% | 97.30% | 96.20% | -3.2 |
| South Africa | COSATU | | 1.8 million | | |
| Spain | CC.OO | | | 45.40% | |
| | UGT | | | 44.80% | |
| | KESK | | | | |
| Turkey | DISK | | | | |
| | HAK-İŞ | | | | |
| | TÜRK-İŞ | | | | |
| Ukraine | FPU | | 75–98% | | |

*Source*: European Industrial Relations Observatory On-line. http://www.eurofound.europa.eu/eiro/. http://en.wikipedia.org/wiki/List_of_federations_of_trade_unions.

**Appendix 4B** Database of Social Pacts in New Democracies

| Country | Year | Pact | Wage Regulation | Employment Regulation | Left government | Labor Power |
|---|---|---|---|---|---|---|
| Argentina | 1994 | 1 | 0.6 | 0.9 | 0 | 1 |
| Argentina | 1997 | 0.6 | 0.6 | 0.9 | 0 | 1 |
| Argentina | 2000 | 0.6 | 0.3 | 0.9 | 0.5 | 1 |
| Bulgaria | 1994 | 1 | 0.6 | 0.9 | 0.5 | 0.4 |
| Bulgaria | 1995 | 0.6 | 0.6 | 0.9 | 0.5 | 0.4 |
| Bulgaria | 1997 | 0.8 | 0.6 | 0.9 | 0 | 0.4 |
| Bulgaria | 1998 | 0.6 | 0.6 | 0.6 | 0 | 0.4 |
| Bulgaria | 2000 | 0.6 | 0.6 | 0.6 | 0 | 0.4 |
| Bulgaria | 2002 | 1 | 0.6 | 0.6 | 0.5 | 0.4 |
| Chile | 1994 | 0.6 | 0.6 | 0.3 | 0 | 1 |
| Czech Republic | 1994 | 0.8 | 0.6 | 0.6 | 0 | 1 |
| Greece | 1994 | 1 | 0.3 | 0.9 | 1 | 0.7 |
| Greece | 1996 | 1 | 0.3 | 0.9 | 1 | 0.7 |
| Greece | 1998 | 1 | 0.3 | 0.9 | 1 | 0.7 |
| Greece | 2000 | 1 | 0.3 | 0.9 | 1 | 0.7 |
| Greece | 2002 | 1 | 0.3 | 0.9 | 1 | 0.7 |
| Greece | 2004 | 0.8 | 0.3 | 0.9 | 1 | 0.7 |
| Hungary | 1994 | 0.6 | 0.3 | 0.6 | 0 | 0.1 |
| Hungary | 1995 | 0.8 | 0.3 | 0.6 | 1 | 0.1 |
| Hungary | 1996 | 0.8 | 0.3 | 0.6 | 1 | 0.1 |
| Hungary | 1997 | 0.8 | 0.6 | 0.6 | 1 | 0.1 |
| Hungary | 1998 | 0.8 | 0.6 | 0.6 | 1 | 0.1 |
| Hungary | 2003 | 0.8 | 0.6 | 0.6 | 1 | 0.1 |
| Korea | 1993 | 0.8 | 0.3 | 0.9 | 0 | 0.4 |
| Korea | 1998 | 1 | 0.3 | 0.9 | 0.5 | 0.4 |
| Korea | 2000 | 0.6 | 0.3 | 0.9 | 0.5 | 0.4 |
| Korea | 2004 | 1 | 0.3 | 0.9 | 0.5 | 0.4 |
| Mexico | 1998 | 0.8 | 0.3 | 0.6 | 1 | 0.7 |
| Mexico | 1999 | 0.8 | 0.3 | 0.6 | 1 | 0.7 |
| Mexico | 2000 | 0.8 | 0.3 | 0.6 | 1 | 0.7 |
| Mexico | 2001 | 0.8 | 0.3 | 0.6 | 0 | 0.7 |
| Mexico | 2002 | 0.8 | 0.3 | 0.6 | 0 | 0.7 |
| Mexico | 2003 | 0.8 | 0.3 | 0.6 | 0 | 0.7 |
| Mexico | 2004 | 0.8 | 0.3 | 0.6 | 0 | 0.7 |
| Philippines | 1998 | 1 | 0.6 | 0.3 | 0.5 | 0.1 |
| Philippines | 2004 | 1 | 0.6 | 0.3 | 0.5 | 0.1 |
| Poland | 1994 | 0.8 | 0.6 | 0.6 | 0.5 | 0.4 |
| Poland | 1995 | 0.8 | 0.6 | 0.6 | 0.5 | 0.4 |
| Poland | 1996 | 0.8 | 0.6 | 0.6 | 1 | 0.4 |
| Poland | 1997 | 0.8 | 0.6 | 0.6 | 1 | 0.4 |
| Poland | 1998 | 1 | 0.6 | 0.6 | 1 | 0.4 |
| Poland | 2001 | 0.6 | 0.6 | 0.6 | 1 | 0.4 |
| Poland | 2003 | 0.6 | 0.6 | 0.6 | 1 | 0.1 |
| Portugal | 1996 | 0.6 | 0.3 | 0.9 | 1 | 0.4 |

Continued

**Appendix 4B** Continued

| Country | Year | Pact | Wage Regulation | Employment Regulation | Left government | Labor Power |
|---|---|---|---|---|---|---|
| Portugal | 1997 | 1 | 0.3 | 0.9 | 1 | 0.4 |
| Portugal | 1998 | 0.6 | 0.3 | 0.9 | 1 | 0.4 |
| Portugal | 1999 | 0.6 | 0.3 | 0.9 | 1 | 0.4 |
| Portugal | 2001 | 1 | 0.3 | 0.9 | 1 | 0.4 |
| Romania | 1995 | 0.8 | 0.6 | 0.9 | 0.5 | 0.1 |
| Romania | 2001 | 0.8 | 0.6 | 0.6 | 1 | 0.1 |
| Romania | 2002 | 0.8 | 0.6 | 0.6 | 1 | 0.1 |
| Romania | 2004 | 0.6 | 0.3 | 0.3 | 1 | 0.1 |
| Russia | 1994 | 0.8 | 0.6 | 0.6 | 0.5 | 1 |
| Russia | 1995 | 0.8 | 0.6 | 0.6 | 0.5 | 1 |
| Russia | 1998 | 0.8 | 0.6 | 0.6 | 0.5 | 1 |
| Russia | 1999 | 0.8 | 0.6 | 0.6 | 0.5 | 1 |
| Russia | 2001 | 0.8 | 0.6 | 0.3 | 0.5 | 1 |
| Russia | 2004 | 0.8 | 0.6 | 0.3 | 0.5 | 1 |
| Slovakia | 1994 | 0.8 | 0.6 | 0.3 | 1 | 1 |
| Slovakia | 1995 | 0.8 | 0.6 | 0.6 | 1 | 1 |
| Slovakia | 1996 | 0.8 | 0.6 | 0.6 | 1 | 1 |
| Slovakia | 2000 | 0.8 | 0.6 | 0.6 | 0.5 | 1 |
| Slovakia | 2003 | 0.6 | 0.3 | 0.3 | 0.5 | 1 |
| South Africa | 1997 | 0.6 | 0.9 | 0.6 | 1 | 1 |
| South Africa | 2002 | 1 | 0.9 | 0.9 | 1 | 1 |
| Spain | 1996 | 1 | 0.6 | 0.6 | 1 | 0.4 |
| Spain | 1997 | 1 | 0.6 | 0.6 | 0 | 0.4 |
| Spain | 1999 | 0.6 | 0.6 | 0.6 | 0 | 0.4 |
| Spain | 2001 | 0.8 | 0.3 | 0.6 | 0 | 0.4 |
| Spain | 2002 | 0.6 | 0.3 | 0.6 | 0 | 0.4 |
| Spain | 2003 | 0.8 | 0.3 | 0.6 | 0 | 0.4 |
| Spain | 2004 | 1 | 0.3 | 0.6 | 0 | 0.4 |
| Turkey | 1997 | 0.6 | 0.6 | 0.3 | 0 | 0.1 |
| Turkey | 2001 | 0.6 | 0.6 | 0.6 | 1 | 0.1 |
| Turkey | 2002 | 0.6 | 0.6 | 0.6 | 1 | 0.1 |
| Turkey | 2003 | 0.6 | 0.6 | 0.6 | 0.5 | 0.1 |
| Ukraine | 1995 | 0.8 | 0.6 | 0.6 | 0.5 | 1 |
| Ukraine | 1997 | 0.8 | 0.6 | 0.6 | 0.5 | 1 |

# Notes

## Introduction

1. The term "new democracies" is used interchangeably in this book with "Third Wave democracies" and "emerging democracies" and is synonymous in many cases with Less Developed Countries (LDCs). Nevertheless, the term refers here to countries that began the transition to a democratic regime on or after 1974—the date most commonly used as the beginning of the Third Wave of democratization—and remained democratic thereafter (Huntington 1991).
2. Originally coined by Thucydides (Canfora1992), this maxim referred to nation states in the international system. In my case, I use it to refer to workers in new democracies.
3. Corporatism in this study refers to a form of policymaking where the state officially incorporates interest groups (i.e., labor and employer organizations) into the policymaking machinery of the state. The state may also be involved in licensing and regulating these groups, effectively co-opting their leadership in the process or circumscribing their ability to challenge state authority. See Schmitter (1974) for a full elaboration of this concept.
4. More formally, I combine within-case and cross-case evidence using what is known as the XY-centered approach to within-case analysis (Lieberman 2005; Rohlfing 2008). In this approach, the starting point and end point within cases are known at the outset. The prime goal of the investigator is thus to uncover other systematic variables whose effect can be estimated in the cross-case portion of the analysis, and causal mechanisms that link X to Y within the cases.
5. Exceptions include Rudra (2002, 2005).

## 1 Industrial Relations after the Third Wave

1. Walton and Seddon (1994: 333–34) document a global trend toward the democratization of authoritarian and one-party regimes in the 1980s and 1990s. This includes nineteen one-party states in Africa and

four continental powers (Brazil and Mexico in Latin America and Nigeria and Algeria in Africa). As of 2005, more than half of the world's nearly 200 countries held regular multiparty elections, more than at any time in history (Gurr and Marshall 2005).
2. Other terms used to denote this phenomenon include "tripartite concertation," "social concertation," and "(neo)-corporatist concertation."
3. This claim jives well with Terry Lynn Karl's (2000) observation that the degree of equality, rather than the level of economic development, may be the best indicator of political stability in democracies.
4. Evidence for Nollert's (1995) modified theory of corporatism, however, is not consistently supported in his analysis. Nollert found that neo-corporatism directly suppresses the more militant forms of protest regardless of the degree of income inequality and economic performance. In other words, the neo-corporatist effect is not strictly an indirect one. As he himself notes, prior to 1968 there was little difference between pluralistic and neo-corporatist polities and, in general, there is little difference in this period between pluralistic states and the moderate neo-corporatist regimes. Only fully developed neo-corporatism appears to have a significant dampening effect on protest.
5. For a useful topical and geographical survey, see Trebilcock (1994).
6. This is the view of the ILO with respect to the reforms carried out in the new democracies of Central and Eastern Europe, Latin America, and South Africa. International Labour Organization (1997: 107).
7. As of 1999, six new democracies had laws/regulations in place banning or restricting some types of unions (ILO 2004; ICFTU 2006). They are Brazil, Chile, Honduras, Latvia, Thailand, and Turkey.
8. This is also true of Schmitter's (1974) notion of "societal corporatism."
9. Other examples of exclusionary corporatism include the bureaucratic authoritarian military regime in Chile (1973–1990), Salazar's *Estado Novo* in Portugal (1932–1974), Franco's regime in Spain (1936–1975), and South Korea's *Yushin* (1972–1980) and Fifth Republic dictatorships (1972–1980, 1981–1988). Inclusionary corporatism imposing high constraints on organized labor include Argentina (before 1976), Brazil (before 1964), Mexico, and Venezuela (1958–1999).
10. This type of corporatism is indistinguishable from Schmitter's notion of state corporatism. See Valenzuela (1989: 448).
11. Statistical Appendix of 1997–1998 World Labour Report, http://www.ilo.org/public/english/dialogue/ifpdial/publ/wlr97/annex/tab31.htm.
12. International Labour Organization (1997: 148–49).
13. International Labour Organization (1997: 158–61).
14. International Labour Organization (1997: 165–69).

15. South Africa, although noted as having registered a neat increase in union membership, had just emerged from dictatorship in 1994.
16. OECD stands for "Organisation for Economic Co-operation and Development."
17. Greskovits has also argued a similar point, namely, that "the exclusionary logic of rapid marketization is in conflict with the participatory logic of democratic politics." See Greskovits (1998: 69).
18. One important exception is Ost's (2000) study of tripartism in Eastern Europe, which labels the experiences of Eastern European countries with corporatist policymaking "illusory corporatism." In his view, labor incorporation has been used to bless a package of exclusionary economic policies that denies the value of concerted policymaking in the first place.

## 2 Democratization and Socioeconomic Security

1. Deyo and Agartan (2003) note that these reforms have been particularly prevalent in developing countries over the past three decades.
2. The data for these figures are taken from the ILO October Inquiry database and standardized so that they may be comparable by country and year and across occupations.
3. See, for example, the Polity IV country reports for 2007, where democracy is taken to mean a Polity score of 6 or more. http://www.systemicpeace.org/polity/polity06.htm.
4. The exception is Peru, which experienced a democratic backslide in the 1990s.
5. In Latin America, it has been estimated that informal labor rose from 44 percent of total employment in 1990 to about 48 percent by the end of the decade (ILO 2004: 140).
6. The remaining five indexes are the Labour Market Security Index (LMSI), the Job Security Index (JSI), the Skills Security Index (SSI), the Work Security Index (WSI), and the Income Security Index (ISI). All seven indexes can be combined into an overall Economic Security Index (ESI).
7. Process indicators measured are the existence of a tripartite board or council, a law allowing nongovernmental organizations to operate to promote workers' interests, the percentage of total employment covered by collective agreements adjusted by the percentage of the workforce in wage and salaried employment, and the share of employees in total employment (ILO 2004: 270).
8. More formally, the coefficient of codetermination (or $R^2$) for the model is 0.25.
9. Wildcat militancy refers to a strike action taken by workers without the authorization of their trade union officials. Alternatively, unions

can experience wildcat cooperation, which refers to workers in a particular firm agreeing to a level of compensation that is lower than that stipulated nationally (Blake 1996; Streeck 1984: 296–97).

## 3 Labor Market Regulation and Industrial Conflict

1. The exceptions are Greece (where the national minimum wage rate is fixed by collective agreement) and Ukraine. See Eyraud and Saget (2005: 18–22).
2. State socialist regimes in Eastern Europe and the former Soviet Union, for example, required all workers to belong to unions until the late 1980s or early 1990s. As a result, the ILO (2004), in constructing its RSI, halves unionization rates for all of these countries. The unionization figures are also adjusted by multiplying the recorded rate (or halving it in the case of the ex-Soviet countries) by the percentage of the workforce in wage and salaried employment.
3. Another way to explain this phenomenon is as follows: if low-skilled workers are going to receive higher wages than their skills command on the open market, then high-skilled workers need to reduce their wage demands for wage pacts to be attractive to employers.
4. Tsebelis and Lange report that participation of the left in government is a better predictor of strike activity than the various measures of corporatism available in the literature. Regressions including only one of these variables come to the same qualitative result, but with a lower fit. Tsebelis and Lange (1995: 118).
5. This relationship is most commonly expressed by the equation $s = a + cP - dP^2 + e$, where $s$ is the level of strike activity, $c$ and $d$ are positive constants, and $P$ is some measure of the power of Labor in different countries. Soskice (1990: 40) concluded, however, that a linear specification best captured the relationship between wage bargaining and unemployment in a number of OECD countries.
6. Rama (2003: 172). In other countries, however, the ability of unions to obtain wage premiums is considerable. Examples include the Philippines and South Africa. See ILO (2004).
7. The correlation between the outcome measure of employment protection as coded in the SES database and the EIU indicator of employment regulation is statistically significant ($r=.53$). Looking instead at formal levels of employment protection, the correlation between the "input" SES measure and the EIU indicator retains its statistical significance ($r=.64$). This suggests not only that the two indicators are highly interchangeable, but that the EIU employment protection measure reflects formal levels of regulation as well as their implementation.

8. I thank Pat Thaker of the EIU Market Indicators and Forecasts bureau for explaining how the score is calculated and providing some relevant examples.
9. Many countries in the developing world set minimum wages too low, or are too lax in enforcing the law for it to have much effect. See Freeman (1992: 126).
10. In general, this cutoff comports well with the judgement of scholars regarding which countries can be classified as democratic and which cannot. Mexico before 1997 and Pakistan after 1999, for example, have polity scores below 6 and hence are not included in the regressions.
11. Schmitter (1981) argues that the relationship between the ideological orientation of the government and the presence of neo-corporatist institutions is not deterministic. In reality, however, the two tend to be highly correlated.
12. This variable was derived from the Database of Political Institutions' "Chief Executive's Party" variable. See Beck et al. (2001).
13. Examples include the Peronist Party in Argentina, the National Revolutionary Movement in Bolivia, Solidarity in Poland, the African National Congress in South Africa, the Institutional Revolutionary Party (PRI) in Mexico, the Spanish Socialist Workers' Party (PSOE), and the Venezuelan Democratic Action (DA). See Burgess (1999).
14. This was the situation in Argentina, and to a lesser extent in Brazil and Uruguay, during the first years of democracy. See Buchanan (1995: 45–46).
15. Korpi (1974) predicts a direct relationship between the balance of power and the going rate of exchange in the labor market.
16. Many researchers consider fixed effects superior to random effects since the former is the best linear unbiased estimator in the presence of correlation between the country indicator variable and other regressors (Hsiao 2003: 35), a fairly common situation in most work in comparative political economy. As an alternative, Beck and Katz (1995) recommend panel-corrected standard errors (PCSE) with a lagged dependent variable. A model with PCSE would not be appropriate, however, since the number of years in the data is ten. This estimation is suitable with time series cross-sectional (TSCS) datasets where the number of time periods is typically greater than twenty.
17. Typical datasets in comparative political economy tend to be highly collinear and not drawn from a random sample (Western and Jackman 1994).
18. This is a necessary step for running a FEVD model. These calculations, however, are not reported here.
19. For the first two models, I use a robust cluster estimator for the covariance matrix.

20. In both the random-effects and fixed-effects cases, the dispersion is the same for all elements in the same group. In the random-effects model, the dispersion varies randomly from group to group, while in the fixed-effects model it can take on any value, since a conditional likelihood is used in which the dispersion parameter drops out of the estimation (Hausman, Hall, and Griliches 1984).
21. As the Korean case in chapter 5 illustrates, safety nets were almost nonexistent in South Korea until the East Asian financial crisis of 1998.

### 4  Labor Market Regulation and Social Dialogue

1. I could only find one published article that presented and analyzed evidence of pact-making for several new democracies. See Blake (1996). For some comparative studies on the subject, see Roxborough (1992) and Przeworski (1991).
2. The motivation for using QCA is in part theoretical, but also practical. With only seventy-eight cases of consummated social pacts, there are not enough observations to perform multiple regression analysis.
3. This framework primarily applies to the analysis of labor responses to neoliberal reforms. Nevertheless, the approach can be extended to the study of industrial relations.
4. In Boolean algebra, the "*" (sometimes omitted) symbolizes the logical operator "AND," "+" the logical operator "OR," and "→" is used to denote a causal relationship.
5. A more explicit discussion of coding rules can be found in Appendix 4A.
6. In the Philippines in 1998, for example, agreements on industrial peace were forged between labor and management covering 85 percent of business firms and 10 regions in the country. "'No Strike, No Lockout' Adopted in 10 Regions," *Manila Standard*, October 14 1998.
7. See, for example, "Government, Unions, and Employers Sign Cooperation Agreement," Bulgarian News Agency BTA, March 26, 2002.
8. Mexican unions voted against the rise in the minimum wage for 2001 proposed by representatives of the government and employers in December 2000 in the National Commission on Minimum Wages. See "Labor-Mexico: Minimum Wage Increase Too Small to Dent Poverty," *Global Information Network*, December 26, 2000. The agreement, however, went into effect on January 1, 2001. In 2001 and 2002, it was the employer representatives that judged the wage increase too high and voted against it. See "CNSM-Salarios,"

*Servicio Universal de Noticias,* December 28, 2001; "Aumentan 4.5% en promedio los minisalarios," *Novedades,* December 20, 2002.
9. In Mexico, for example, the National Commission on Minimum Wages (Conapros), a body comprised of representatives of state, business, and labor, votes on yearly increases in the minimum wage. Labor's interests are represented by the Mexican Workers Confederation (CTM), one of the world's biggest trade unions holding approximately 55 percent of the country's collective bargaining agreements. Minimum wages are crucial in a country in which 57 percent of workers had no social benefits, while 46 percent were employed under a verbal contract. "Minimum Wage Increase Too Small to Dent Poverty," *Global Information Network,* December 26, 2000.
10. Typically, instances of the outcome do not have any causal conditions in common. If they do, however, the goal is to have high coverage for a single condition or high coverage for alternate conditions (joined by logical or). I thank Charles Ragin for bringing this point to my attention.
11. This represents the "complex" (or detailed) solution. In our analysis no further simplification is possible.
12. Set theoretic coverage gauges empirical relevance or importance. The way the solution coverage is calculated exhibits some conceptual similarities to the meaning of the coefficient of codetermination ($R^2$) in regression analysis (Ragin 2006: 301).
13. For a treatment of this question in the case of established democracies, see Baccaro and Simoni 2008.
14. The strike data for these two countries is also available for the entire period of analysis. For the Philippines, coverage ends in 2000, and for South Africa, in 1998, only four years after the transition to democracy.

## 5 Protest and Social Dialogue in South Korea

1. South Koreans worked an average of 53.8 hours a week, had the biggest gender differential in pay (women earning only 44 percent of male salaries in 1980), and had a rate of fatal injuries more than double that of Singapore, Hong Kong, Argentina, Mexico, the United States, and Japan (Buchanan and Nicholls 2004: 61).
2. By the late 1980s, chaebol owners and their families had become a de facto ruling elite. Their supply of political funding, ownership of much of the mass media, and social ties based on school, region, and intermarriage provided them with considerable influence in policymaking (Kwon and O'Donnell 2001: 24).

3. According to Ogle (1990: 99), the protests had reached such a level of intensity that the primary manufacturer of tear gas was reported to have received the highest income in the country that year.
4. "The Price of Democracy," *Far Eastern Economic Review*, January 29, 1988.
5. See Articles 13.1 and 15.
6. Article 26.
7. Article 32.
8. "The late blooming of the South Korean labor movement," *Monthly Review*, New York, Jul/Aug 1997.
9. National Statistical Office. http://www.nso.go.kr/eng2006/emain/index.html.
10. "Organized Teachers retreat in clash with government," *Far Eastern Economic Review*, November 4, 1993.
11. Kim Young Sam should have opposed a merger with his rival power bloc, but the two-thirds majority suited his desire to run for president in 1993.
12. "Kim Young-sam Makes Reconciliation Approach to Dissidents," *Yonhap News*, April 1, 1993.
13. There were a few exceptions, such as the transportation sector (e.g., the taxi and bus industries) having regional-level bargaining practices and the textile sector having sectoral-level bargaining practices.
14. The discussion that follows is largely based on Tae (2002).
15. "AFL Protests Korean Unionists Arrest & Toy Worker Conditions," *AFL-CIO News*, January 5, 1996.
16. Access to cheap credit was seen as a threat to Korea's egalitarian social structure as well as its global economic competitiveness.
17. "Rough Sailing Expected Over Labor Talks," *Korea Herald*, June 13, 1996.
18. Korea's five main economic organizations included the Federation of Korean industries (FKI), the Korean Employers' Federation (KEF), the Korea Chamber of Commerce and Industry (KCCI), the Korea Foreign Trade Association (KFTA), and the Korea Federation of Small Business (KFSB).
19. They included, inter alia, mutual participation and cooperation, respect for mutual autonomy, vitality of labor markets and balanced development among sectors, and enhancement of national competitiveness.
20. The government did not show any intention to amend the related "Political Fund Act" and the "Act on the Election of Public Officials and the Prevention of Election Malpractices" (Statutes of the Republic of Korea, vol. 1 [Constitution, National Assembly, Election and

Political Parties, Administration, Public Officials and Foreign Affairs]).
21. In effect, the majority of the nation's unions would be unable to afford union dues, which had been limited to a maximum 2 percent of total wages (Koo 2002: 67).
22. According to a survey conducted by the *Hankyoreh*, 78 percent of respondents thought the government drafts of bills were far more favorable to management than to labor. *Hankyoreh*, December 11, 1996.
23. "Unions Poised to Start Strike to Protest Labor Law Reform," *Yonhap News*, December 4, 1996.
24. "Objection to Passage of Labor Reform Bill within Year Reaffirmed," *Yonhap News*, December 11, 1996.
25. Act No. 5473, December 24, 1997.
26. There was a slight difference of opinion between the President's Office—represented by Senior Secretary Park Se Il—and NKP's chairman Lee Hong Ku over this postponement.
27. It required employers to receive mandatory approval from a central or local Labor Relations Commission prior to layoffs though.
28. "Trade Union Confederation Instructs General Strike," *Yonhap News*, December 26, 1996.
29. "Unionists Threaten Wider Strike, Defying Crackdown," *Yonhap News*, January 6, 1997.
30. "Public Sector Trade Unions to Stage Strikes, Jan.13," *Yonhap News*, December 31, 1996.
31. Strikes in the transportation sector, however, were suspended by union leaders in consideration of inconvenience to citizens.
32. As part of an effort to mollify workers and the public, the government in February 1997 disclosed a plan to enact a special law designed to improve the quality of life and the welfare of workers.
33. "KCTU to Launch Strikes Only Wednesdays to Reduce Economic Loss," *Yonhap News*, January 18, 1997.
34. Labor Standards Act (Act No. 5309), March 13, 1997. http://www.lmg.go.kr/english/sub03/sub03_2.asp.
35. "Labor Groups Likely to Form Political Force," *Korea Herald*, March 31, 1997.
36. Kim Dae Jung drew support from the lower classes in urban and rural areas. His populist appeals have inspired workers and mobilized their political support.
37. These included, among others, liberalization of foreign investment in the stock market, increases in the ceiling on aggregate foreign ownership in firms from 26 percent to 55 percent by the end of 1998; foreign equity purchases of Korean domestic banks; foreign purchases of Korean money market investments and corporate bonds; elimination

of all government-directed lending; an end to all subsidized credit and tax privileges; elimination of all restrictions on foreign borrowing by corporations; and liberalization of the trade regime.
38. http://www.lmg.go.kr/.
39. Act No. 5510, February 20, 1998. http://www.lmg.go.kr/english/sub03/sub03_3.asp.
40. "KCTU to Be Legalized Next Month," *Korea Times*, March 15, 998.
41. "Unionists Go on Strike after Talks with Government Fail," *Yonhap News*, May 27, 1998.
42. "Unionists Start Strike, Warn Bigger Protests Will Follow," *Yonhap News*, July 22, 1998.
43. "Hyundai Motor Co.'s Unionized Workers Stages Demos in Seoul," *Yonhap News*, July 27, 1998.
44. "Trade Unions Refuse Labor Committee Talks, Plans to Hold Rally," *Yonhap News*, July 10, 1998.
45. "KCTU Bolts Tripartite Panel Wed., Demanding End to Restructuring," *Yonhap News*, February 24, 1999.
46. The Teachers' Labor Union Act was designed to allow teachers, who were considered government employees, the right to unionize and bargain collectively. "Finally, the Government Gives in to Recognize the KCTU," *KCTU News*, November 23, 1999.
47. "Third-term Three-way Panel on Labor Affairs Meets Again Wednesday," *Yonhap News*, September 1, 1999.
48. Others included policy direction for development and reform in the financial sector (July 12, 2000); reduction of working hours (October 23, 2000); the Basic Law for Workers' Welfare (October 23, 2000); regulation of financial holding companies and merger activities (December 21, 2000); and improvement in vocational training programs (July 31, 2001).
49. This section is largely based on research conducted in the archives of Yonhap news agency in Seoul in the summer of 2003.
50. Even without the Saturday off, if a worker does use all of her available leave, she is actually working 38 hours per week, according to the KEF report. On average, workers work for 44.6 hours a week in Taiwan, 37.4 hours in the United States, 42.9 hours in Germany, and 36.3 hours in Japan.
51. The KEF argued that the cut in working hours would result in a wage increase of 14.4 percent.
52. Atypical workers were defined as employed at least one month per year (temporary workers), working more than eighteen hours per week (part-time workers) or working less than 30.8 hours per week (day workers). See Yang (2006: 222).
53. *Dong-a Ilbo* daily, September 5, 2006.

## 6 Protest and Social Dialogue in Democratic Chile

1. Edwards and Lustig (1997: 2) state that "[i]t is no exaggeration to say that the labor market has been forgotten in Latin America's economic reform." For further evidence of the continued salience of labor market regulation in Latin America, see Cook (1998) and Murillo (2005).
2. The number of ILO conventions ratified by Latin American and East Asian countries up to December 2004 is as follows: Argentina, 72; Brazil, 90; Colombia, 59; Mexico, 78; Peru, 71; Indonesia, 17; Malaysia, 34; Singapore, 23; Thailand, 14. This compares to 14 for the United States. Many European countries, on the other hand, had ratified most of them; for example: France, 124; Germany, 83; Spain, 129; Sweden, 93. See the International Labour Organization Database of International Labour Standards http://www.ilo.org/ilolex/english/index.htm.
3. In 1996, the poorest quintile of the population enjoyed 3.4 percent of per capita GNP, while the richest quintile made out with 61.3 percent. This compares to 4.4 percent and 59.9 percent, respectively, in 1990. "El País ha Disfrutado de un Crecimiento Económico Envidiable, pero con Alto Costo Social," *Reuters—Noticias Latinoamericanas*, December 8, 1999.
4. They were restored in 1986.
5. Biglaiser (2002: 3) claims that Chile became the first developing country to orient its economy toward the market. Pollack (1999: 197) argues that nowhere was the new economic and political model applied so vigorously as in Chile. Ffrench-Davis (2002: 29) characterizes the program as exceptional in its purity, depth, extensiveness of coverage, and duration.
6. Prior to 1981, the state had subsidized the health system for workers by paying the difference between contributions made by employees and employers to the National Health Service.
7. Roberts (1998: 82) notes that the Chilean right has historically been able to recognize and defend its interests, but never before have these interests been embedded in such a distinctive and all-encompassing ideological vision as they are today under neoliberalism.
8. See "La Constitución, la Ley Electoral y el Consejo de Seguridad Marcaron los Últimos 10 Años," *La Vanguardia*, December 7, 1999.
9. "Chile Politics: Constitutional Reform Is Enacted," *Economist Intelligence Unit*, October 28, 2005.
10. The Chilean left has had more extensive experience with efforts to deepen democracy than any other in Latin America, and perhaps no other left has been so thoroughly shaped by the successes and failures of such efforts. See Roberts (1998: 86).

11. A revisionist view defends the impact of popular protest on the democratic transition (Oxhorn 1995), and it remains true that the 1988 plebiscite defeated Pinochet's plans to remain in power for another eight years.
12. A smaller leftist coalition, the PAIS or *Partido Amplio de Izquierda Socialista*, also clinched a few seats. The remaining seats were taken by the *Democracia y Progreso* pact, an electoral alliance formed by RN and UDI and later renamed *Unión por el Progreso de Chile*.
13. This new alliance made the Socialists the first party with Marxist roots to assume major national-level governmental responsibilities during Latin America's contemporary wave of democratization. See Roberts (1998: 84).
14. In this unique majority system, which governs Chile's congressional elections, political parties or groupings form pacts and permit slates (two candidates per slate), from which two senators and two deputies are elected from each district. By requiring each party to obtain two-thirds of the vote in each district for the successful election of its two candidates to the legislature, this system gives the opposition disproportionate representation in Congress.
15. Despite losing this battle, the SOFOFA remained by far the most powerful member of the CPC and continued to pose a major obstacle at nearly every stage of negotiating the Accord's implementation.
16. Law 19.069 on Workers' Organizations and Collective Negotiations.
17. Barrett (2001: 567). See Law 19.049 on Labor Confederations.
18. July 11 is the anniversary of the 1971 strikes at El Teniente mine. See Frías (1995: 69).
19. "Médicos Chilenos Realizan Huelgas por Mejores Salarios," *Reuters—Noticias Latinoamericanas*, October 27, 1994.
20. "Law on Associations for Public Administration Employees," 19,296/ February, 28, 1994.
21. "Lider Sindical Pronuncia Discurso en Medio de Protestas," *Reuters—Noticias Latinoamericanas*, May 1, 1995.
22. In a survey administered to 1,240 people in twenty-nine cities, it was revealed that 60 percent of wage-earners preferred collective wage negotiations and 83 percent considered strikes had legitimate causes. The majority of those surveyed were also against replacing workers during periods of strike. The majority also thought that the fear of dismissal explained the decline in unionization in Chile. "Trabajadores Chilenos Creen que Leyes Favorecen a Empresarios," *Reuters—Noticias Latinoamericanas*, August 7, 1995.
23. Between 1993 and 1995, this figure had increased to 24.8 percent of the total workforce. As of 1995, about 3 million workers remained uncovered by collective negotiations. See Frías (1996: 216).

NOTES 169

24. "Crisis Política en Coalición Chilena de Gobierno," *Reuters—Noticias Latinoamericanas*, April 22, 1996.
25. "Masiva Manifestación de Trabajadores en Chile," *Reuters—Noticias Latinoamericanas*, November 10, 1995.
26. "Trabajadores de la Salud Paralizan Labores en Chile," *Reuters—Noticias Latinoamericanas*, August 28, 1996.
27. "Maestros y Trabajadores de Salud Chilenos Protestan por Salarios," *Reuters—Noticias Latinoamericanas*, August 27, 1996.
28. "Concluye Prolongada Huelga de Mineros Carboníferos en Chile," *Reuters—Noticias Latinoamericanas*, July 26, 1996.
29. "Mineros del Carbón Toman Dos Ministerios Chilenos," *Reuters—Noticias Latinoamericanas*, June 21, 1996.
30. "Accord Ends Conflict Over Mine Closure," *Inter Press Service*, May 12, 1997.
31. Edwards, Sebastian, "Thanks, Mr. Hoffa, but Chile has Plenty of Labor Laws," *the Wall Street Journal*, January 14, 2000.
32. "Frei Culpa a Derecha por Fracaso de Reforma Laboral en Chile," *Reuters—Noticias Latinoamericanas*, December 2, 1999.
33. February 17, 1999.
34. "Peor Tasa de Desempleo en Chile en Once Años, 10.8 por ciento," *Reuters—Noticias Latinoamericanas*, July 28, 1999.
35. The industrialists' association, Sofofa, calculated that payroll costs would rise by up to 13 percent in a firm employing thirty-five people with an average monthly wage of Ps200000, and by up to 18 percent in a firm employing twenty workers with an average wage of Ps150000. See "Chile economy—New law revises many aspects of labor market," the Economist Intelligence Unit, November 14, 2002.
36. "CUT and Lagos Clash on Labor Issues," *Chile Information Project*, May 2, 2002.
37. "Reunion clave tendrán CPC, CUT y gobierno," *Diario Financiero*, December 18, 2002.
38. "Anuncia Central Obrera Chilena 'Independencia' ante próximo gobierno," Agencia Mexicana de Noticias, September 22, 2005.

### Conclusion

1. Figure 2.5 also showed, however, that Mexico has very high levels of formal voice representation compared to its formal level of employment regulation. The opposite is the case for Portugal.
2. Minimum wages on average were 20 percent lower in 1995 than in 1980. See Tokman (2002: 142).
3. The political role assumed by umbrella labor confederations allows affiliate unions to concentrate attention on industry-specific economic

and work-related issues. Conversely, national labor confederations serve as "amplifiers" of local union demands. In so doing, they serve as agents of class consciousness, collective solidarity, and sectoral mobilization, rather than as national economic agents of a particular occupational category (Buchanan 1995: 72).
4. In Latin America, democratic governments introduced nine constitutional changes and six labor code reforms throughout the 1980s and 1990s (Tokman 2002).

### Appendix

1. http://countryindicators.bvdep.com/cgi/template.dll?product=103&user=ipaddress
2. http://laborsta.ilo.org/.
3. http://econ.worldbank.org/WBSITE/EXTERNAL/EXTDEC/EXTRESEARCH/0,,contentMDK:20649465~pagePK:64214825~piPK:64214943~theSitePK:469382,00.html.
4. http://www.systemicpeace.org/polity/polity4.htm.
5. http://unstats.un.org/unsd/methods/icp/gdp/gdp01_htm.htm.
6. World Development Indicators Online http://devdata.worldbank.org/dataonline/.
7. http://pwt.econ.upenn.edu/.
8. *The Korea Herald*, "Two Labor Groups Engage in War of Nerves over Membership Tallies," April 22, 2000.
9. The only exception is Russia, which had a Polity score of 4 in the late 1990s. It is included in this analysis because under Yeltsin it was generally regarded as a new democracy.
10. In Greece, National General Collective Agreements, which cover most of the economy for two-year periods, have been agreed to since 1994. Similarly, a General Agreement signed in December 1995 between representatives of trade unions, employers, and the government of the Russian Federation covered the 1996–97 period. Two more General Agreements covered the 1998–99 and 2000–01 periods, signed, respectively, on January 27, 1998 and December 16, 1999. The Agreement of December 20, 2001 covered a period of three years. The last Agreement signed on December 29, 2004 was for the 2005–2007 period.
11. It is important to note that the twenty-three cases that have a score of .5 on the Left government (L) set are excluded from the analysis. Since the software automatically drops cases with this score, one alternative would be to assign these cases scores slightly above or below the .5 threshold. The raw data, however, does not allow such fine-grained calibration. In this situation, it is preferable to limit the analysis to those cases where partisanship can be validly inferred.

12. Some prominent studies consulted include Avdagic (2005); Burgess (1999, 2004); Cook (2007); Kubicek (1999); Kuruvilla and Erickson (2002); Myant et al. (2000); Murillo (2000, 2001); Nelson (1991); Robertson (2004); Royo (2002); and Zambarloukou (2006). See also EIRO online http://eurofound.europa.eu/eiro/.
13. The only exception is Mexico, where the power of the country's largest confederation, the Confederation of Mexican Workers, is reduced by average union size and the presence of rival confederations active in some geographic areas. Although the CTM was one of the essential pillars of the Institutional Revolutionary Party (or PRI), its influence decreased dramatically after the PRI lost the 2000 presidential elections. As a result, Mexico receives a fuzzy score of .7.

# References

Alemán, José A. 2005. "Protest and Democratic Consolidation: A Korean Perspective." *International Journal of Korean Studies* IX (1): 71–90.
———. 2009. "Labour Market Dualism and Industrial Relations in Europe." *Industrial Relations Journal* 40 (3): 252–72.
Arce, Moises, and Paul T. Bellinger Jr. 2007. "Low Intensity Democracy Revisited: The Effects of Economic Liberalization on Political Activity in Latin America." *World Politics* 60 (1): 97–121.
Avdagic, Sabina. 2005. "State-Labour Relations in East Central Europe: Explaining Variations in Union Effectiveness." *Socio-Economic Review* 3 (1): 25–53.
Baccaro, Lucio, and Chang-Hee Lee. 2003. "Strengthening Industrial Relations and Social Dialogue in the Republic of Korea." http://www.ilo.org/public/english/dialogue/ifpdial/downloads/papers/korea.pdf.
Baccaro, Lucio, and Marco Simoni. 2008. "Policy Concertation in Europe: Understanding Government Choice." *Comparative Political Studies* 41 (10): 1323–48.
Barrett, Patrick S. 2001. "Labour Policy, Labour-Business Relations and the Transition to Democracy in Chile." *Journal of Latin American Studies* 33 (3): 561–97.
Beck, George, Alberto Clarke, Philip Keefer Groff, and Patrick Walsh. 2001. "New Tools in Comparative Political Economy: The Database of Political Institutions." *World Bank Economic Review* 15 (1): 165–76.
Beck, Nathaniel, and Jonathan N. Katz. 1995. "What to do (and Not to do) with Time-Series Cross-Section Data." *American Political Science Review* 89 (3): 634–47.
Bellin, Eva Rana. 2000. "Contingent Democrats: Industrialists, Labor, and Democratization in Late-Developing Countries." *World Politics* 52 (2): 175–205.
———. 2002. *Stalled Democracy: Capital, Labor, and the Paradox of State-Sponsored Development.* Ithaca: Cornell University Press.
Biglaiser, Glen. 2002. "Privatization and Democracy." *Comparative Political Studies* 35 (1): 83.

Blake, Charles H. 1994. "Social Pacts and Inflation Control in New Democracies: The Impact of Wildcat Cooperation in Argentina and Uruguay." *Comparative Political Studies* 27 (3): 381–401.

———. 1996. "The Politics of Inflation Fighting in New Democracies." *Studies in Comparative International Development* 31 (2): 37–57.

Boix, Carles. 2000. "Partisan Governments, the International Economy, and Macroeconomic Policies in Advanced Nations, 1960–93." *World Politics* 53 (1): 38–73.

Borisov, Vadim, and Simon Clarke. 2006. "The Rise and Fall of Social Partnership in Postsocialist Europe: The Commonwealth of Independent States." *Industrial Relations Journal* 37 (6): 607–29.

Botero, Juan, Simeon Djankov, Rafael La Porta, Florencio Lopez-de-Silanes, and Andrei Shleifer. 2004. "The Regulation of Labor." *Quarterly Journal of Economics* 119 (4): 1339–82.

Bramble, Tom, and Neal Ollett. 2007. "Corporatism as a Process of Working Class Containment and Roll-Back: The Recent Experiences of South Africa and South Korea." *Journal of Industrial Relations* 49 (4): 569–89.

Brandl, Bernd, and Franz Traxler. 2005. "Industrial Relations, Social Pacts and Welfare Expenditures: A Cross-National Comparison." *British Journal of Industrial Relations* 43 (4): 635–58.

Bresser Pereira, Luiz Carlos, Jose Maria Maravall, and Adam Przeworski, eds. 1993. *Economic Reforms in New Democracies: A Social Democratic Approach*. Cambridge: Cambridge University Press.

Bronstein, Arturo S. 1995. "Societal Change and Industrial Relations in Latin America: Trends and Prospects." *International Labour Review* 134 (2): 163–87.

———. 1997. "Labor Law Reform in Latin America: Between State Protection and Flexibility." *International Labour Review* 136 (1): 5–26.

Buchanan, Paul G. 1995. *State, Labor, Capital: Democratizing Class Relations in the Southern Cone*. Pittsburgh: University of Pittsburgh Press.

Buchanan, Paul G., and Kate Nicholls. 2003. *Labour Politics in Small Open Democracies: Australia, Chile, Ireland, New Zealand, and Uruguay*. New York: Palgrave Macmillan.

Buchanan, Paul G., and Kate Nicholls. 2004. "Where Dragons Falter: Labor Politics and the Democratization of Civil Society in South Korea and Taiwan." In *Growth and Governance in Asia*, ed. Yochiro Sato. Honolulu: Asia Pacific Center for Security Studies, 59–86.

Burgess, Katrina. 1999. "Loyalty Dilemmas and Market Reform: Party-Union Alliances Under Stress in Mexico, Spain, and Venezuela." *World Politics* 52 (1): 105–34.

———. 2004. *Parties and Unions in the New Global Economy*. Pittsburgh: University of Pittsburgh Press.

Calmfors, Lars, and John Driffill. 1988. "Centralization and Wage Bargaining." *Economic Policy* 3 (1): 13–61.
Cameron, David R. 1984. "Social Democracy, Corporatism, Labour Quiescence, and the Representation of Economic Interests in Advanced Capitalist Society." In *Order and Conflict in Contemporary Capitalism: Studies in the Political Economy of Western European Nations*, ed. John H. Goldthorpe. Oxford: Claredon Press, 143–78.
Canfora, Luciano. 1992. *Tucidide e l'impero: la presa di Melo*. Roma-Bari: Laterza.
Carbonaro, William. 2006. "Cross-National Differences in the Skills-Earnings Relationship: The Role of Labor Market Institutions." *Social Forces* 84 (3): 1819–42.
Cazes, Sandrine, and Alena Nesporova. 2001. "Labour Market Flexibility in the Transition Countries: How Much is Too Much?" *International Labour Review* 140 (3): 293–325.
Choi, Jang-jip. 1993. "Political Cleavages in South Korea." In *State and Society in Contemporary Korea*, ed. Hagen Koo. Ithaca: Cornell University Press, 13–50.
Collier, David, and Ruth Berins Collier. 1991. *Shaping the Political Arena: Critical Junctures, the Labor Movement, and Regime Dynamics in Latin America*. Princeton, NJ: Princeton University Press.
Collier, Ruth Berins. 1999. *Paths Toward Democracy: Working Class and Elites in Western Europe and South America*. New York: Cambridge University Press.
Collier, Ruth Berins, and David Collier. 1979. "Inducements Versus Constraints: Disaggregating 'Corporatism.'" *The American Political Science Review* 73 (4): 967–86.
Collier, Ruth Berins, and James Mohoney. 1997. "Adding Collective Actors to Collective Outcomes: Labor and Recent Democratization in South America and Southern Europe." *Comparative Politics* 29 (3): 285–303.
Compston, Hugh. 2003. "Beyond Corporatism: A Configurational Theory of Policy Concertation." *European Journal of Political Research* 42 (6): 787–809.
Cook, Maria Lorena. 1998. "Toward Flexible Industrial Relations? Neo-Liberalism, Democracy, and Labor Reform in Latin America." *Industrial Relations* 37 (3): 311–37.
———. 2007. *The Politics of Labor Reform in Latin America: Between Flexibility and Rights*. University Park, Pennsylvania: The Pennsylvania State University Press.
Córdova, Efrén. 1996. "The Challenge of Flexibility in Latin America." *Comparative Labor Law Journal* 17 (2): 314–37.
Coppedge, Michael. 1999. "Thickening Thin Concepts and Theories—Combining Large N and Small in Comparative Politics." *Comparative Politics* 31 (4): 465–76.

Crouch, Colin. 1982. *Trade Unions: The Logic of Collective Action*. London: Fontana Paperbacks.
Crouch, Colin. 2006. "Neo-Corporatism and Democracy." In *The Diversity of Democracy: Corporatism, Social Order and Political Conflict*, ed. Colin Crouch and Wolfgang Streeck. Northampton, MA: Edward Elgar, 46–70.
Crowley, Stephen. 2004. "Explaining Labor Weakness in Post-Communist Europe: Historical Legacies and Comparative Perspective." *Eastern European Politics and Societies*, 18 (3): 394–429.
Deyo, Frederic C. 1987. "State and Labor: Modes of Political Exclusion in East Asian Development." In *The Political Economy of the New Asian Industrialism*, ed. Frederic C. Deyo. Cornell University Press: Ithaca, 182–202.
———. 1989. *Beneath the Miracle: Labor Subordination in the New Asian Industrialism*. Berkeley: University of California Press.
Deyo, Frederic C., and Kaan Agartan. 2003. "Markets, Workers and Economic Reforms: Reconstructing East Asian Labor Systems." *Journal of International Affairs* 57 (1): 55–79.
Doorenspleet, Renske. 2005. *Democratic Transitions: Exploring the Structural Sources of the Fourth Wave*. Boulder: Lynne Rienner Publishers.
Ebbinghaus, Bernhard, and Anke Hassel. 2000. "Striking Deals: Concertation in the Reform of Continental Welfare States." *Journal of European Public Policy* 7 (1): 44–62.
Ebbinghaus, Bernhard, and Bernhard Kittel. 2005. "European Rigidity Versus American Flexibility? The Institutional Adaptability of Collective Bargaining." *Work and Occupations* 32 (2): 163–95.
Eder, Mine. 1997. "Shop Floor Politics and Labor Movements: Democratization in Brazil and South Korea." *Critical Sociology* 23 (2): 3–31.
Edwards, Sebastian, and Alejandra Cox Edwards. 2002. "Social Security Privatization Reform and Labor Markets: The Case of Chile." *Economic Development and Cultural Change* 50 (2): 465–89.
Edwards, Sebastian, and Nora Lustig, eds. 1997. *Labor Markets in Latin America*. Washington, D.C.: Brookings Institute.
Ekiert, Grzegorz, and Jan Kubik. 1998. "Contentious Politics in New Democracies: East Germany, Hungary, Poland, and Slovakia, 1989–93." *World Politics* 50 (4): 547–81.
———. 1999. *Rebellious Civil Society: Popular Protest and Democratic Consolidation in Poland, 1989–1993*. Ann Arbor: University of Michigan Press.
Encarnación, Omar G. 1997. "Social Concertation in Democratic and Market Transitions: Comparative Lessons from Spain." *Comparative Political Studies* 30 (4): 387–419.
Esping-Andersen, Gøsta. 1990. *Three Worlds of Welfare Capitalism*. Princeton: Princeton University Press.

Esping-Andersen, Gøsta, and Marino Regini, eds. 2000. *Why Deregulate Labour Markets?* Oxford: Oxford University Press.
Etchemendy, Sebastián. 2004. "Repression, Exclusion, and Inclusion: Government-Union Relations and Patterns of Labor Reform in Liberalizing Economies." *Comparative Politics* 36 (3): 273–312.
Eyraud, Francois, and Catherine Saget. 2005. *The Fundamentals of Minimum Wage Fixing.* Geneva: International Labour Office.
Ffrench-Davis, Ricardo. 2002. *Economic Reforms in Chile: From Dictatorship to Democracy.* Ann Arbor: University of Michigan Press.
Flanagan, Robert J. 1999. "Macroeconomic Performance and Collective Bargaining: An International Perspective." *Journal of Economic Literature* 37 (3): 1150–75.
———. 2006. *Globalization and Labor Conditions: Working Conditions and Workers Rights in a Global Economy.* New York: Oxford University Press.
Flora, Peter, Franz Kraus, and Winfried Pfenning. 1987. *State, Economy, and Society in Western Europe 1815–1975, Vol. II: Growth of Industrial Societies and Capitalist Economies.* London: Macmillan Press.
Foweraker, Joe, and Todd Landman. 1997. *Citizenship Rights and Social Movements: A Comparative and Statistical Analysis.* Oxford: Oxford University Press.
Frank, Volker. 2002. "The Elusive Goal in Democratic Chile: Reforming the Pinochet Labor Legislation." *Latin American Politics and Society* 44 (1): 35–70.
Franzosi, Roberto. 1994. *The Puzzle of Strikes: Class and State Strategies in Postwar Italy.* Cambridge University Press: Cambridge.
Freeman, Richard B. 1992. *Labor Market Institutions and Policies: Help or Hindrance to Economic Development?* Washington, D.C. ed.: World Bank.
Freeman, Richard B., and Oostendorp, Remco H. 2005. "Occupational Wages Around the World Database." *National Bureau of Economic Research* http://www.nber.org/oww/.
Frías, Patricio. 1995. "Sindicalismo y Desarrollo De Acción Contestataria." In *Economía y Trabajo en Chile 1993–1994*, ed. Roberto Urmeneta. Santiago: Chile: Programa de Economía y Trabajo (PET), 57–74.
———. 1996. "Desarrollo Del Sindicalismo Chileno, 1995–1996." In *Informe Anual, 1995–1996* Anonymous Santiago, Chile: Programa de Economia del Trabajo (PET), 203–21.
Garrett, Geoffrey. 1998. *Partisan Politics in the Global Economy.* Cambridge: Cambridge University Press.
Geddes, Barbara. 2003. *Paradigms and Sand Castles: Theory Building and Research Design in Comparative Politics.* Ann Arbor: University of Michigan Press.

Gereffi, Gary, and Donald L. Wyman, eds. 1990. *Manufacturing Miracles: Paths of Industrialization in Latin America and East Asia.* Princeton, NJ: Princeton University Press.

Glyn, Andrew. 2006. *Capitalism Unleashed: Finance, Globalization, and Welfare.* Oxford: Oxford University Press.

Golden, Miriam, Michael Wallerstein, and Peter Lange. 1999. "Postwar Trade-Union Organization and Industrial Relations in Twelve Countries." In *Continuity and Change in Contemporary Capitalism*, ed. Herbert Kitschelt, Peter Lange, Gary Marks and John D. Stephens. Cambridge: Cambridge University Press, 194–230.

Goldthorpe, John H., ed. 1984. *Order and Conflict in Contemporary Capitalism: Studies in the Political Economy of Western European Nations.* Oxford: Oxford University Press.

González Santibánez, Cristián. 1998. "Notas Sobre Empleo Precario y Precarización Del Empleo En Chile." In *Economía y Trabajo en Chile 1997–1998*, ed. Margarita Fernandez. Santiago: Chile: Programa de Economía del Trabajo (PET), 51–85.

Greskovits, Bela. 1998. *The Political Economy of Protest and Patience: East European and Latin American Transformations Compared.* Budapest: Central European University Press.

Grote, Jurgen, and Philippe Schmitter. 2003. "The Renaissance of National Corporatism: Unintended Side-Effect of European Economic and Monetary Union, Or Calculated Response to the Absence of European Social Policy?" In *Renegotiating the Welfare State: Flexible Adjustment through Corporatist Concertation*, ed. Frans van Waarden and Gerhard Lehmbruch. Florence: Routledge, 279–302.

Gurr, Ted Robert, and Monty G. Marshall. 2005. *Peace and Conflict 2005: A Global Survey of Armed Conflicts, Self-Determination Movements, and Democracy.* http://www.cidcm.umd.edu/inscr/pc05print.pdf: Center for International Development and Conflict Management (CIDCM), University of Maryland.

Haagh, Louise, and David Bravo. 2004. "Ideological Marketization and Policy Learning in Chile: The Case of Unemployment Insurance." In *Learning from Foreign Models in Latin American Policy Reform*, ed. Kurt Weyland. Baltimore: John Hopkins University Press, 166–95.

Hassel, Anke. 2006. *Wage Setting, Social Pacts and the Euro: A New Role for the State.* Amsterdam: Amsterdam University Press.

Hausman, Jerry, Bronwyn H. Hall, and Zvi Griliches. 1984. "Econometric Models for Count Data with an Application to the Patents-R & D Relationship." *Econometrica* 52 (4): 909–38.

Heckman, James, and Carmen Pagés-Serra. 2000. "The Cost of Job Security Regulation: Evidence from Latin American Labor Markets." *Economia* 1 (1): 109–54.

———, eds. 2004. *Law and Employment: Lessons from Latin America and the Caribbean.* Chicago: University of Chicago Press.

Hewitt, Kenneth. 2001. "Between Pinochet and Kropotkin: State Terror, Human Rights and the Geographers." *Canadian Geographer Toronto* 45 (3): 338–55.

Hibbs, Douglas A. 1977. "Political Parties and Macro-Economic Policy." *American Political Science Review* 71 (4): 1467–87.

———. 1987. *The Political Economy of Industrial Democracies.* Cambridge, MA: Harvard University Press.

Hicks, Alexander M. 1999. *Social Democracy and Welfare Capitalism: A Century of Income Security Politics.* Ithaca, NY: Cornell University Press.

Honeybone, Anthony. 1997. "Introducing Labour Flexibility: The Example of New Zealand." *International Labour Review* 136 (4): 493–507.

Hsiao, Cheng. 2003. *Analysis of Panel Data.* 2nd ed. New York: Cambridge University Press.

Hyman, Richard. 2001. "Trade Union Research and Cross-National Comparison." *European Journal of Industrial Relations* 7 (2): 203–32.

Iankova, Elena A. 2002. *Eastern European Capitalism in the Making.* New York: Cambridge University Press.

Im, Hyug Baeg. 1999. "From Affiliation to Association: The Challenge of Democratic Consolidation in Korean Industrial Relations." In *Corporatism and Korean Capitalism*, ed. Dennis I. McNamara. New York: Routledge, 75–94.

International Confederation of Free Trade Unions. 2006. *Annual Survey of Violations of Trade Union Rights.* Brussels: ICFTU. http://www.icftu.org/www/pdf/survey06/Survey06-EN.pdf.

International Labour Organization. 1997. *World Labour Report: Industrial Relations, Democracy and Social Stability.* Geneva: International Labour Office.

———. 2000. *World Labour Report: Income Security and Social Protection in a Changing World.* Geneva: International Labour Office.

———. 2004. *Economic Security for a Better World.* Geneva: International Labour Office.

International Monetary Fund. 1994. *World Economic Outlook.* Washington: IMF.

Ishikawa, Junko. 2003. "Key Features of National Social Dialogue: A Social Dialogue Resource Book." http://www.ilo.org/public/english/dialogue/ifpdial/downloads/papers/key.pdf.

Itzigsohn, Jose. 2000. *Developing Poverty: The State, Labor Market Deregulation, and the Informal Economy in Costa Rica and the Dominican Republic.* University Park: Penn State Press.

Karl, Terry Lynn. 2000. "Economic Inequality and Democratic Instability." *Journal of Democracy* 11 (1): 149–56.

Katzenstein, Peter J. 1985. *Small States in World Markets: Industrial Policy in Europe*. Ithaca, NY: Cornell University Press.

Keefer, Philip, and David Stasavage. 2003. "The Limits of Delegation: Veto Players, Central Bank Independence and the Credibility of Monetary Policy." *American Political Science Review* 97 (3): 407–23.

Kenworthy, Lane. 2001. "Wage-Setting Measures: A Survey and Assessment." *World Politics* 54 (1): 57–98.

Kim, Jin Kyoon. 2000. "Rethinking the New Beginning of the Democratic Union Movement in Korea: From the 1987 Great Workers' Struggle to the Construction of the Korean Trade Union Council (Chunnohyup) and the Korean Confederation of Trade Unions (KCTU)." *Inter-Asia Cultural Studies* 1 (3): 491–502.

Kim Park, MiKyoung. 1997. "Economic Hardships, Political Opportunity Structure and Challenging Actions: A Time Series Analysis of South Korean Industrial Disputes, 1979–1991." *Asian Perspective* 21 (2): 147–77.

Kim, Wonik. 2007. "Social Insurance Expansion and Political Regime Dynamics in Europe, 1880–1945." *Social Science Quarterly* 88 (2): 494–514.

King, Gary, Robert O. Keohane, and Sidney Verba. 1994. *Designing Social Inquiry: Scientific Inference in Qualitative Research*. Princeton: Princeton University Press.

Kong, Tat Yan. 2004. "Neo-Liberalization and Incorporation in Advanced Newly Industrialized Countries: A View from South Korea." *Political Studies* 52 (1): 19–42.

Koo, Hagen. 2000. "The Dilemmas of Empowered Labor in Korea: Korean Workers in the Face of Global Capitalism." *Asian Survey* 40 (2): 227–50.

———. 2001. *Korean Workers: The Culture and Politics of Class Formation*. Ithaca: Cornell University Press.

———. 2002. *Labor Market Reforms in South Korea*. University of California at Los Angeles ed. Korea Economic Institute of America.

Korpi, Walter. 1974. "Conflict, Power and Relative Deprivation." *The American Political Science Review* 68 (4): 1569–78.

———. 1983. *The Democratic Class Struggle*. London: Routledge and Kegan Paul.

Korpi, Walter, and Michael Shalev. 1979. "Strikes, Industrial Relations and Class Conflict in Capitalist Societies." *The British Journal of Sociology* 30 (2): 164–87.

———. 1980. "Strikes, Power and Politics in the Western Nations, 1900–1976." In *Political Power and Social Theory: A Research Annual*, ed. Maurice Zeitlin. vol. 1 ed. Greenwich, Connecticut: JAI Press Inc., 301–334.

Kubicek, Paul. 1999. "Organized Labor in Postcommunist States: Will the Western Sun Set on it, Too?" *Comparative Politics* 32 (1): 83–102.

# REFERENCES

Kurtz, Marcus. 2004a. *Free Market Democracy and the Chilean and Mexican Countryside*. New York: Cambridge University Press.
———. 2004b. "The Dilemmas of Democracy in the Open Economy: Lessons from Latin America." *World Politics* 56 (2): 262–302.
Kuruvilla, Sarosh, and Christopher L. Erickson. 2002. "Change and Transformation in Asian Industrial Relations." *Industrial Relations* 41 (2): 171–228.
Kwon, Seung-Ho, and Michael O'Donnell. 2001. *The Chaebol and Labour in Korea: The Development of Management Strategy in Hyundai*. London; New York: Routledge.
Lange, Peter and Garrett, Geoffrey. 1985. "The Politics of Growth: Strategic Interaction and Economic Performance in the Advanced Industrial Democracies, 1974–1980." *The Journal of Politics* 47 (3): 792–827.
Lee, Cheol-Soo. 2002. "Law and Labor-Management Relations in South Korea: Advancing Industrial Democratization." In *Law and Labor Market Regulation in East Asia*, ed. Sean Cooney, Tim Lindsey, Richard Mitchell and Ying Zhu, 215–245. New York: Routledge.
Lee, Sung-Hee. 2004. "An Overview of Industrial Relations: Changes in Industrial Relations from 1987 to 2002." In *Labor in Korea 1987~2002*, ed. Won-duck Lee. Seoul: Korea Labor Institute, 37–68 http://gw.kli. re.kr/emate-gw/issue.nsf/allview/5C909D041738A8B249256EB7002 0C1CB/$FILE/Labor%20in%20Korea%201987%202002.pdf.
Lee, Won-duck, and Byoung-hoon Lee. 2002. "Industrial Relations: Recent Changes and New Challenges." In *Labor in Korea*, ed. Won-duck Lee. Seoul: Korea Labor Institute, 1–20 http://222.110.238.9/pub/docu/ kr/AI/ZA/AIZA2002AAF/AIZA-2002-AAF.PDF.
Lehmbruch, Gerhard. 1979. "Consociational Democracy, Class Conflict, and the New Corporatism." In *Trends Toward Corporatist Intermediation*, ed. Philippe C. Schmitter and Gerhard Lehmbruch. Beverly Hills, CA: Sage, 58–75.
Lehmbruch, Gerhard, and Philippe Schmitter. 1982. *Patterns of Corporatist Policy-making*. Beverly Hills, California: Sage Publications.
Levitsky, Steven, and Lucan A. Way. 1998. "Between a Shock and a Hard Place: The Dynamics of Labor-Backed Adjustment in Poland and Argentina." *Comparative Politics* 30 (2): 171–92.
Lieberman, Evan S. 2005. "Nested Analysis as a Mixed-Method Strategy for Comparative Research." *American Political Science Review* 99 (3): 435–52.
Mackie, J. L. 1965. "Causes and Conditions." *American Philosophical Quarterly* 2 (4): 245–64.
Mahoney, James. 2008. "Toward a Unified Theory of Causality." *Comparative Political Studies* 41 (4–5): 412–36.

Marshall, Adriana. 1999. "Wage Determination Regimes and Pay Inequality: A Comparative Study of Latin American Countries." *International Review of Applied Economics* 13 (1): 23-39.

McGuire, James W. 1999. "Labor Union Strength and Human Development in East Asia and Latin America." *Studies in Comparative International Development* 33 (4): 3-34.

McNamara, Dennis L. 1999. "Comparative Corporatism." In *Corporatism and Korean Capitalism*, ed. Dennis L. McNamara. New York: Routledge, 9-25.

Mo, Jongryn. 1996. "Political Learning and Democratic Consolidation: Korean Industrial Relations, 1987-1992." *Comparative Political Studies* 29 (3): 290-311.

Murillo, Maria Victoria. 2000. "From Populism to Neoliberalism: Labor Unions and Market Reforms in Latin America." *World Politics* 52 (2): 135-74.

———. 2001. *Labor Unions, Partisan Coalitions, and Market Reforms in Latin America*. New York: Cambridge University Press.

———. 2005. "Partisanship Amidst Convergence: The Politics of Labor Reform in Latin America." *Comparative Politics* 37 (4): 441-58.

Myant, Martin, Brian Slocok, and Simon Smith. 2000. "Tripartism in the Czech and Slovak Republics." *Europe-Asia Studies* 52 (4): 723-39.

Nelson, Joan M. 1991. "Organized Labor, Politics, and Labor Market Flexibility in Developing Countries." *The World Bank Research Observer* 6 (1): 37-56.

Nollert, Michael. 1995. "Neocorporatism and Political Protest in the Western Democracies: A Cross-National Analysis." In *The Politics of Social Protest: Comparative Perspectives on States and Social Movements*, ed. Jenkins, J. Craig and Klandermans, Bert. Minneapolis: University of Minnesota Press, 138-64.

Ogle, George E. 1990. *South Korea: Dissent within the Economic Miracle*. London and New Jersey: Zed Books Ltd.

Olson, Mancur. 1965. *The Logic of Collective Action: Public Goods and the Theory of Groups*. Boston: Harvard University Press.

———. 1982. *The Rise and Decline of Nations: Economic Growth, Stagflation, and Social Rigidities*. New Haven: Yale University Press.

Orenstein, Mitchell A., and Lisa E. Hale. 2001. "Corporatist Renaissance in Post-Communist Central Europe?" In *The Politics of Labor in a Global Age*, ed. Christopher Candland and Rudra Sil. Oxford University Press: Oxford, 258-82.

Organisation for Economic Co-operation and Development. 2004. "OECD Employment Outlook 2004: Reassessing the OECD Jobs Strategy." http://www.oecd.org/document/62/0,2340,en_2649_33927_319351 02_1_1_1_1,00.html.

Oskarsson, Sven. 2003. "The Fate of Organized Labor: Explaining Unionization, Wage Inequality, and Strikes across Time and Space." Ph.D. Department of Government, Uppsala University.

Ost, David. 2000. "Illusory Corporatism in Eastern Europe: Tripartism in the Service of Neoliberalism." *Politics & Society* 28 (4): 503–30.

Oxhorn, Philip. 1994. "Where did all the Protesters Go? Popular Mobilization and the Transition to Democracy in Chile." *Latin American Perspectives* 21 (3): 49–68.

———. 1995. *Organizing Civil Society: The Popular Sectors and the Struggle for Democracy in Chile*. University Park, PA: Pennsylvania State University Press.

Pagés, Carmen. 2004. "A Cost-Benefit Approach to Labor Market Reform." *Economic Review* 89 (2): 67–85.

Pempel, T. J. 2002. "Labor Exclusion and Privatized Welfare: Two Keys to Asia Capitalist Development." In *Models of Capitalism: Lessons for Latin America*, ed. Evelyne Huber. University Park: Penn State University Press.

Pempel, T. J., and Keiichi Tsunekawa. 1979. "Corporatism without Labor: The Japanese Anomaly." In *Trends Towards Corporatist Intermediation*, ed. Philippe C. Schmitter and Gerhard Lehmbruch. Beverly Hills: Sage, 231–70.

Pizzorno, Alessandro. 1978. "Political Exchange and Collective Identity in Industrial Conflict." In *The Resurgence of Class Conflict in Western Europe Since 1968*, ed. Colin Crouch and Alessandro Pizzorno. London: Macmillan, 277–98.

Plümper, Thomas, and Vera E. Troeger. 2005. *The Estimation of Rarely Changing Variables in Panel Data with Unit Effects*. Annual Meeting of the American Political Science Association ed. Washington, D.C.: September 1–5:.

———. 2007. "Efficient Estimation of Time-Invariant and Rarely Changing Variables in Finite Sample Panel Analyses with Unit Fixed Effects." *Political Analysis* 15 (2): 124–39.

Plümper, Thomas, Vera E. Troeger, and Philip Manow. 2005. "Panel Data Analysis in Comparative Politics: Linking Method to Theory." *European Journal of Political Research* 44 (2): 327–54.

Polanyi, Karl. 1944. *The Great Transformation*. Boston, MA: Beacon Press.

Pollack, Marcelo. 1999. *The New Right in Chile, 1973–1997*. New York: St. Martin's Press.

Portes, Alejandro. 1994. *The Informal Economy and its Paradoxes*. Princeton: Princeton University Press.

Przeworski, Adam. 1980. "Material Bases of Consent: Economics and Politics in a Hegemonic System." In *Political Power and Social Theory I*, ed. Maurice Zeitlin. Greenwich, CT: JAI Press.

Przeworski, Adam. 1991. *Democracy and the Market: Political and Economic Reforms in Eastern Europe and Latin America*. Cambridge: Cambridge University Press.
———. 1992. "The Game of Transition." In *Issues in Democratic Consolidation: The New South American Democracies in Comparative Perspective*, ed. Scott Mainwaring, Guillermo O'Donnell, and J. Samuel Valenzuela. Notre Dame: University of Notre Dame Press, 105–52.
———, ed. 1995. *Sustainable Democracy*. Cambridge ed. Cambridge University Press.
Przeworski, Adam, and Wallerstein, Michael. 1982. "The Structure of Class Conflict in Democratic Capitalist Societies." *The American Political Science Review* 76 (2): 215–38.
———. 1986. "Popular Sovereignty, State Autonomy, and Private Property." *Archives Européennes de Sociologie* 27 (2): 215–59.
R. Michael Alvarez, Geoffrey Garrett, and Peter Lange. 1991. "Government Partisanship, Labor Organization, and Macroeconomic Performance." *The American Political Science Review* 85 (2): 539–56.
Ragin, Charles C. 2000. *Fuzzy-set Social Science*. Chicago: University of Chicago Press.
———. 2006. "Set Relations in Social Research: Evaluating their Consistency and Coverage." *Political Analysis* 14 (3): 291–310.
Rama, Martin. 2003. "Globalization and the Labor Market." *The World Bank Research Observer* 18 (2): 159–86.
Rhodes, Martin. 2001. "The Political Economy of Social Pacts: Competitive Corporatism and European Welfare Reform." In *The New Politics of the Welfare State*, ed. Paul Pierson. Oxford: Oxford University Press, 165–94.
Roberts, Kenneth M. 1998. *Deepening Democracy? The Modern Left and Social Movements in Chile and Peru*. Stanford, California: Stanford University Press.
Robertson, Graeme. 2004. "Leading Labor: Unions, Politics, and Protest in New Democracies." *Comparative Politics* 36 (3): 253–72.
Rodrik, Dani. 1999. "Democracies Pay Higher Wages." *The Quarterly Journal of Economics* 114 (3): 707–38.
Rohlfing, Ingo. (2008). What You See and What You Get: Pitfalls and Principles of Nested Analysis in Comparative Research. *Comparative Political Studies*, 41(11), 1492–1514.
Roxborough, Ian. 1992. "Inflation and Social Pacts in Brazil and Mexico." *Journal of Latin American Studies* 24 (3): 639–64.
Royo, Sebastián. 2002. "'A New Century of Corporatism?' Corporatism in Spain and Portugal." *West European Politics* 25 (3): 77–104.
Rudra, Nita. 2002. "Globalization and the Decline of the Welfare State in Less-Developed Countries." *International Organization* 56 (2): 411–45.

———. 2005. "Are Workers in the Developing World 'Winners' Or 'Losers' in the Current Era of Globalization?" *Studies in Comparative International Development* 40 (3): 29–64.

———. 2008. *Globalization and the Race to the Bottom in Developing Countries: Who Really Gets Hurt?* New York: Cambridge University Press.

Rueda, David. 2005. "Insider-Outsider Politics in Industrialized Democracies: The Challenge to Social Democratic Parties." *American Political Science Review* 99 (1): 61–74.

Sandoval, Salvador A. M. 1998. "Social Movements and Democratization: The Case of Brazil and the Latin Countries." In *From Contention to Democracy*, ed. Marco G. Guigni, Doug McAdam, and Charles Tilly. Lanham: Rowman & Littlefield Publishers, Inc., 169–201.

Schmitter, Philippe. 1974. "Still the Century of Corporatism?" *Review of Politics* 36 (1): 85–131.

———. 1981. "Interest Intermediation and Regime Governability in Contemporary Western Europe and North America." In *Organizing Interests in Western Europe: Pluralism, Corporatism, and the Transformation of Politics*, ed. Suzanne Berger. Cambridge: Cambridge University Press, 287–330.

———. 1985. "Neo-Corporatism and the State." In *The Political Economy of Corporatism*, ed. Wyn P. Grant. London: Macmillan, 32–62.

Seidman, Gay W. 1994. *Manufacturing Militance: Workers' Movements in Brazil and South Africa, 1970–1985*. Berkeley, CA: University of California Press.

Shadlen, Kenneth C. 2004. *Democratization Without Representation: The Politics of Small Industry in Mexico*. University Park: Penn State Press.

Siaroff, Alan. 1999. "Corporatism in 24 Industrial Democracies: Meaning and Measurement." *European Journal of Political Research* 36 (2): 175–205.

Siegel, Nico A. 2005. "Social Pacts Revisited: 'Competitive Concertation' and Complex Causality in Negotiated Welfare State Reforms." *European Journal of Industrial Relations* 11 (1): 107–26.

Silver, Beverly J. 2003. *Forces of Labor: Workers' Movements and Globalization since 1870*. Cambridge; New York: Cambridge University Press.

Song, Ho Keun. 1999. *Labor Unions in the Republic of Korea: Challenge and Choice*. Geneva: International Labour Organization. http://www-ilo-mirror.cornell.edu/public/english/bureau/inst/download/dp10799.pdf.

———. 2000. *Labor Unions in the Republic of Korea: Challenge and Choice*. Geneva: International Labour Organization. http://www.hartford-hwp.com/archives/55a/311.html.

Soskice, David. 1990. "Wage Determination: The Changing Role of Institutions in Advanced Industrialized Countries." *Oxford Review of Economic Policy* 6 (4): 36–61.

Standing, Guy. 2008. "Economic Insecurity and Global Casualisation: Threat Or Promise?" *Social Indicators Research* 88 (1): 15–30.
Streeck, Wolfgang. 1984. "Neo-Corporatist Industrial Relations and the Economic Crisis in West Germany." In *Order and Conflict in Contemporary Capitalism: Studies in the Political Economy of Western European Nations*, ed. John H. Goldthorpe. Oxford: Clarendon Press, 291–314.
Streeck, Wolfgang, and Lane Kenworthy. 2005. "Theories and Practices of Neo-Corporatism." In *Handbook of Political Sociology*, ed. Thomas Janoski, Robert R. Alford, Alexander Hicks, and Mildred A. Schwartz. New York: Cambridge University Press, 441–60.
Swank, Duane H., and Cathie Jo Martin. 2001. "Employers and the Welfare State." *Comparative Political Studies* 34 (8): 889–923.
Tae, Sun Hak. 2002. *The Political Economy of Democratic Consolidation: Dynamic Labour Politics in South Korea*. Kwangju: Chonnam National University Press.
Tokman, Victor. 2002. "Jobs and Solidarity: Challenges for Labor Market Policy in Latin America." In *Models of Capitalism: Lessons for Latin America*, ed. Evelyne Huber. Pennsylvania: The Pennsylvania State University Press, 159–94.
Torres, Raymond. 2008. *World of Work Report 2008: Income Inequalities in the Age of Financial Globalization*. Geneva: International Labour Organization (International Institute for Labour Studies).
Traxler, Franz. 1995. "Farewell to Labour Market Associations? Organized Versus Disorganized Decentralization as a Map for Industrial Relations." In *Organized Industrial Relations in Europe: What Future?*, ed. Colin Crouch and Franz Traxler. Avebury, Hants, England; Brookfield, VT: Aldershot, 3–19.
———. 2003. "Bargaining, State Regulation and the Trajectories of Industrial Relations." *European Journal of Industrial Relations* 9 (2): 141–61.
Trebilcock, Anne. 1994. *Towards Social Dialogue: Tripartite Cooperation in National Economic and Social Policy-Making*. Geneva: International Labour Office.
Tsebelis, George, and Peter Lange. 1995. "Strikes Around the World: A Game Theoretic Approach." In *The Workers of Nations: Industrial Relations in a Global Economy*, ed. Sanford M. Jacoby. Oxford: Oxford University Press, 101–26.
Valenzuela, J. Samuel. 1989. "Labor Movements in Transitions to Democracy: A Framework for Analysis." *Comparative Politics* 21 (4): 445–72.
Vogel, Ezra F., and David L. Lindauer. 1997. "Toward a Social Compact for South Korean Labor." In *The Strains of Economic Growth: Labor Unrest and Social Dissatisfaction in Korea*, ed. David L. Lindauer. Cambridge, MA: Harvard Institute for International Development, 93–121.

Wade, Robert. 1990. *Governing the Market: Economic Theory and the Role of Government in East Asian Industrialization*. Princeton: Princeton University Press.

Wallerstein, Michael, Miriam Golden, and Peter Lange. 1997. "Unions, Employers' Associations, and Wage-Setting Institutions in Northern and Central Europe, 1950–1992." *Industrial & Labor Relations Review* 50 (3): 379–401.

Walton, John, and David Seddon. 1994. *Free Markets and Food Riots: The Politics of Global Adjustment*. Oxford: Blackwell.

Western, Bruce. 1991. "A Comparative Study of Corporatist Development." *American Sociological Review* 56 (3): 283–94.

———. 1997. *Between Class and Market: Postwar Unionization in the Capitalist Democracies*. Princeton: Princeton University Press.

———. 2001. "Bayesian Thinking about Macrosociology." *American Journal of Sociology* 107 (2): 353–78.

Western, Bruce, and Simon Jackman. 1994. "Bayesian Inference for Comparative Research." *The American Political Science Review* 88 (2): 412–23.

Wiarda, Howard J. 1997. *Corporatism and Comparative Politics: The Other Great "Ism"*. Armonk, NY: M.E. Sharpe.

Wilthagen, Ton, and Frank Tros. 2004. "The Concept of 'flexicurity': A New Approach to Regulating Employment and Labour Markets." *Transfer* 10 (2): 166–86.

Woldendorp, Jaap J. 1995. "Neo-Corporatism as a Strategy for Conflict Regulation in the Netherlands (1970–1990)." *Acta Politica* 30 (2): 121–51.

Wood, Adrian S. 1994. *North-South Trade, Employment, and Inequality: Changing Fortunes in a Skill-Driven World*. New York: Oxford University Press.

Wooldridge, Jeffrey M. 2002. *Econometric Analysis of Cross Section and Panel Data*. Cambridge, MA: MIT Press.

Yang, Jae-jin. 2006. "Corporate Unionism and Labor Market Flexibility in South Korea." *Journal of East Asian Studies* 6 (2): 205–31.

Zambarloukou, Stella. 2006. "Collective Bargaining and Social Pacts: Greece in Comparative Perspective." *European Journal of Industrial Relations* 12 (2): 211–29.

# Index

Africa, 13, 73
Allende, Salvador (1908–1973), 118–19, 122
alliances (union-government), 30–1, 47, 68, 74, 76
  *see also* power resources theory
Argentina, 27, 32, 48, 68, 69, 72, 139–40
Asia, 13, 18, 49, 73, 104
atypical work, 93, 108
  in the form of fixed term contracts, 16, 61, 100, 108, 111
  *see also* temporary work
Australia, 27
Austria, 27
autocracy, 11, 27
  and exclusionary corporatism, 14, 16, 19, 34, 78, 79, 81, 83, 84, 104
  and repression of labor, 3, 17, 81, 83, 84, 87, 117
  and wage compensation, 11, 25, 52, 56
  *see also* bureaucratic authoritarianism, 79, 92
Aylwin, Patricio (1918–), 124–6

bargaining, 3, 12, 18, 21, 28, 29, 33, 43, 44, 45, 47, 68, 73, 76, 79, 92, 93, 96, 101, 102, 104, 122, 123, 130, 131
  and labor power, 11, 17, 18, 20, 21, 43, 45, 68, 96, 132

  wage bargaining, 9, 16, 18, 44, 46, 89, 90
  *see also* collective bargaining
Belgium, 27
benefits
  unemployment related, *see under* unemployment
  wage related, *see under* wages
  work related, 11, 12, 20, 23, 28, 34, 36, 38, 41, 47, 62, 65, 66, 76, 83, 95, 108, 130
boycotts, *see under* industrial relations
Brazil, 27, 32, 49, 68, 140
Bulgaria, 27, 32, 140
business community, 29, 93, 96, 99, 119, 121
  *see also* employers, managers
business conglomerates, 79, 81, 82, 87, 102, 130
  *see also* chaebol

Canada, 27
Central Unitaria de Trabajadores (CUT), *see under* Chile
chaebol, 82, 83, 99, 100, 101, 102, 107, 109
  *see also* business conglomerates
Chile
  Central Unitaria de Trabajadores (CUT), 116, 121, 122
  Christian Democratic Party (PDC), 131

Chile—*Continued*
  Communist Party, 120, 121, 128
  Concertación (de Partidos por la
    Democracia), 9, 115, 120–2,
    124, 125, 126, 127, 128, 129,
    132, 133, 134
  Confederación de Producción y
    Comercio (CPC), 122, 123,
    124, 125, 126, 128
  Corporación del Cobre
    (Codelco), 125
  Federation of Chilean Industry
    (SOFOFA), 123, 129
  labor laws, 124
  National Workers Command
    (CNT), 119, 120, 122
  Productive Development Forum,
    127, 132
  Railroads of the State, 125
  Renovación Nacional (RN), 121
  Socialist Party, 120, 133
  Unidad Popular Government
    (1970–1973), 119
  Union Demócrata Independiente
    (UDI) of Chile, 121
Christian Democratic Party (PDC),
  *see under* Chile
class compromises, *see under*
  corporatism
collective bargaining, 1, 2, 12, 15,
  17, 18, 33, 43, 44, 47, 48, 71,
  72, 86, 90, 92, 93, 94, 95, 101,
  107, 116, 117, 124, 125, 130,
  131, 133
Communist Party, *see under* Chile
Concertación (de Partidos por la
  Democracia), *see under* Chile
Confederación de Producción y
  Comercio (CPC), *see under* Chile
coordinated market economies
  (CMEs), 15
Corporación del Cobre (Codelco),
  *see under* Chile
corporatism
  and class compromises, 2, 12, 20,
    22, 42, 61, 62, 112, 144

and commodification *v.*
  decommodification of labor
  market outcomes, 4, 59
and consultation involving
  labor, employers and the
  government, 12, 32, 43, 73,
  76, 123, 125
exclusionary, 14, 16, 19, 34, 78,
  79, 81, 83, 84, 104
inclusionary, 14, 16, 18, 19,
  34, 78
and interest group cooperation,
  4, 6, 8, 14, 29, 32, 38, 41, 43,
  47, 65, 66, 67, 68, 71, 74, 75,
  76, 77, 89, 94, 96
and negotiations involving
  labor, employers and the
  government, 1, 8, 12, 18, 22,
  42, 47, 62, 75, 76, 84, 89, 90,
  92, 93, 97, 98, 101, 103, 107,
  117, 122, 125, 126, 128, 129,
  131, 133
and policymaking, 2, 3, 4, 11,
  13, 14, 15, 17, 19, 20, 21, 22,
  28, 29, 30, 31, 33, 35, 41, 62,
  71, 81
and political exchanges, 47, 108
and political inclusion of
  organized labor, 21, 31, 42,
  62, 116
and political process, 3, 14, 17,
  21, 33, 42, 72
and political representation, 3, 4,
  6, 11, 12, 19, 21, 33, 37, 47,
  78, 99, 104, 119
and social dialogue, 2, 3, 9, 13,
  18, 20, 21, 22, 43, 65, 66, 71,
  75, 76, 77, 79, 81, 84, 87, 88,
  108, 109, 111, 115, 122, 132,
  137–8
  societal, 17, 43
  state, 17, 44
and tripartism, 67, 77, 129, 138
*v.* pluralism, 12, 15, 30
*see also* neo-corporatism
Czech Republic, 27, 32, 139–40

democracy
  emerging democracies, 1, 2, 3, 4, 5, 8, 9, 15, 17, 25, 30, 31, 32, 38, 45, 66
  established (industrialized) democracies, 2, 4, 7, 8, 12, 13, 19, 20, 25, 26, 27, 29, 30, 32, 38, 41, 46, 76
  and wage compensation, 11, 25, 52, 56
  *see also* democratization (Third Wave of)
Democratic Justice Party, *see under* Korea (South)
Democratic Liberal Party (DLP), *see under* Korea (South)
democratization (Third Wave of), 1, 2, 4, 6, 7, 8, 11, 15, 19, 25, 27, 34, 38, 49, 79, 87, 92, 111, 116, 119
  *see also* democracy
Denmark, 27
developing countries, 1, 2, 9, 18, 34, 44, 45, 49, 92
Dominican Republic, 27

East Asia, 9, 115
  Newly Industrialized Countries (NICs), 14, 59
Eastern Europe, 9, 18, 21, 30, 62, 75
economic development, 8, 37, 42, 46, 49, 53, 57, 80, 81, 90
economic growth, 52, 60, 116
economic reforms, 1, 12, 18, 31, 88, 100, 101–2, 106
Ecuador, 32, 139–40
EIU Market Indicators and Forecasts database, 47, 48, 49
employers, 1, 2, 3, 5, 8, 12, 18, 19, 20, 21, 22, 28, 29, 32, 37, 41, 42, 43, 47, 48, 51, 58, 61, 65, 66, 67
  *see also* business community, managers
employment
  deregulation, 51, 54, 55, 59, 60

Protection Security Index (EPSI), 33–4, 35, 37, 48, 78
  regulation, 16, 22, 37, 42, 48–9, 54, 70, 71, 73, 74, 75, 76, 78, 79, 92
  security, 18, 33, 35, 36, 37, 78, 81
Estonia, 27, 32

Federation of Chilean Industry (SOFOFA), *see under* Chile
Federation of Korean Trade Unions (FKTU), *see under* Korea (South)
Asian financial crisis of 1997, 99, 104, 108
Finland, 27
fixed-term contracts, *see under* atypical work
flexibility
  and automatic layoffs in South Korea, 98
  combination with security (or flexicurity), 144
  of employment, 20, 59, 66
  of labor market regulations, 2, 9, 15, 16, 18, 20, 35, 42, 49, 78, 82, 93, 98, 99, 115, 116, 126, 133
foreign direct investment (FDI), 52, 55, 60
France, 27
freedoms (civil and political), 34, 87
  and inclusionary corporatism 14, 16, 18, 19, 34, 78
Frei, Eduardo (1942–), 127, 130, 131

general strikes, *see under* industrial relations
Germany, 27
Gini coefficient, 19, 38, 67
  *see also* income inequality
globalization, 7, 18, 30, 56, 88, 99
governments
  behavior of conservative governments, 8, 46, 50, 55, 56, 59, 62, 92

governments— *Continued*
behavior of left governments, 5, 9, 30, 31, 45, 46, 47, 50, 54, 55, 56, 59, 60, 62, 66, 68, 69, 70, 71, 73, 74, 75, 76, 79, 80, 92, 116, 121, 127, 134
involvement in labor policy, 16, 44, 48, 59
Great Workers' Struggle, *see under* Korea (South)
Greece, 9, 27, 32, 33, 48, 139–40

Honduras, 27, 32, 37
Hungary, 27, 32, 139–40
Hyundai, 86, 91, 102, 103, 106
Hyundai Heavy Industries union, 91, 101

import substitution industrialization (ISI), 146
income inequality, 12, 19, 37, 83, 92, 104
*see also* Gini coefficient
industrial relations
boycotts, 96, 127
general strikes, 72, 88, 92, 96, 100, 101, 107, 116, 120, 134
industrial conflict, 8, 9, 21, 41, 43, 50, 58, 60, 62, 65, 84
and labor protest, 4–5, 12, 22, 50, 68, 76, 80, 83, 97, 101, 106, 109, 119, 130, 134
'no work, no pay' principle, 94, 95, 98, 103
slowdowns, 22
and social concertation, 50, 77, 80, 87, 90, 91, 116, 120, 125, 126
strikes, 3, 20, 22, 37, 41, 45, 46, 51, 52, 53, 56, 58, 59, 60, 61, 68, 76, 77, 79, 80, 82, 83, 85, 86, 87, 91, 95, 97, 98, 99, 101, 106, 109, 110, 111, 121, 125, 126, 127, 128, 129, 130
wildcat cooperation, 160
wildcat militancy, 37, 68, 83, 97, 159

inflation, 29, 41, 51, 52, 110, 116, 124, 134
interest representation
and corporatism, 2, 8, 12–15, 17, 20, 22, 28, 29, 30, 31, 36, 37, 42–4, 75, 79, 81, 83, 84
interest groups, 6, 13, 25, 29, 45, 138, 157
and monopoly of association, 14, 29, 43, 67, 68
International Labor Organization (ILO), 22, 43, 93, 105, 106, 110, 115, 132
International Monetary Fund (IMF), 77
investors, 1, 56
Ireland, 27
Italy, 27

Japan, 4, 27, 87
job security, 4, 9, 52, 81, 88, 101, 111, 120, 126, 145
*see also* security *under* employment

Kim Dae Jung (1925–2009), 99, 100, 102, 106, 108
Kim Jong Pil (1926–), 87
Kim Young Sam (1927–), 88, 90, 91, 93, 94, 96, 100
Korea (South)
Democratic Justice Party, 84
Democratic Liberal Party (DLP), 87
Federation of Korean Trade Unions (FKTU), 82, 83, 84, 85, 87, 88, 89, 90, 92, 94, 96, 97, 98, 100, 101, 103, 104, 106, 107
Fifth Republic (1980–1987), 82–3
Great Workers' Struggle, 91
Korea Congress of Independent Industrial Trade Union Federations (KCIIF), 88
Korea Trade Union Congress (KTUC), 88, 89, 90, 91

Korean Central Intelligence
  Agency (KCIA), 82, 83
Korean Confederation of Trade
  Unions (KCTU), 90, 91, 92,
  94, 95, 96, 97, 98, 100, 101,
  102, 103, 104, 105, 106, 107,
  109, 110
Korean Employers' Federation
  (KEF), 87, 105
  and labor laws, 86, 87, 92, 93,
    94, 98, 99, 101, 103
  Labor Standards Act, 98, 99, 101
  Millennium Democratic Party,
    102, 108
  Ministry of Labor (MOLA), 91,
    95, 101, 102
  National Assembly, 96, 97, 98,
    101, 102
  National Congress for New
    Politics (NCNP), 97
  New Democratic Republican
    Party (NDRP), 87
  New Korea Party (NKP), 97
  Presidential Commission on
    Industrial Relations Reform
    (PCIRR), 94, 95
  Reunification Democratic Party
    (RDP), 87
  Sixth Republic (1987–), 82, 84, 86
  Trade Union Act, 85, 86
  Tripartite Commission, 103, 104,
    105, 106
  United Liberal Democrats
    (ULD), 97
Korea Trade Union Congress
  (KTUC), *see under* Korea
  (South)
Korean War, 81–2

labor
  codes, 13, 31, 77, 79, 82, 83, 84,
    86, 87, 93, 99, 103, 116, 121,
    122, 124, 126, 128, 130, 131,
    132, 133
  compensation, 6, 8, 19, 21, 25, 27,
    41, 50, 52, 56–7, 90, 108, 126, 142

  confederations, 12, 22, 30, 34,
    37, 43, 68, 72, 124, 127, 152
  conflict, 1, 2, 6, 20, 22, 28, 42,
    52, 56, 58–9, 65, 76, 82, 125
  force (size), 18, 42, 53, 54, 55,
    58, 60, 61, 62, 79
  laws, 16, 19, 48, *see also* codes
  militancy (or quiescence), 3, 4, 9,
    28, 41, 46, 47, 57, 61, 84, 85,
    86, 87, 126
  power, 45–6, 51, 55, 56, 57, 59,
    60, 71, 73
  productivity, 52–3, 54, 55, 56–7,
    60, 61
  protest, *see under* industrial
    relations
labor market
  deregulation, 19, 111, *see also*
    wage deregulation *under* wages
  insiders *v.* outsiders, 61, *see also*
    formal *v.* informal sector under
    workers
  institutions, 2, 3, 12, 22, 31, 41,
    42, 43, 50, 61
  regimes, 13, 14, 16, 17, 19, 34
  regulations, 2, 3, 5, 7, 8, 13,
    15–17, 19, 20, 22, 25, 28, 31,
    35, 37, 38, 41, 42, 46, 47, 50,
    54, 56, 57, 58, 61, 62, 65, 66,
    67, 77, 82, 99, 115, 116
Labor Strength Index (LSI), 44, 45
Laborsta database, 58, 85
Lagos, Ricardo (1938–), 132–3
Latin America, 3, 9, 13, 15, 18, 19,
    31, 38, 44, 49, 69, 73, 80, 115,
    137, 138, 141, 142

managers, 1, 95, 101, 107, 110
  *see also* business community,
    employers
market liberalization, 25, 27, 32, 158
Mexico, 27, 32, 48, 69, 78, 79, 140
  Confederation of Mexican
    Workers (CMT), 171
  Millennium Democratic Party, *see
    under* Korea (South)

Ministry of Labor (MOLA), see under Korea (South)
National Congress for New Politics (NCNP), see under Korea (South)
National Workers Command (CNT), see under Chile
neo-corporatism, 12, 158
  see also corporatism
neoliberal policies, 15, 31, 116–19, 132, 134
  see also economic reforms, market liberalization
Netherlands, 27
New Zealand, 27
Newly Industrialized Countries (NICs), 79
Nicaragua, 27
Norway, 27

Occupational Wages around the World (OWW) database, 25
Organization for Economic Cooperation and Development (OECD), 19, 27, 30, 38, 48, 93, 94, 105, 111

pacts (social), 8, 52, 65, 66, 67, 69, 70, 71, 72, 73, 74, 75, 76, 77, 82, 90, 91, 127
  comprehensive, 71, 72, 74, 127
  single issue, 72, 74, 75
  tripartite wage agreements, 69, 72, 74, 92
Panama, 32
Park Chung Hee (1917–1979), 82
Partido Socialista (PS), a.k.a. Socialist Party, see under Chile
partisan competition, 68
payroll taxes, 62, 133
Peru, 27, 139–40
Philippines, 13, 19, 27, 32, 48, 79, 140–1

Pinochet, Augusto (1915–2006), 116, 119–20, 121, 134
pluralism, see under corporatism
Poland, 27, 49, 69, 140
polarization (executive-legislative), 50–1, 55, 60
political representation of labor, see under corporatism
  see also democracy
Portugal, 9, 27, 32, 33, 37, 48, 140
power resources theory, 5, 31, 34
  see also alliances (union-government)
privatizations, 118, 121, 126, 130
protest demonstrations, 22, 83, 84, 130
  see also industrial conflict, riots

Qualitative Comparative Analysis (QCA), 65, 69

Representation Security Index (RSI), 33, 47
repression, 3, 17, 81, 83, 84, 87, 117
Rhee Syngman (1875–1965), 82
riots, 22
  see also industrial conflict, under industrial relations protest demonstrations
Roh Moo Hyun (1946–2009), 108–11
Roh Tae Woo (1932–), 84
Russia, 27, 32, 69, 139–40

Slovakia, 27, 32, 139–40
Slovenia, 27
slowdowns, see under industrial relations
small and medium sized enterprises (SMEs), 92, 103
social concertation, see under industrial relations
  see also social dialogue

social cooperation, 47, 65, 66, 67, 68, 71, 74, 75, 76, 77
  *see also* corporatism
social dialogue, *see under* corporatism
social policy, 13, 29, 32, 41, 71, 101, 118, 121
Socio-Economic Security (SES) database, 25, 31–3, 37, 47, 48, 49, 58
South Africa, 13, 27, 32, 48, 49, 139–40
Spain, 9, 19, 27, 32, 33, 37, 48, 68, 69, 79, 139–40
strikes, *see under* industrial conflict
  *see also* conflict *under* labor
Sweden, 27, 167

Taiwan, 27, 139
temporary work, 16, 34, 61, 94, 95, 102, 104, 105, 107, 108, 131, 135
  *see also* atypical work
Thailand, 27, 32, 37, 78, 139–40
trade openness, 53, 56, 59
trade unions, *see under* unions
tripartism, *see under* corporatism
Turkey, 27, 32, 72, 140

Ukraine, 27, 32, 48, 139–40
unemployment, 4, 29, 46, 52, 55, 71, 82, 89, 90, 99, 101, 102, 103, 108, 110, 111, 118, 120, 128, 131, 133, 134
  benefits, 4, 89, 90, 101, 108, 128, 133
unionization, 16, 18, 19, 33, 34, 44, 45, 70, 85, 88, 124, 125, 127, 128, 134
unions
  alliances with government, *see* alliances (union-government)
  leadership, 3, 85, 87, 91, 96, 104, 109, 116, 128

membership, 18, 44, 79, 81, 85, 96, 111
  rates, 18, 19, 33, 44, 45
  trade unions, 3, 8, 11, 17, 18, 21, 22, 28, 32, 34, 80, 82, 90, 91, 93, 101, 104, 144–5
  union competition, 46, 68, 69
unit labor costs, *see under* wages
United Kingdom, 27
United Liberal Democrats (ULD), *see under* Korea (South)
United States, 15, 27
Uruguay, 27, 68

voice representation, 8, 19, 34, 36, 37, 38, 44, 47, 78, 80
  *see also* political representation

wages
  minimum wage, 42, 47, 51, 72, 85, 116, 118, 123, 124, 125, 126, 132, 134
  monthly wage, 8, 25, 27, 133
  real wages, 4, 49, 51, 87, 102, 118, 142
  unit labor costs, 50, 54, 55, 57, 58
  wage costs, 8, 22, 41, 42, 43, 49, 50, 51, 52, 54, 55, 56, 57, 61, 92, 105
  wage deregulation, 51, 54, 55, 59, 60
  wage growth, 12, 56, 61, 91, 103
  wage moderation, 8, 42, 51, 55, 56, 57, 59, 61, 65, 67, 110
  wage regulation, 8, 47, 48, 49, 57, 71, 73, 74, 116
  wage restraint, 44, 52, 101
Western Europe, 2, 3, 4, 20, 62, 138, 141, 142
wildcat cooperation, *see under* industrial relations
wildcat militancy, *see under* industrial relations

workers
    blue collar, 45, 92, 97
    female, 27, 83, 105
    formal sector, 18, 27, 31, 44
    health, 126, 129
    informal sector, 27, 47, 116
    miners, 130
    public sector, 4, 69, 72, 101, 103, 126
    teachers, 87, 93, 95, 96, 97, 98, 102, 130
    white collar, 86, 88, 92, 93, 97
    *see also* atypical work
workers' councils, 16, 110
working conditions, 57, 108, 117, 124

The manufacturer's authorised representative in the EU is Springer Nature Customer Service Centre GmbH, Europaplatz 3, 69115 Heidelberg, Germany. If you have any concerns regarding our products, please contact ProductSafety@springernature.com

Printed and bound by CPI Group (UK) Ltd, Croydon, CR0 4YY
23/03/2026
02076459-0013